FROM BETHLEHEM TO CALVARY

The Initiations of Jesus

by

ALICE A. BAILEY

LUCIS PUBLISHING COMPANY
113 University Place, 11th Floor
P.O. Box 722, Cooper Station
New York, N.Y. 10276

LUCIS PRESS LTD.
3 Whitehall Court
Suite 54
London SW1A 2EF
England

First printing, 1937
Third printing, 1968 (Revised)
Eighth printing, 1989 (4th Paperback Edition)

ISBN 0-85330-107-7

The publication of this book is financed by the Tibetan Book Fund which is established for the perpetuation of the teachings of the Tibetan and Alice A. Bailey.

This Fund is controlled by the Lucis Trust, a tax-exempt, religious, educational corporation.

The Lucis Publishing Company is a non-profit organisation owned by the Lucis Trust.   No royalties are paid on this book.

This title is also available in a
clothbound edition.

It has been translated into Dutch, French, German, Greek, Italian, Portuguese and Spanish. Translation into other languages is proceeding.

MANUFACTURED IN THE UNITED STATES OF AMERICA
By FORT ORANGE PRESS, INC., Albany, N.Y.

FROM BETHLEHEM TO CALVARY

The Initiations of Jesus

BOOKS BY ALICE A. BAILEY

DEDICATED TO

M. VICTOR FOX

IN AFFECTIONATE RECOGNITION
OF COMRADESHIP IN SERVICE
AND OF AN UNDERSTANDING HEART

THE GREAT INVOCATION

From the point of Light within the Mind of God
    Let light stream forth into the minds of men.
    Let Light descend on Earth.

From the point of Love within the Heart of God
    Let love stream forth into the hearts of men.
    May Christ return to Earth.

From the centre where the Will of God is known
    Let purpose guide the little wills of men —
    The purpose which the Masters know and serve.

From the centre which we call the race of men
    Let the Plan of Love and Light work out
    And may it seal the door where evil dwells.

Let Light and Love and Power restore the Plan on Earth.

"The above Invocation or Prayer does not belong to any person or group but to all humanity. The beauty and the strength of this Invocation lies in its simplicity, and in its expression of certain central truths which all men, innately and normally, accept — the truth of the existence of a basic Intelligence to Whom we vaguely give the name of God; the truth that behind all outer seeming, the motivating power of the universe is Love; the truth that a great Individuality came to earth, called by Christians, the Christ, and embodied that love so that we could understand; the truth that both love and intelligence are effects of what is called the Will of God; and finally the self-evident truth that only through *humanity* itself can the Divine Plan work out."

ALICE A. BAILEY

Foreword

This book goes out with the earnest wish that its effect may be wholly constructive and result in a deepening of our belief in Christ and a broader recognition of the work which He came to initiate. Many years of work as an evangelist and as a teacher in the field of Christian principles, and a difficult cycle in which I faced the problem of my own relation to Christ and to Christianity, have brought me to two definitely clear and clean cut recognitions: first, a recognition of the reality of the Individuality of Christ and of His Mission; and secondly, a recognition that the development of the Christ Consciousness and the Christ Nature in individual man, and in the race as a whole, carries with it the solution of our world problem. Most heartily do I endorse the words of Arthur Weigall when he says:

"Yet the Jesus of History as distinct from the Jesus of Theology, remains 'the way, the truth, and the life'; and I am convinced that concentration upon the historic figure of our Lord and upon His teaching can alone inspire in this Twentieth Century that fervent adherence and service which in former ages could be obtained from the average layman by the expounding of theological dogmas, the threat of hell, and the performance of elaborate rites and cere- monies."[1]

The kingdom of God is now in process of rapid formation, as all those with forward-seeing vision and a realisation of the rapidly emerging beauty and divinity of man can bear testi- mony. We are passing through the transition period between the old age and the new, and the true mission of Christ, so deeply and frequently obscured by theological implications and disputations, embodies in itself the coming revelation. The development of humanity guarantees the recognition of Christ and His work and its participation, consciously, in the kingdom of God.

[1] *The Paganism in Our Christianity,* by Arthur Weigall, p. 16.

The conscious evocation of the Christ Life in the human heart and our rapid integration into the kingdom of God are the immediate tasks ahead, embodying our responsibility, opportunity and destiny.

In closing, I would like to offer my grateful thanks to Mr. William Cummings and Mr. Alan Murray for the willing and intelligent help they have given me. They have made the writing of this book possible.

From Bethlehem to Calvary

Of those who sought my crib at Bethlehem
Heeding a voice and following a star,
How many walked with me to Calvary?
It was too far.

Glory surrounded that once mangered babe,
And hope for men who struggled with their loss.
But hope, fulfilled, came through my thorny crown
And through my cross.

Truth was my sword and pain the accolade
Which I bestowed on those who followed on,
A tethered ass the charger which I chose
To ride upon.

Gone was the glory, then, of Bethlehem,
The gifts of Kings and Magi from the East;
Gone were the multitudes and only twelve
Were at the feast

Of humble bread served in the upper room
Where that sad cup was passed from hand to hand
In token of my love for all mankind
Within the land.

When, at Gethsemane, I prayed alone
That a more bitter cup might be withdrawn,
Ye could not watch with me one little hour
Until the Dawn!

So many sought my crib at Bethlehem
Heeding a voice and following a star,
But only Simon walked to Calvary—
It was too far.

H. Le Gallienne.

Reprinted with the kind permission of
The New York Times and the Author.

CHAPTER ONE

Introductory Remarks on Initiation

KEY THOUGHT

"There is a human desire for God; but there is also a Divine desire for man. God is the supreme idea, the supreme concern and the supreme desire of man. Man is the supreme idea, the supreme concern and the supreme desire of God. The problem of God is a human problem. The problem of man is a Divine problem. . . . Man is the counterpart of God and His beloved from whom He expects the return of love. Man is the other person of the Divine mystery. God needs man. It is God's will not only that He should Himself exist, but man also, the Lover and beloved."

Wrestlers with Christ, by Karl Pfleger, p. 236.

CHAPTER ONE

Introductory Remarks on Initiation

1

WE are in process of passing from one religious age into another. The spiritual trends of today are steadily becoming more defined. The hearts of men have never been more open to spiritual impression than they are at this time, and the door into the very centre of reality stands wide open. Paralleling, however, this significant development is a trend in the counter direction, and materialistic philosophies and doctrines of negation are becoming increasingly prevalent. To many, the whole question of the validity of the Christian religion remains to be determined. Claims are made that Christianity has failed and that man does not need the Gospel story with its implications of divinity and its urge to service and sacrifice.

Is the Gospel story historically true? Is it a mystical tale of great beauty and of real teaching value but nevertheless of no vital import to the intelligent men and women of today, who pride themselves on their reasoning powers and upon their independence of ancient mental trammels and of old and dusty traditions? As to the perfection of the portrayed character of Christ there is never any question. The enemies of Christianity admit His uniqueness, His basic profundity and His understanding of the hearts of men. They recognise the intelligence of His ideas and sponsor them in their own philosophies. The developments which the Carpenter of Nazareth brought about in the fabric of human life, His social and economic ideals, and the beauty of the civilisation which could be founded upon the ethical teaching of the

3

Sermon on the Mount are frequently emphasised by many who refuse to recognise His mission as an expression of divinity. From the rational point of view, the question as to the historical accuracy of His story remains as yet unsolved, though His teaching upon the Fatherhood of God and the brotherhood of man is endorsed by the best minds of the race. Those who can move in the world of ideas, of faith and of living experience testify to His divinity and to the fact that He can be approached. But such testimony is often passed over lightly as being mystical, futile and incapable of proof. Individual belief is, after all, of no value to anyone except to the believer himself, or as it tends to increase testimony until the total assumes such proportions that it eventually becomes proof. To fall back upon the "way of belief" can be indicative of a living experience, but it can also be a form of self-hypnotism and a "way of escape" from the difficulties and problems of daily life. The effort to understand, to experiment, to experience and to express what is known and believed is frequently too difficult for the majority, and they then fall back upon a belief which is based upon the testimony of the trusted, as the easiest way out of the impasse.

The problem of religion and the problem of orthodox Christianity are not one and the same thing. Much that we see around us today of unbelief and criticism, and the negation of our so-called truths, is based upon the fact that religion has been largely superseded by creed, and doctrine has taken the place of living experience. It is this living experience which is the keynote of this book.

Perhaps another reason why humanity at this time believes so little, or questions so unhappily what is believed, may be the fact that theologians have attempted to lift Christianity out of its place in the scheme of things and have overlooked its position in the great continuity of divine revelation. They have endeavoured to emphasise its uniqueness, and to regard it as an isolated and entirely separated expression of spiritual religion. They thereby destroy its background, remove its foundations, and make it difficult for the steadily developing mind of man to accept its presentation. Yet St. Augustine tells us that "that which is called the Christian religion existed among the ancients, and never did not exist from the beginning of the human race until Christ came in the flesh, at which time the true religion, which already existed, began to be called Christianity."[1] The Wisdom which expresses relationship to God, the rules of the road which guide our wandering footsteps back to the Father's home, and the teaching which brings revelation have ever been the same, down the ages, and are identical with that which Christ taught. This body of inner truths and this wealth of divine knowledge have existed since time immemorial. It is the truth which Christ revealed; but He did more than this. He revealed in Himself and through His life history what this wisdom and knowledge could do for man. He demonstrated in Himself the full expression of divinity, and then enjoined upon His disciples that they should go and do likewise.

In the continuity of revelation, Christianity enters upon its cycle of expression under the same divine law which governs all manifestation—the Law of Cyclic Appearance. This revelation passes through the phases of all form-manifestation, or appearance, then growth and development, and finally (when the cycle draws towards its close) crystallisation and a gradual but steady emphasis of the letter and the form, till the death of that form becomes inevitable and wise. But the spirit remains to live on and take to itself new forms. The Spirit of Christ is undying, and as He lives to all eternity, so that which He incarnated to demonstrate must also live. The cell in the womb, the stage of littleness, the development of the child into the man—to all this He submitted Himself, and underwent all the processes which are the destiny of every son of God. Because of this submission and because He "learned obedience by the things which he suffered,"[2] He could be trusted to reveal God to man, and (may we say it?) the divine in man to God. For the Gospels

---

[1] Quoted by W. Kingsland in *Religion in the Light of Theosophy*.
[2] *Hebrews*, V, 8.

show us that continuously Christ called forth this recognition from the Father.

The great continuity of revelation is our most priceless possession, and into it the religion of Christ must, and does, fit. God has never left Himself without witness, and He never will. The place of Christianity as the fulfilment of the past and as a stepping-stone to the future, is often forgotten, and this perhaps is one of the reasons why people speak of a failing Christianity, and look forward to that spiritual revelation which seems so sorely needed. Unless this continuity is emphasised and the place of the Christian faith in it, revelation may come and pass unrecognised.

"There was," we are told, "in every ancient country having claims to civilisation, an Esoteric Doctrine, a system which was designated WISDOM, and those who were devoted to its prosecution were first denominated sages, or wise men. . . . Pythagoras termed this system . . . the Gnosis or Knowledge of things that are. Under the noble designation of WISDOM, the ancient teachers, the sages of India, the magians of Persia and Babylon, the seers and prophets of Israel, the hierophants of Egypt and Arabia, and the philosophers of Greece and the West, included all knowledge which they considered as essentially divine; classifying part as esoteric and the remainder as exterior."[3]

We know much of the exoteric teaching. Orthodox and theological Christianity is founded on it, as are all the orthodox formulations of the great religions. When, however, the inner wisdom teaching is forgotten and the esoteric side is ignored, then the spirit and the living experimental experience disappear. We have been occupied with the details of the outer form of the faith, and have sadly forgotten the inner meaning which carries life and salvation to the individual and also to humanity. We have been busy fighting over the non-essentials of traditional interpretation and have omitted to teach the secret and the technique of the Christian life. We have over-emphasised the doctrinal and dogmatic aspects, and have deified the letter, whilst all the time the soul

---

[3] *The Secret Doctrine*, by H. P. Blavatsky, Vol. III, p. 55.

of man was crying out for the spirit of life, which the letter veiled. We have agonised over the historical aspects of the Gospel narrative, over the time element, and over the verbal accuracy of the many translations, while failing to see the real magnificence of Christ's accomplishment and the significant teaching it holds for the individual and for the race. The drama of His life and its practical application to the lives of His followers have been lost to sight in the undue importance attached to certain phrases which He is supposed to have uttered, whilst that which He expressed in His life, and the relationships which He emphasised and regarded as implicit in His revelation have been totally ignored.

We have fought over the historical Christ, and thus fighting, have lost sight of His message of love to all beings. Fanatics quarrel over His words, and fail to remember that He *was* "the Word made flesh." We argue about the Virgin Birth of the Christ, and forget the truth which the Incarnation is intended to teach. Evelyn Underhill points out in her most valuable book, *Mysticism,* that "The Incarnation, which is for popular Christianity synonymous with the historical birth and earthly life of Christ, is for the mystic not only this but also a perpetual cosmic and personal process."

Scholars spend their lives in proving that the whole story is only a myth. It should, however, be pointed out that a myth is the summarised belief and knowledge of the past, handed down to us for our guidance and forming the foundation of a newer revelation, and that it is a stepping-stone to the next truth. A myth is a valid and proven truth which bridges, step by step, the gap between the past gained knowledge, the present formulated truth, and the infinite and divine possibilities of the future. The ancient myths and the old mysteries give us a sequential presentation of the divine message as it went forth from God in response to the need of man, down the ages. The truth of one age becomes the myth of the next, but its significance and its reality remain untouched, and require only re-interpretation in the present.

We are free to choose and to reject; but let us see to it that we choose with eyes opened by that sagacity and wisdom which are the hall mark of those who have penetrated a considerable way along the path of return. There is life and truth and vitality in the Gospel story yet to be re-applied by us. There is dynamic and divinity in the message of Jesus. Christianity is, for us today, a culminating religion. It is the greatest of the later divine revelations. Much of it, since its inception two thousand years ago, has come to be regarded as myth, and the clear outlines of the story have dimmed and have come frequently to be regarded as symbolic in their nature. Yet behind symbol and myth stands reality—an essential, dramatic and practical truth.

Our attention has been engrossed by the symbol and by the outer form, whilst the meaning has remained obscured and fails sufficiently to affect our lives. In our myopic study of the letter we have lost the significance of the Word itself. We need to get behind the symbol to that which it embodies, and to shift our attention away from the world of outer forms to that of inner realities. Keyserling points this out in these words:

"The process of shifting levels from the letter to the inner meaning in the matter of spiritual attitudes can be clearly set forth by one single proposition. *It consists in 'seeing through' the phenomenon.* Every living phenomenon is, first and last, a symbol; for the essence of life is meaning. But every symbol which is the ultimate expression of a state of consciousness is in itself transparent for another deeper one, and so on into eternity; for all things in the sense-connexion of life are inwardly connected, and their depths have their roots in God.

"Therefore, no spiritual form can ever be an ultimate expression; every meaning, when it has been penetrated, becomes automatically a mere letter-expression of a deeper one, and herewith the old phenomenon takes on a new and different meaning. Thus, Catholicism, Protestantism, Greek-Catholic, Islamism and Buddhistic religiousness can in principle continue, on the plane of this life, what they were and yet signify something entirely new."[4]

[4] *The Recovery of Truth,* by Hermann Keyserling, pp. 91-92.

The only excuse for this book is that it is an attempt to penetrate to that deeper meaning underlying the great events in the life of Christ, and to bring into renewed life and interest the weakening aspiration of the Christian. If it can be shown that the story revealed in the Gospels has not only an application to that divine Figure Which dwelt for a time among men, but that it has also a practical significance and meaning for the civilised man today, then there will be some objective gained and some service and help rendered. It is possible that today—owing to our more advanced evolution and the ability to express ourselves through more finely developed shades of consciousness—we can appropriate the teaching with a clearer vision and a wiser use of the indicated lesson. This great *Myth* belongs to us—for let us be courageous and use this word in its true and right connotation. *A myth is capable of becoming a fact in the experience of an individual, for a myth is a fact which can be proven.* Upon the myths we take our stand, but we must seek to re-interpret them in the light of the present. Through self-initiated experiment we can prove their validity; through experience we can establish them as governing forces in our lives; and through their expression we can demonstrate their truth to others. This is the theme of this book, dealing as it does with the facts of the Gospel story, that fivefold sequential myth which teaches us the revelation of divinity in the Person of Jesus Christ, and which remains eternally truth, in the cosmic sense, in the historical sense, and in its practical application to the individual. This myth divides itself into five great episodes:

1. The Birth at Bethlehem.
2. The Baptism in Jordan.
3. The Transfiguration on Mount Carmel.
4. The Crucifixion on Mount Golgotha.
5. The Resurrection and Ascension.

Their significance for us and their re-interpretation in modern terms is our task.

A point of crisis and of culmination has been reached in the history of man, and man owes this to the influence of Christianity. As a member of the human family, he has reached a level of integration unknown in the past, except in the case of a select few in every nation. He is, as the psychologists have indicated, a sum total of physical organisms, of vital force, of psychical states or emotional conditions, and of mental or thought reactions. He is now ready to have indicated to him his next transition, development or unfoldment. Of this he is expectant, standing in readiness to take advantage of the opportunity. The door into a world of higher being and consciousness stands wide open; the way into the kingdom of God has been clearly pointed out. Many in the past have passed into that kingdom and awakened there to a world of being and of understanding which is, to the multitude, a sealed mystery. The glory of the present moment lies in the fact that many thousands stand thus prepared, and (given the needed instruction) could be initiated into the mysteries of God. A new unfoldment in consciousness is now possible; a new goal has arisen and governs the intentions of many. We are, as a race, definitely on our way towards some new knowledge, some fresh recognitions, and some deeper world of values. What happens on the outer plane of experience is indicative of a similar happening in a more subtle world of meaning. For this we must prepare.

We have seen that the Christian revelation unified in itself the teachings of the past. This, Christ Himself pointed out when He said, "Think not that I am come to destroy the law or the prophets: I am not come to destroy, but to fulfil."[5] He embodied all the past, and revealed the highest possibility to man. The words of Dr. Berdyaev, in *Freedom and the Spirit,* throw light on this:

"The Christian revelation is universal, and everything analogous to it in other religions is simply a part of that revelation. Christianity is not a religion of the same order as the others; it is, as Schleiermacher said, the religion of religions. What does it matter if within

[5] *St. Matt.,* V, 17.

Christianity, supposedly so different from other faiths, there is nothing original at all apart from the coming of Christ and His Personality; is it not precisely in this particular that the hope of all religions is fulfilled?"[6]

Each great period of time and each world cycle will have— through the loving-kindness of God—its religion of religions, synthesising all the past revelations and indicating the future hope. The world expectancy today shows that we stand on the verge of a new revelation. It will be a revelation which will in no way negate our divine spiritual heritage, but will add the clear vision of the future to the wonder of the past. It will express what is divine but has been hitherto unrevealed. It is therefore possible that an understanding of some of the deeper significances of the Gospel story may enable the modern seeker to grasp the wider synthesis.

Some of these deeper implications were touched upon in a book published many years ago, entitled *The Crises of the Christ*, by that veteran Christian, Dr. Campbell Morgan. Taking the five major episodes in the life of the Saviour, around which the entire Gospel narrative is built, he gave them a wide and general application, leaving one with the realisation that Christ had not only passed through these dramatic experiences, in deed and in truth, but had left us with the definite command that we should "follow His steps."[7] Is it not possible that these great facts in the experience of Christ, these five personalised aspects of the universal myth, may have for us, as individuals, more than an historical and personal interest? Is it not possible that they may embody some experience and some initiated undertaking through which many Christians may now pass, and thus obey His injunction to enter into new life? Must we not all be born again, baptised into the Spirit, and transfigured upon the mountain top of living experience? Does not the crucifixion lie ahead for many of us, leading on to the resurrection and the ascension? And is it not also pos-

---

[6] *Freedom and the Spirit*, by Nicholas Berdyaev, pp. 88-89.
[7] *I Peter*, II, 21.

sible that we have interpreted these words in too narrow a
sense, with too sentimental and ordinary an implication,
whereas they may indicate to those who are ready a special
way and a more rapid following in the footsteps of the Son
of God? This is one of the points which concern us and
with which this book will attempt to deal. If this more
intensive meaning can be found, and if the drama of the
Gospels can become in some peculiar way the drama of those
souls who are ready, then we shall see the resurrection of
the essentials of Christianity and the revivifying of the form
which is so rapidly crystallising.

2

It is of interest to recall that other teachings besides that
of Christianity have emphasised these five important crises
that occur, if so desired, in the life of those human beings
who take their stand upon their essential divinity. Both
the Hindu teaching and the Buddhist faith have emphasised
them as evolutionary crises which we may not ultimately
escape; and a right understanding of the interrelation of
these great world religions may eventually bring about a
truer understanding of all of them. The religion of the
Buddha, though preceding that of the Christ, expresses the
same basic truths, but phrases them in a different manner,
which can help us nevertheless to a larger interpretation of
Christianity.

"Buddhism and Christianity find their origins respectively in two
inspired moments of history: the life of the Buddha, and the life of
Christ. The Buddha gave his doctrine to enlighten the world:
Christ gave his life. It is for Christians to discern the doctrine. Per-
haps in the end the most valuable part of the doctrine of the
Buddha is its interpretation of his life."[8]

The teaching of Lao-Tzu can also serve the same purpose.
Religion must eventually be composite, gathered from many

[8] *Religion in the Making*, by A. N. Whitehead, p. 55.

sources and composed of many truths. Yet it is legitimate to feel that if one had to choose, at this time, *one* faith, one might choose Christianity, and for this specific reason: the central problem of life is to lay hold upon our divinity and to make it manifest. In the life of Christ we have the most complete and perfect demonstration and example of divinity lived successfully on earth, and lived—as most of us have to live—not in retirement, but in the full tide of storm and stress.

Exponents of all faiths are today meeting to discuss the possibility of finding a platform of such universality and truth that upon it all men may unite, and on which the coming world religion may be based. This may perhaps be found in a clearer interpretation and understanding of these five outstanding episodes, and in their practical and unique relationship not only to the individual but to humanity as a whole. This realisation will bind us more definitely to the past, anchoring us in the truth that was; it will indicate to us our immediate goal and duty, which when understood will enable us to live more divinely, to serve more adequately, and thus to bring the will of God into fruition on earth. It is their inner meaning and our individual relation to them that are of importance.

There is nothing but a valuable gain to us, an enriching of our consciousness, when we realise the unity, and at times the uniformity of the teaching as it is given in both the East and the West. For instance, the fourth event in Christ's life, the Crucifixion, finds a parallel in the fourth initiation of the Oriental teaching which is called the Great Renunciation. There is an initiation, called in the Buddhist terminology the "entering of the stream," and there is in the life of Jesus an episode which we call the "baptism in Jordan." The story of Christ's birth at Bethlehem can be paralleled in practically every detail in the lives of earlier messengers from God. These proved facts should surely evoke from us the recognition that though there are many messengers there is only one Message; but this recognition in no way detracts from the unique task of the Christ and the unique function which He came forth to fulfil.

It is interesting also to bear in mind that these two outstanding Individualities, the Buddha and the Christ, have set Their seal upon both hemispheres—the Buddha being the Teacher for the Orient, and Christ the Saviour of the Occident. Whatever may be our personal conclusions as to Their relations to the Father in Heaven or to each other, the fact stands out past all controversy that They gave the revelation of divinity to Their particular civilisations, and that in a most significant manner They worked together for the eventual benefit of the race. Their two systems are interdependent, and Buddha prepared the world for the message and the mission of Christ.

Both embodied in Themselves certain cosmic principles, and by Their work and sacrifice certain divine potencies poured through and upon mankind. The work done by the Buddha, and the message which He sounded, stimulated intelligence into wisdom. Wisdom is a cosmic principle, and a divine potency. This the Buddha embodied.

But love came to the world through Christ, and He, through His work, transmuted emotion into Love. As "God is Love," the comprehension that Christ revealed the love of God makes clear the magnitude of the task He undertook —a task far beyond the powers of any teacher or messenger who had preceded Him. The Buddha, when He achieved illumination, "let in" a flood of light upon life and upon our world problems, and this intelligent understanding of the causes of world distress He endeavoured to formulate into the Four Noble Truths. These are, as most of us well know:

1. That existence in the phenomenal universe is inseparable from suffering and from sorrow.

2. That the cause of suffering is desire for existence in the world of phenomena.

3. That cessation of suffering is brought about by eradicating all desire for existence in this universe of phenomena.

4. That the way to the cessation of suffering is by treading the noble Eightfold Path, wherein are expressed right belief, right intentions, right speech, right actions, right living, right endeavour, right-mindedness and right concentration.

He provided a structure of truth, of dogma and of doctrine which has enabled many thousands, down the centuries, to see the light. Today Christ and His disciples are occupied (as they have been for two thousand years) with the same task of bringing enlightenment and salvation to men; blows are being struck at the world illusion, and the minds of humanity are arriving, *en masse,* at an increasing clarity of thought. Through the message, therefore, of the Buddha, man can, for the first time, grasp the cause of his eternal discontent, of his constant distaste and dissatisfaction, and of his endless nostalgia. From the Buddha he can learn that the way of release is to be found in detachment, dispassion and discrimination. These are the first steps on the road to Christ.

Through the message of Christ three general concepts emerged into the racial consciousness:

First, that the individual, as an individual, is of value. This was a truth which the general Eastern doctrine of rebirth had tended to negate. Time was long; opportunity would endlessly recur; the evolutionary process would do its work. Let mankind therefore drift as a whole with the tide, and eventually all would be well. Hence the general attitude of the East was failure to emphasise the supreme value of any individual. But Christ came and emphasised the work of the individual, saying, "Let your light so shine before men, that they may see your good works."[9]

Second, the opportunity was presented to the race as a whole to take a tremendous step forward, to undergo the "new birth" or take the first initiation. This we shall deal with in our next chapter.

[9] *St. Matt.,* V, 16.

The third concept which was taught by the Christ was that which embodied the technique of the new age, which was to come when individual salvation and the new birth had been properly grasped. This was the message or command to love our neighbour as ourselves.[10] Individual effort, group opportunity, and identification with each other—this was the message of the Christ.

In the teaching of the Buddha we have the three ways in which the lower nature can be changed and prepared to be a conscious expression of divinity. Through *detachment* man learns to withdraw his interest and his consciousness from the things of the senses, and to turn a deaf ear to the calls of the lower nature. Detachment imposes a new rhythm upon the man. Through learning the lesson of *dispassion* he becomes immune to the suffering of the lower nature as he detaches his interest from secondary things and the non-essentials, and centres it upon the higher realities. Through the practice of *discrimination* the mind learns to select the good, the beautiful and the true. These three practices, leading to a changed attitude towards life and reality, will, when held sanely, bring in the rule of wisdom and prepare the disciple for the Christ life.

Upon this racial teaching follows the work of the Christ with humanity, resulting in an understanding of the value of the individual and his self-initiated efforts at release and illumination, with the final objective of group love and group good. We learn to perfect ourselves in consonance with Christ's injunction, "Be ye therefore perfect,"[11] in order to have somewhat to contribute to the group good, and in order to serve Christ perfectly. Thus that spiritual reality, spoken of by St. Paul as "Christ in you, the hope of glory,"[12] is released in man and can manifest in full expression. When a sufficient number of people have grasped this ideal, the entire human family can stand for the first time before the portal

[10] *St. Matt.,* XIX, 19.
[11] *St. Matt.,* V, 48.
[12] *Col.,* I, 27.

perfect = all-embracing

which leads to the Path of Light, and the life of Christ will flower forth in the human kingdom. Personality then fades out, dimmed by the glory of the soul, which, like the rising sun, disperses the darkness, reveals the life-situation, and irradiates the lower nature. It leads to group activity, and self, as we usually understand it, disappears. This is already happening. The final result of the work of the Christ can be seen portrayed for us in His words to be found in St. John XVII, which it would be of value to all of us to read.

Individuality, Initiation, Identification—in these terms the message of the Christ can be expressed. This He epitomised when on earth in the words: "I and my Father are one."[13] *That great Individuality, the Christ, through the process of the five great Initiations, gave to us a picture of the stages and method whereby identification with God can be brought about.* This sentence gives us the keynote of the entire Gospel story, and constitutes the theme of this book.

The interrelation of the work of the past and of the present, as given to us by the great Teacher of the East and by the Saviour of the West, can be expressed as follows:

The Buddha . . . The Method . . . Detachment.
                                   Dispassion.
                                   Discrimination.

The Christ . . . . The Result . . . . Individualism.
                                      Initiation.
                                      Identification.

Christ lived His life in that small but significant strip of land which we call Palestine, the Holy Land. He came to prove to us the possibility of individual attainment. He emerged (as all the Teachers throughout the ages seem to have done) out of the Orient, and worked in that country which seems like a bridge between the Eastern and Western hemispheres, separating two most different civilisations. Modern thinkers would do well to remember that Christianity is a bridging religion. Herein lies its great importance. Christi-

[13] *St. John*, X, 30.

anity is the religion of that transitional period which links the era of self-conscious individualistic existence to a future group-conscious unified world.   It is outstandingly a religion of cleavage, demonstrating to man his duality, and thus laying the foundation for his effort to achieve unity or at-one-ment.   The realisation of this duality is a most needed stage in man's unfoldment, and the purpose of Christianity has been to reveal this; also to point out the warfare between the lower and the higher man, between carnal man and spiritual man, united in one person, and to emphasise the necessity for that lower man to be saved by the higher.   This, St. Paul points out in the words so familiar to all of us: ". . . to make in himself, of twain, one new man, so making peace; and that he might reconcile both unto God in one body, having slain the enmity in himself."[14]   This was His divine mission, and this is the lesson of the Gospel narrative.

Christ therefore not only unified in Himself the past "law and the prophets," but He also provided that presentation of truth which could bridge the gap between Eastern belief and philosophy and our Western materialism and scientific attainment, both of them divine expressions of reality.   At the same time He demonstrated to human beings the perfection of the task which each man could carry forward within himself, bridging that essential duality which is his nature, and bringing about that at-one-ment of the human and the divine which it is the task of all religions to aid.   Each of us has to make "of twain, one new man, so making peace," for peace is unity and synthesis.

But the lesson and message which Christ brought to individual man He brought also to the nations, holding before them the hope of future world unity and world peace.   He came at the beginning of that astronomical age which we call "the Piscean age" because, during this period of approximately two thousand years, our sun is passing through that sign in the zodiac which we call Pisces, or the Fishes.   Hence the frequent references to fishes, and the appearance of the

[14] *Eph.*, II, 15, 16, Marginal Reading.

symbol of the fish in Christian literature, including the New Testament. This Piscean age comes between the previous Jewish dispensation (the two thousand years wherein the sun was passing through the sign Aries, the Ram) and the Aquarian age into which our sun is now in process of transiting. These are astronomical facts, for I am not here speaking of astrological conclusions. In the period when the sun was in Aries, we find the frequent appearance of the ram or the scapegoat in the Old Testament teaching, and the keeping of the Passover feast. In the Christian age we use the fish symbology, even to eating fish on Good Friday. The symbol of the Aquarian age, as it appears in all the ancient zodiacs, is that of a man bearing a jar of water. The message of that age is one of unity, communion and our relationship as brothers, because we are all the children of the one Father. To this age Christ pointed in His instructions to His disciples when He told them to go into the city, and said: "When ye are entered into the city, there shall a man meet you, bearing a pitcher of water; follow him into the house where he entereth in."[15] This they did, and the great and holy feast of communion was later held in that house. The reference is undoubtedly to the future period wherein we enter into that house in the zodiac which is called "the Water-carrier," and wherein also we shall all sit at the same table, and hold communion one with another. The Christian dispensation comes between the two great world cycles, and just as Christ consummated in Himself the message of the past, and gave the teaching for the present, so He also pointed to that future of unity and understanding which is our inevitable goal. We are today at the end of the age, and entering the period of Aquarian unity, as He foretold. The "upper room" is a symbol of that high point of achievement towards which we are, as a race, rapidly moving. Some day the great Communion Service will be held, of which every communion service is the forecast. We are slowly passing into this new sign. For more than two thousand years its potencies and

[15] *St. Luke*, XXII, 7, 10.

forces will play upon the race and will establish the new
types, foster the new expansions of consciousness, and lead
man on to a practical realisation of brotherhood.

It is interesting to note how it was that the energies play-
ing upon our planet when the sun was in Aries, the Ram,
produced in religious symbology the emphasis of the goat or
ram, and how in our present age of Pisces, the Fishes, those
influences have coloured our Christian symbology so that the
fish preponderates in our New Testament and in our eschatological symbology. The new incoming rays, energies and
influences must surely be destined to produce equal effects,
not only in the realm of physical phenomena but also in the
world of spiritual values. The atoms of the human brain
are being "awakened" as never before, and those millions of
cells which, we are told, are to be found inactive and dor-
mant in the human brain may be brought into functioning
activity, bringing with them that intuitive insight which will
recognise the coming spiritual revelation.

Today the world is re-orienting itself to the newer influences, and in the processes of re-adjustment a period of temporary chaos is inevitable. Christianity will not be superseded. It will be transcended, its work of preparation being
triumphantly accomplished, and Christ will again give us
the next revelation of divinity. If all that we now know of
God is all that can be known, the divinity of God is but a
limited matter. What the new formulation of truth will be,
who can say? But the light is slowly pouring into men's
hearts and minds, and in this lighted radiance they will vision the new truths and arrive at a fresh enunciation of the
ancient wisdom. Through the lens of the illumined mind
man will shortly see aspects of divinity hitherto unknown.
May there not be qualities and characteristics of the divine
nature which are as yet totally unrecognised and unknown?
Can there not be revelations of God utterly unprecedented,
and for which we have no words or adequate means of expression? The ancient mysteries, so shortly to be restored,
must be re-interpreted in the light of Christianity, and re-

adapted to meet modern need, for we can now enter into the Holy Place as intelligent men and women, and not as children looking on at dramatic stories and procedures in which we, as individuals, play no conscious part. Christ enacted for us the dramatic story of the five initiations, and urged us to follow in His steps. For this the past era has prepared us, and we can now pass intelligently into the kingdom of God through the process of initiation. The fact that the *historical* Christ existed and walked on earth is the guarantee to us of our own divinity and our ultimate achievement. The fact of the *mythic* Christ, appearing again and again down the ages, proves that God has never left Himself without witness and that always there have been those who have achieved. The fact of the *cosmic* Christ, manifest as the urge towards perfection in all the kingdoms of nature, proves the fact of God and is our eternal hope. Humanity stands at the portals of initiation.

3

Always there have been temples and mysteries and holy places where the true aspirant could find what he sought, and the needed instruction as to the way he should go. The prophet of old said:

". . . a highway shall be there, and a way, and it shall be called the way of holiness; the unclean shall not pass over it, for he shall be with them; the wayfaring men, though fools, shall not err therein."[16]

It is a way that leads from that which lies without to that which dwells within. It reveals, step by step, the hidden life which every form and symbol veils and hides. It assigns to the aspirant certain tasks which lead to his understanding, and produces an inclusiveness and wisdom which meet his deeply sensed need. He passes from the stage of enquiry to what the Tibetans call "straight knowledge." Upon that path

[16] *Isaiah*, XXXV, 8, Marginal Reading.

vision and hope give place to realisation. Initiation after initiation is undergone, each one leading the initiate nearer to the goal of complete unity. Those who in the past thus worked, agonised and attained, constitute a long chain, reaching out of the remotest past into the present, for the initiates are still with us and the door still stands wide open. Through the agency of this hierarchy of achievement, men are lifted, step by step, up the long ladder reaching from earth to heaven, to stand eventually before the Initiator and in that high moment to find that it is the Christ Himself Who thus greets them—the familiar Friend Who, having prepared them by example and precept, now receives them into the presence of God. Such has ever been the experience, the uniform experience down the ages, of all seekers. Revolting in the East from the wheel of rebirth, with its constantly re-iterated suffering and pain, or revolting in the West from the apparent monstrous injustice of the one sorrowful life which the Christian allots himself, men have turned within to find the light and peace and release so ardently desired.

Christ gives us a definite picture of the entire process in His own life story, built around those major initiations which are our universal heritage and the glorious (and for many) the immediate opportunity. These are:

1. The Birth at Bethlehem, to which Christ called Nicodemus, saying, "Except a man be born again, he cannot see the kingdom of God."[17]

2. The Baptism in Jordan. This is the baptism to which John the Baptist referred us, telling us that the baptism of the Holy Spirit and of fire must be administered to us by Christ.[18]

3. The Transfiguration. There perfection is for the first time demonstrated, and there the divine possibility of such perfection is proven to the disciples. The command

[17] *St. John,* III, 3.
[18] *St. Matt.,* III, 1.

goes forth to us, "Be ye therefore perfect even as your Father which is in heaven is perfect."[19]

4. The Crucifixion. This is called the Great Renunciation, in the Orient, with its lesson of sacrifice and its call to the death of the lower nature. This was the lesson which St. Paul knew and the goal towards which he strove. "I die daily," he said, for only in the practice of death daily undergone can the final Death be met and endured.[20]

5. The Resurrection and Ascension, the final triumph which enables the initiate to sing and to know the meaning of the words: "Oh death, where is thy sting? Oh grave, where is thy victory?"[21]

Such are the five great dramatic events of the mysteries. Such are the initiations through which all men must some day pass. Humanity stands today upon the path of probation. The way of purification is being trodden by the masses, and we are in process of purging ourselves from evil and materialism. When this process is completed, many will find themselves ready to make preparation for the first of the initiations, and to undergo the new Birth. The disciples of the world are preparing for the second initiation, the Baptism, and for this must come a purification of the emotional desire nature and a dedication of the desire nature to the life of the soul. The initiates of the world are facing the Transfiguration initiation. Mind control and right orientation towards the soul, with a complete transmutation of the integrated personality, lies ahead of them.

There is much foolishness talked these days in connection with initiation, and the world is full of people who are claiming to be initiates. They fail to remember that no initiate makes any claim or speaks about himself. Those who claim to be initiates give denial to their claim in so doing. Disciples and initiates are taught to be inclusive in their thoughts

---

[19] *St. Matt.*, V, 48.
[20] *I Cor.*, XV, 31.
[21] *I Cor.*, XV, 55.

and non-separative in their attitudes. They never set themselves apart from the rest of humanity by asserting their
status and thus automatically placing themselves upon a
pedestal. Nor are the requirements, as stated in many of
the esoteric books, quite as simple as they are made out to
be. To read some of them, one would think that as long as
the aspirant has achieved a measure of tolerance, of kindness,
devotion, sympathy, idealism, patience and perseverance he
has fulfilled the major requirements. These are indeed primary essentials, but to these qualities must be added an intelligent understanding and a mental unfoldment which will
lead to a sane and intelligent cooperation with the plans for
humanity. It is the balance of head and heart that is required, and the intellect must find its complement and expression in and through love. This needs a most careful
re-proclaiming. Love and sentiment and devotion are often
confused with each other. Pure love is an attribute of the
soul and is all-inclusive, and it is in pure love that our relation to God and to each other consists. "For the love of
God is broader than the measure of man's mind, and the
heart of the Eternal is most wonderfully kind"—so runs the
old hymn, and thus is expressed that love which is the attribute of Deity and also the hidden attribute of every son of
God. Sentiment is emotional and unstable; devotion can
be fanatical and cruel; but love blends and fuses, understands
and interprets and synthesises all form and all expressions, all
causes and all races, into one flaming heart of love, knowing
no separateness, no division and no disharmony. To bring
about this divine expression in our daily life takes the utmost
that is in us. To be an initiate takes every power of every
aspect of one's nature. It is no easy task. To face the inevitable tests with which one will assuredly be confronted
as one treads the path Christ trod, takes courage of the rarer
kind. To cooperate sanely and wisely with God's Plan and
to merge one's will in the divine Will must call into activity
not only the deepest love of one's heart, but the keenest decisions of the mind.

Initiation might be regarded as a great experiment. There was perhaps a time, when this process of unfoldment was instituted, that it became possible to enact upon earth certain inner processes known at that time only to the few. Then that which was within could be put into symbolic form for the teaching of the "little ones," and could later be undergone openly and expressed for us upon earth by the Son of God, the Christ. Initiation is a living process, and through that process all who duly discipline themselves and voluntarily acquiesce may pass, scrutinised and aided by that band of initiates and knowers who are the guides of the race, and who are known to us under many names in different parts of the world and in different ages. They are called in the West, Christ and His Church, the Elder Brothers of Humanity. Initiation is therefore a reality and not a beautiful and rather easily attained vision, as so many occult and esoteric books seem to claim. Initiation is not a process which a man undergoes when he joins certain organisations, and which can be understood only by joining such groups. It has nothing to do with societies, esoteric schools and organisations. All that they can do is to teach the aspirant certain well known and basic "rules of the road," and then leave him to understand or not, as his earnestness and development permit, and to pass on through the portal as his equipment and destiny allow. The Teachers of the race, and the Christ, Who is the "Master of all the Masters and the Teacher alike of angels and of men," are not more interested in these organisations than They are in any movement in the world today which carries illumination and truth to men. The initiates of the world are to be found in every nation, in every church, and in every group where men of good will are to be found working, and where world service is rendered. The modern so-called esoteric groups are not the custodians of the teaching of initiation, nor is it their prerogative to prepare man for this unfoldment. The best of them can only prepare men for that stage in the evolutionary process which is called "discipleship." The reason why this is sadly the case, and why initiation seems so far away from the membership of most of the groups who claim an insight into the initiation processes, is that they have not laid the needed emphasis upon that mental illumination which perforce lights the way to the Gate leading to the "Secret Place of the Most High." They have laid the emphasis upon personality devotion to the Masters of the Wisdom, and to their own organisation leaders; they have stressed adherence to authoritative teaching and rules of life, and have not primarily emphasised adherence to the still small voice of the soul. The way to the place of initiation and to the Centre where Christ may be found is the way of the soul, the lonely way of self-unfoldment, of self-effacement and of self-discipline. It is the way of mental illumination and intuitive perception.

Initiation is the revelation of love, of the second great aspect of divinity, expressing itself in wisdom. This expression is found in its fulness in the life of Christ. He revealed to us the nature of essential love, and then told us to love. He demonstrated to us what divinity is, and then told us to live divinely. In the New Testament this unfolding life of living divine love is held before us in three ways, each progressive in its definition of experience, and each giving us the sequence of the revelation of Christ in the human heart. There is first of all the phrase "Christ in you, the hope of glory."[22] This is the stage which precedes and immediately follows the new birth, the Birth at Bethlehem. It is the stage towards which the masses of men are slowly but steadily working, and it is the immediate goal for many of the aspirants in the world today. Secondly, there is the stage which is called that of a full-grown man in Christ, indicating an increased experience of the divine life and a deeper unfoldment of the Christ consciousness in the human being. Towards this the disciples of the world are now oriented. Then there is the stage of achievement, referred to by St. Paul in the following terms, "Till we all come, in the unity of the faith and of the knowledge of the Son of God, unto

[22] *Col.*, I, 27.

a perfect man, unto the measure of the stature of the fulness of Christ."[23]

Initiation is therefore a graded and realised series of expansions of consciousness, a steadily increasing awareness of divinity and of all its implications. Many so-called initiates today believe themselves to have reached this status because some occult leader or some psychic seer has told them that it is so; yet within themselves they know nothing of the process whereby they can pass (as Masonry teaches) through that mysterious door, between the two great pillars, in their search for light; they have no conscious knowledge of that self-initiated programme which has to be followed in full waking consciousness, being realised simultaneously by the indwelling divine soul and the mind and brain of the man in physical life. These expansions of consciousness progressively reveal to man the quality of his higher and his lower nature; it is this realisation which marks St. Paul as one of the first initiates to attain that status under the Christian dispensation. Read what he says about this revelation of his duality:

"I know that in me [that is, in my flesh] dwelleth no good thing: for to will is present with me; but how to perform that which is good I find not.

"For the good that I would, I do not: but the evil which I would not, that I do.

"For I delight in the law of God after the inward man:

"But I see another law in my members, warring against the law of my mind, and bringing me into captivity to the law of sin which is in my members.

"Oh, wretched man that I am! who shall deliver me from the body of this death?

"I thank God through Jesus Christ our Lord."[24]

Only through the revelation of the Christ within each human being can this at-one-ment be made. Only through the new birth, the baptism of spirit and of fire, and the transfiguration of the nature can deliverance be found, can unity

[23] *Eph.*, IV, 13.
[24] *Romans,* VII, 18-25.

with God be achieved. Only through the sacrifice of humanity, which is the essence of the crucifixion, can the resurrection be undergone.

What is true of the individual will be true ultimately of the entire human family. The plan for humanity concerns man's *conscious* unfoldment. As mankind grows in wisdom and knowledge, and as the civilisations come and go, each bringing its needed lesson and its high point of attainment, men as a group approach the gate which leadeth unto life. All modern discovery, all psychological studies and knowledge, all group activity and all scientific achievement, as well as all real occult knowledge, are spiritual in nature, and these are aids to that expansion of consciousness which will make of mankind the Great Initiate. Just as soon as human beings can grasp in a large synthesis the necessity of entering more definitely into the world of true meaning and of value, we shall see the mysteries becoming universally recognised. The new values will be seen and the new techniques and methods of living will be evolved as a result of this perception. There are signs that this is already happening, that the destruction going on around us and the tearing down of the ancient institutions—political, religious and social—are only preparatory to this undertaking. We are on our way to "that which is within," and many voices are today proclaiming this.

We are on that path of transition (can we call it the Path of Discipleship?) which will lead us into a new dimension, into the interior world of true fact and right energy. It is a world in which only the spiritual body can function and only the eye of spirit can see. It cannot be perceived by those whose inner perception is unawakened and whose intuition sleeps. When the spiritual body begins to be organised and to grow, and when the eye of wisdom slowly opens and trains itself to see truly, then there will come the indications that the Christ, latent in each son of God, is beginning to control and to lead man into the world of spiritual being, true meaning and essential values. This world is the kingdom of God, the world of souls, and—when manifested—is that expression of divine life which we can call the fifth kingdom in nature. But it cannot yet be generally perceived. It is through the process of initiation that this world stands revealed.

Before initiation can be given, the significance of the above ideas must be grasped, and certain great developments are necessarily presupposed. These requirements can be seen working out in the life of every disciple at this time, and, for those who have eyes to see, they can be seen actively bringing changes in the race.

Aspiration is a basic requirement, both in the individual and in the race. Today humanity aspires to great heights, and this aspiration is responsible for the great national movements seen in so many countries. At the same time, individual disciples are striving anew towards illumination, incited thereto by their longing to meet world need. Spiritual selfishness, which has been such a characteristic of aspirants in the past, has to be transcended and transmuted into love of man and a sharing in the "fellowship of Christ's sufferings."[25] Self must be lost to sight in service. Service is rapidly becoming the keynote of the time, and one of the incentives in racial endeavour. The meeting of disaster and the undergoing of painful experiences is ever the lot of the individual disciple. It is becoming obvious that the world disciple, humanity itself, is now deemed worthy of such a testing. This universality of difficulty, in every department of human life and excluding no group, indicates that mankind as a whole is being prepared for initiation. There is purpose underlying what is happening today. The birth pangs of the Christ within the race have begun, and the Christ will be born in the "House of Bread" (which is the meaning of the word "Bethlehem"). The implications of our present world pain and suffering are too obvious to need further explanation. There is purpose underlying all world affairs at this time, and there is reward at the end of the way. Some day, sooner perhaps than many may think, the portals of initiation will open wide to the suffering world disciple (as they have ever

[25] *Phil.,* III, 10.

opened in the past to individuals), and humanity will enter
into a new Kingdom and stand before that mysterious Presence Whose light and wisdom shone forth before the world
through the Person of Christ, and Whose voice was heard
at each of the five crises through which Christ passed. Then
will mankind enter into the world of causes and of knowing.
We shall dwell in the inner world of reality, and the outer
appearance of physical living will be known to be only symbolic of inner conditions and happenings. Then we shall
begin to work and live as those who are initiate in the mysteries, and our lives will be regulated from the realm of reality where Christ and His Disciples of all time (the Church
invisible) guide and control human affairs.

The goal which They have in view and the end towards
which They are working has been summed up for us in a
commentary upon an ancient Tibetan scripture. The words
are as follows:

"All beauty, all goodness, all that makes for the eradication of
sorrow and ignorance upon earth must be devoted to the one Great
Consummation. Then when the Lords of Compassion shall have
spiritually civilised the Earth and made of it a Heaven, there will
be revealed to the Pilgrims the Endless Path, which reaches to the
heart of the universe. Man, then no longer man, will transcend
Nature, and impersonally, yet consciously, in at-one-ment with all
the Enlightened Ones, help to fulfil the Law of the Higher Evolution, of which *Nirvana* is but the beginning."[26]

Such is our goal. Such our glorious objective. How can
we progress towards this consummation? What is the first
step that we must take? In the words of an unknown poet:

"When thou canst see
Beneath the outer seeming
The causes which to all effects give birth,
When thou canst feel, in warmth of sunlight streaming
The Love of God, encircling all the earth,
Then know thyself initiate in the Mysteries
The wise men ever deemed of greatest worth."

[26] *Tibetan Yoga and Secret Doctrines,* by W. Y. Evans-Wentz, p. 12.

CHAPTER TWO

The First Initiation . . . The Birth at Bethlehem

KEY THOUGHT

"Except a man be born again, he cannot see the kingdom of God."

(St. John, III, 3.)

CHAPTER TWO

The First Initiation . . . The Birth at Bethlehem

1

In our discussion of these five major initiations we shall seek to do three things. First, we shall endeavour to realise that Christianity is the flower and the fruitage of the religions of the past, being the last to be given out, with the exception of the Mohammedan religion. We have seen that the emphasis of the Christian religion has been laid upon the unit in the human family, and also upon the unique mission of Christ Himself. Christ came to teach the supreme value of the individual, as I have already indicated in the previous chapter.[1]

It would appear that the emphasis laid by the followers of Mohammed upon the fact of God, the Supreme, the One and Only, was in the nature of a balancing pronouncement, coming forth as it did in the fifteenth century, in order to safeguard man from forgetfulness of God, as he drew nearer to his own latent and essential divinity as a son of the Father. The study of the relationships of these different faiths, and the manner in which they prepare for and complement each other, is of the deepest interest. This our Western theologians have often forgotten. Christianity may and does preserve secret within itself the sacred teaching, but it inherited that teaching from the past. It may personalise itself through the instrumentality of the greatest of the divine Messengers, but the way of that Messenger had been prepared before-

[1] See p. 15.

hand, and He had been preceded by other great Sons of God. His word may be the life-giving Word for our Western civilisation, and may embody the salvation which had to be brought to us, but the East had its own teachers, and each of the past civilisations upon our planet had had its divine Representative.   As we consider the message of Christianity and its unique contribution, let us not forget the past, for if we do we shall never understand our own faith.

Secondly, we must remember to think in terms of the whole and to realise that the great expansions of consciousness to which we shall constantly refer have their universal parallels.   Some of these unfoldments in the race lie in past racial history.   Some lie ahead.   One lies immediately possible in the present.   As man's physical and mechanical equipment develops to meet his expanding consciousness, he is gradually led to experience more and more of the divine Immanence, to perceive more of the divine Transcendence, and to register with an increasingly illumined awareness the revelation which is sequentially presented for his education and his cultural growth.

Today we stand at the very verge of the birth hour of the racial Christ, and out from the darkness of the womb of matter the Christ child can enter into the light of the kingdom of God. Another crisis is upon us, and for this Christ has prepared the race, for when He was born at Bethlehem, it was not simply the birth of another divine Teacher and Messenger, but the appearing of an Individual Who not only summed up in Himself the past achievement of the race, but Who was also the forerunner of the future, embodying in Himself all that it was possible for humanity to achieve. The appearance of Christ in the cave at Bethlehem was the inauguration of the possibility of a new cycle of spiritual unfoldment for the race, as well as for the individual.

Finally, we shall consider these unfoldments from the standpoint of the individual, and study those episodes related in the Gospel story which vitally concern the individual human being who, approaching the end of the long and weary way of evolution, is ready to re-enact the same drama in his own experience. To him there comes the opportunity to pass from the stage of the new birth to that of the final resurrection, via the steep path of Mount Golgotha. In his innermost nature he must learn to understand the words of Christ, "Ye must be born again,"[2] and to express the death unto life which is the outstanding message of St. Paul.[3]

Each of us must sooner or later prove this for himself, because "living religious experience is the only legitimate way to the comprehension of dogmas."[4] Only by following the example of those who have achieved can we ourselves learn the meaning of achievement. Only by our living divinely can our hidden divinity find true expression. This involves a practical self-application which brings its own reward but which must at first be entered upon blindly.

The history of humanity is therefore the history of this individual search for divine expression and light, and for the ultimate achievement of the new birth which releases a man into the service of the kingdom of God. Down the ages, individuals throughout the world have passed through these five expansions of consciousness, and have entered into a deeper life of fuller, richer service. Step by step, their sense of divinity has grown, and their awareness of the divine Life, immanent in nature, has led them to the recognition of the paralleling truth of God transcendent. God in the individual, and God in Christ. God in all forms, and God the informing life of the cosmos, and yet a God Who consciously informs a universe as well as a man and the minutest atom of substance. The evolution of this recognition of divinity in man has been gradual and slow, but at certain points in racial history (as in the history of the individual man) critical moments have been reached, and crises have emerged and have been transcended, each definite initiation leaving the

[2] *St. John*, III, 7.
[3] *I Cor.*, XV, 31.
[4] Pavel Florensky, quoted in *The Recovery of Truth*, by Hermann Keyserling, p. 80.

race with an expanded understanding. Today mankind is being prepared for just such a transition, and for the refocussing of the human consciousness in a higher dimension and in a richer field of experience. Humanity is ready to step on to a higher rung of the evolutionary ladder. Faced with a situation so peculiar and an experience so unparalleled, our present chaotic bewilderment need cause no surprise. We are trembling on the verge of another step forward; we are ready for another initiation; we are on the point of widening our horizon, and passing through an open door into a larger room. All that is transpiring is no indication of failure, of senseless confusion and blind upheaval. It is rather a process of temporary destruction for further rebuilding, and is but a correspondence in the racial life to those tests and trials which are always the lot of the disciple preparing for initiation. For this, Christianity has prepared numbers of the race. The new interpretation and the next revelation are imminent.

This coming revitalisation of the essential and inner nature of humanity, with the consequent reorganisation of world affairs and of human life, is already sensed and awaited by the thinkers of the race, and they constantly isolate the present opportunity. The expectancy in the race is assuming vital proportions.

In the words of an ancient Mexican aphorism, "Always in the centre shall come a new Word." Every form has its positive centre of life. Every organism is constructed around a central nucleus of power. There is a centre in our universe from which the Word went forth, bringing into being our organised solar system as we now have it, and the planet on which we live, with its myriad forms of life.

"In the beginning was the Word, and the Word was with God, and the Word was God.

"The same was in the beginning with God.

"All things were made by Him, and without Him was not anything made that was made.

"In Him was life; and the life was the light of men.

"He was in the world, and the world was made by Him, and the world knew Him not."[5]

What is thus true of the Whole is true also of the part. Each civilisation, as an expression of the human consciousness, has had its Word. Two thousand years ago a Word was for us "made Flesh," and around that dynamic centre of spiritual life our Western world revolves. Whether we accept this fact or question it matters not, as far as the results are concerned, for as Dr. Schweitzer tells us:

"The historical foundation of Christianity, as rationalism, liberalism, and modern theology count it, exists no longer—which, however, is not to say that Christianity has therefore lost its historical foundation. The work which historical theology believed it must carry out, and which it sees falling to pieces at the very moment when completion was near, is only the terra cotta veneer of the true indestructible, historical foundation, which is independent of any historical knowledge and proof—simply because it is there, it exists.

"Jesus is something to our world because a mighty stream of spiritual influence has gone forth from Him and has penetrated our age also. This fact will be neither shaken nor confirmed by an historical knowledge."[6]

Always the Word has sounded out which has enabled the race to see and recognise its next step. The Christ enabled man to hear this in the past; He will enable man to do so again today. Some day, as all Masons know, these Words which have been spoken periodically will be superseded by a WORD which is known among them as the "Lost Word." When that Word is finally spoken humanity will be enabled to climb to the final peak of human achievement. The hidden divinity will then shine forth in its glory, through the medium of the race. The height of material achievement has perhaps been reached. Now comes the opportunity for that subtle divine Self to manifest through the agency of the experience which we call the "new birth,"

[5] *St. John,* I, 1, 2, 3, 4, 10.
[6] *The Mystery of the Kingdom of God,* by Albert Schweitzer, pp. 28, 29.

and which Christianity has ever taught. The effect of all that is now transpiring upon earth is to bring to the surface that which is hidden within the human heart, and to unveil to our eyes the new vision. Then we can pass through the gateway of the New Age into a world which will be characterised by newer awareness, a deeper understanding of the vital realities, and a truer and higher standard of values. The Word must again sound forth from the centre—the Centre in the Heavens, and the centre in every human heart. Each individual soul must hear it for itself alone. Each of us has to pass through that experience wherein we know ourselves to be a "Word made Flesh," and until the Bethlehem experience is a part of our individual consciousness as souls, it remains a myth. It can become a fact—the major fact in the experience of the soul.

I cannot here enter into a definition of the word "soul." An extract from a book by Dr. Bosanquet expresses the idea in terms which link it up with individual experience, and yet preserve the cosmic implications in their beauty. An isolated soul is an impossibility. He says:

"The Soul—I use the term in the most general sense to mean the centre of experience which as a microcosm has acquired or is acquiring a character of its own and a relative persistence—the soul is not to be contrasted as a detached agent either with its constituent externality on the one hand or with the life of the absolute on the other. Our idea has been throughout . . . that *the soul is a range of externality 'come alive' by centring in mind.* And when we speak of the soul as a will creatively moulding circumstance, this is another expression for the microcosm, including the centre which its circumstances stand around, remoulding and reshaping itself. It is, on the other hand, a thread or fibre of the absolute life, . . . a stream or tide within it of varying breadth, intensity, and separateness from the great flood within which it moves."[7] [The italics are mine. A. A. B.]

What this soul is, when unveiled and manifested (even through the limitations of the flesh), Christ made clear to us.

[7] *The Value and Destiny of the Individual,* by B. Bosanquet, p. 129.

The partial in us is complete in Him, a fact in full expression. He has linked us to Himself through His perfected humanity; He has linked us to God through His expressed divinity.

Two thoughts must therefore be borne in mind by all of us at this time if we are not to be submerged in the apparent world chaos and thus lose our perspective. One is that *each age provides its way out.* This, Christ meant when He said, "I am the way, the truth and the life."[8] He knew that He synthesised in Himself the soul of the past and the spirit of the future. And what is true of Him is true also of the teaching He gave. In Christianity the past is comprised and its best religious elements are included.

The soul of man stands at the gates of revelation, and he must learn that this revelation will come through himself perfected. Browning expressed this in the well-known lines:

> "Thus he dwells in all
> From life's minute beginnings, up at last
> To man—the consummation of this scheme
> Of being, the completion of this sphere
> Of life: whose attributes had here and there
> Been scattered o'er the visible world before,
> Asking to be combined, dim fragments meant
> To be united in some wonderous whole,
> Imperfect qualities throughout creation,
> Suggesting some one creature yet to make,
> Some point where all those scattered rays should meet
> Convergent in the faculties of man.
>
> . . . .
>
> When all the race is perfected alike
> As man, that is; all tended to mankind,
> And, man produced, all has its end thus far:
> But in completed man begins anew
> A tendency to God. Prognostics told
> Man's near approach; so in man's self arise
> August anticipations, symbols, types

[8] *St. John*, XIV, 6.

Of a dim splendour ever on before
In that eternal circle life pursues.
For men begin to pass their nature's bound,
And find new hopes and cares which fast supplant
Their proper joys and griefs; they grow too great
For narrow creeds of right and wrong, which fade
Before the unmeasured thirst for good: while peace
Rises within them ever more and more.
Such men are even now upon the earth,
Serene amid the half-formed creatures round
Who should be saved by them and joined with them."[9]

Man the human being, a soul in incarnation, is on the verge of taking that step forward which will bring about that first of the great unfoldments which we call "the new birth." Once that has been undergone, the life of the infant Christ will increase, and the momentum set up will carry him forward along that Way which leads from one high peak of attainment to another, until he himself becomes an illumined Light-bearer, and one who can light the way for others. The illuminati have ever led the race forward; the knowers, mystics and saints have ever revealed to us the heights of racial and individual possibility.

The Way from the Birth at Bethlehem to the Crucifixion Mount is a hard and a difficult one, but it is trodden with joy by the Christ and by those whose consciousness has been attuned to His. The joy of physical life is changed into the joy of understanding, and new values, new desires and a new love replace the old.

The Birth at Bethlehem marked the beginning of the long way of tragedy of the Saviour. It made Him "a man of sorrows, and acquainted with grief."[10] It was the beginning of the end, and marked His initiation into higher states of consciousness. This is apparent in the Gospel story.

[9] *Paracelsus*, by Robert Browning.
[10] *Isaiah*, LIII, 3.

2

Before we take up a definite consideration of these great initiations, it might be of value to touch upon one or two points in connection with the subject as a whole. So much peculiar and unsound teaching on the matter is being given out at this time, and so wide is the general interest, that a measure of clear thinking is badly needed, and attention should be called to certain factors which are frequently overlooked. It might be asked at this point, "Who is the initiator? Who is eligible to stand before Him and to pass through an initiation?"

It cannot be too clearly emphasised that the first initiator with whom a man has to deal is, ever and always, his own soul. Many esoteric schools and teachers direct their teaching and their aspirants towards some great Master Who is supposed to prepare them for this step, and without Whom no progress is possible. They forget that it is not possible for such a Master even to contact a man in this relationship until he has made a clear and definite contact with his own soul. It is on the level of awareness which is that of the soul itself that those who can help are to be found, and until we have, as individuals, penetrated into that state, it is not possible for us to be brought into intelligent touch with those who normally function there. Initiation relates to consciousness and is merely a word which we use to express the transition which man can make out of the consciousness of the fourth or human kingdom, into the fifth or spiritual kingdom, the kingdom of God. Christ came to reveal the way into that kingdom.

This initiating soul, as we have already seen, is called by many names in the New Testament, and in the other religions it is called by a terminology suited to the time and temperament of the aspirant. Where the Christian disciple speaks of "Christ in you, the hope of glory,"[11] the Oriental disciple may speak of the Self or the Atman. The modern

[11] *Col.*, I, 27.

schools of thought speak of the ego, or the higher self, the real man, or the spiritual entity, whilst in the Old Testament reference is made to the "Angel of the Presence." A long list of these synonyms could be compiled, but for our purpose we shall confine ourselves to the word "soul" because of its wide use in the West.

The immortal soul in man prepares him for the first initiation, for it is this soul which manifests upon earth as the "infant Christ" and appears in man. This is the new birth. That which has been slowly gestating in man comes at last to birth, and the Christ, or soul, is born consciously. *Always* the germ of the living Christ has been present, though hidden, in every human being. But in due time and season the infant soul makes its appearance, and the first of the five initiations is made possible. The work proceeds, and the Christ-life unfolds and develops in the man until the second and third initiations take place. At that time, as many believe, we are initiated through the instrumentality of the Christ, and in full waking consciousness the initiate stands in His Presence and sees Him face to face. Browning expresses this truth in the great poem *Saul* when he says:

"Oh, Saul, it shall be
A Face like my face that receives thee; a Man like to me
Thou shalt love and be loved by, for ever: A Hand like this hand
Shall throw open the gates of new life to thee!
See the Christ stand!"

After the third initiation, the Transfiguration, when the personality has been subordinated to the soul, or the indwelling Christ, and the glory of the Lord can shine forth through the medium of the flesh, we are faced with the supreme achievement of the Crucifixion and the Resurrection. Then, we are told, that mysterious Being, spoken of in the Old Testament as Melchizedek, and as the Ancient of Days, will play His part and initiate us into the still higher mysteries. Of Him we are told that:

"This Melchizedek, King of Salem, Priest of the Most High God

. . . was, in the first place, as His Name means, King of Righteousness, and besides that, King of Salem (that is King of Peace). Being without father or mother or ancestry, having neither beginning of days nor end of life . . . He remains a priest in perpetuity."[12]

He is the One Who receives the initiate and superintends the higher transitions of consciousness which are the reward of the tests triumphantly undergone. He is the One Whose "star shines forth" when the initiate enters into light.

There are therefore three initiators: first, a man's own soul, then the Christ of history, and finally the Ancient of Days, the one in Whom "we live, and move, and have our Being."[13] These ideas are interesting when we realise that out of the five initiations there are three which seem, and naturally so, to be of supreme importance. In the life of Christ there are episodes which represent great points of attainment, all climaxing cycles and initiating new ones. These are the first initiation, the Birth; the third initiation, the Transfiguration; and the fifth, the Resurrection. There is in nature some mysterious value which is connected with the first, the third, and the fifth—the beginning, the middle point and the climaxing consummation. As has been pointed out, "it is the intervals, not only between the base note, the major third and the perfect fifth, or those which distinguish the quaver from the semi-quaver, which enable us to build up a symphony or song." Between these high points, in the intervals of which the details are given us in the Gospel story, the work is carried on which makes the later achievements possible. We are primarily considering in this book the technique of the entrance into the kingdom of God. That kingdom exists, and birth into it is as inescapable as birth into the human family. The process is a sequential proceeding from gestation until, in "the fulness of time," the Christ Child is born; the soul begins to manifest on earth, and the life of the disciple and initiate begins. He passes from stage

[12] *Hebrews,* VII, 1-4, Weymouth Translation.
[13] *Acts,* XVII, 28.

to stage until he has mastered all the laws of the spiritual kingdom. Through birth, service and sacrifice the initiate becomes a citizen of that kingdom, and this is as much a natural process connected with his inner life as are the physical processes in their connection with his outer life as a human being. These two go on together, but the inner reality eventually comes into manifestation through the sacrifice of the human to the divine.

The initiate is not simply a good man. The world is full of good men who are probably a long way from being initiates. Neither is the initiate a well-meaning devotee. He is a man who has added a sound intellectual understanding to the basic qualifications of a sound moral character and devotion. Through discipline he has co-ordinated his lower nature, the personality, so that it is a "vessel meet for the master's use,"[14] that master being his own soul. He knows that he walks in a world of illusion, but is training himself whilst doing this to walk in the light of the soul, realising that in service to his fellowmen and in forgetfulness of self he prepares himself to stand before the portal of Initiation. Upon that path he meets those who, like himself, are learning to be citizens of the kingdom.

This has been the knowledge and the message of all true Christians down the centuries, and their united testimony bears witness to the reality of the kingdom, to the fact that those who seek it truly can find it, and that those who make enquiry as to its existence shall not be disappointed. The way into the kingdom is found by questioning and answering, by seeking and finding, and by the obedience to that inner voice which can be heard when all other voices are stilled.

When that voice is heard we come to a consciousness of the possibilities ahead and take the initial step towards that first initiation which leads to Bethlehem, there to find and meet with Christ. Within ourselves we find God. In the cave of the heart the divine life can be felt throbbing. Man discovers himself to be one of a vast number who have undergone the

[14] *II Timothy*, II, 21.

same experience, and through the process of initiation he gives birth to the Christ. The "infant life," newborn into the kingdom of God, starts on the struggle and the experience which will lead him step by step from one initiation to another till he too has attained. Then he also becomes a teacher and an expression of divinity, and follows in the footsteps of the Saviour, serving the race, sounding the needed note, and helping others to reach the point he has reached. The path of service and co-operation with the divine will become the purpose of his life.

Not all initiates can reach the altitude which Christ reached. His was a unique and cosmic mission. But experience of each stage of illumination, as portrayed in the Gospel story, is possible to the disciples of the world. Therefore, in summing up these ideas concerning the new birth into the kingdom, which at this time faces so many, it must be borne in mind that:

"At the first great Initiation the Christ is born in the disciple. It is then that he realizes for the first time *in himself* the outpouring of the divine Love, and experiences that marvellous change which makes him feel himself to be one with all that lives. This is the 'Second Birth,' and at that birth the heavenly ones rejoice, for he is born into 'the kingdom of heaven,' as one of the 'little ones,' as a 'little child,'—the names ever given to the new Initiates. Such is the meaning of the words of Jesus, that a man must become a little child to enter into the Kingdom."[15]

The same writer points out in another place that:

"The 'second birth' is another well-recognised term for Initiation; even now in India the higher castes are called 'twice-born,' and the ceremony that makes them twice-born is a ceremony of Initiation—mere husk truly, in these modern days, but the 'pattern of things in the heavens.'[16] When Jesus is speaking to Nicodemus he states that 'Except a man be born again, he cannot see the kingdom of God,' and this birth is spoken of as that 'of water and the Spirit,'[17] this is the first Initiation; a later one is that 'of the Holy

[15] *Esoteric Christianity,* by Annie Besant, pp. 185, 286, 53, 54.
[16] *Hebrews,* IX, 23.
[17] *St. John,* III, 3.5.

Ghost and fire,'[18] the baptism of the Initiate in his manhood, as the first is that of birth, which welcomes him as the 'Little Child' entering the kingdom.[19] How thoroughly this imagery was familiar among the mystics of the Jews is shown by the surprise evinced by Jesus when Nicodemus stumbled over His mystic phraseology: 'Art thou a master of Israel, and knowest not these things?' "[20]

Facing these possible heights of attainment stand the disciples of the world at this time. Here also stands the weary world disciple, humanity as a whole, worn and distraught, bewildered and restless, yet conscious of divine potentialities and great dreams, visions and ideals which evoke a hope and a refusal to be defeated and are the guarantee of eventual success. The voice of all the world Saviours and the example of the Christ indicate to humanity the Way that must be trodden. This leads away from the superficial and the material, from the world of unreality to the world of reality. "Man has had enough of a life cut off from its religious centre, and a quest for a new religious balance, a spiritual deepening will begin; in no order of his activity can he carry on any longer merely on the surface, a purely external life."[21] Deep calls unto deep, and from out the darkness of those depths, and through pain and suffering, the Christ child will emerge, and humanity as a whole will stand ready to make the great transition into the kingdom of God. Man can now pass on into the kingdom and commence making spiritual history. Up to the present, history has been preparatory. The race is only today, for the first time ready to take the great step on to the path of discipleship and of purification which precedes the path of initiation. Individuals have ever emerged out of the rank and file and lifted themselves to the pinnacles of attainment, and so climbed the mountain of initiation. But today this becomes possible for the many. The voice of those who have achieved, the clarion call of those who are

[18] *St. Matt.*, III, 11.
[19] *St. Matt.*, XVIII, 3.
[20] *St. John*, III, 10.
[21] *The End of Our Time*, by Nicholas Berdyaev, p. 59.

initiate in the mysteries of the kingdom of God, make the new step possible. The moment is unique and urgent. The call is to the individual but also, for the first time in history, it is sounded in the ears of the crowd, because the crowd is ready to respond.

Such is the situation now. The voices of these individuals who have entered into the kingdom call to the multitude today in no uncertain terms, and the issue is sure, though to some the initiating of humanity may seem a slow process. Old truths enunciated by the world Teachers and Saviours are in process of re-interpretation, to meet the ancient needs in new terms and in a more vital way. Those Leaders who mould the spirits of men are holding the doors wide open, and through them mankind will be obliged to pass, rapidly if it will listen, but inevitably, whether it now hears or no.

Our theme therefore gradually emerges in our consciousness. We can see that it must be approached from two major angles. We shall study these five initiations of Jesus from the angle, first of all, of the individual aspirant, so that it may become apparent that, as children of God, we can all participate in what the Christ went through. One of the interesting things which appear as we study the life of Christ and note how the divine Plan for that life was progressively registered in His consciousness, is that at first He only dimly sensed what He had to do. The ideas developed as He grew older. After the first initiation, the Birth at Bethlehem, His words to His mother were, "Wist ye not that I must be about my Father's business?"[22] He knew that He was ordained to work and to serve, but the specifications of that work were only later made clear to His mind. He simply recognised a Plan, and to that Plan He dedicated Himself. This must also be done by those who follow in His steps.

The second initiation, that of the Baptism, then took place. Christ had achieved manhood, and this attainment was followed immediately by a definite and conscious rejection of evil. Recognition of work to be done must be succeeded

[22] *St. Luke,* II, 49.

by the purification of the one who must thus work, and a demonstration must be given of that purification and freedom from evil. This, Christ gave in the victory of the three temptations. Then, only after this evidenced preparation, do we read that He proceeded to teach.[23]

Recognition and preparation for participation in the divine Plan was next followed by dedication to that Plan. After the Transfiguration He entered into a full realisation of what lay ahead for Him, and He defined it clearly to His disciples, saying:

". . . the Son of man must suffer many things, and be rejected of the elders and chief priests and scribes, and be slain, and be raised the third day. . . . If any man will come after me, let him deny himself, and take up his cross daily, and follow me."[24]

Then we read later in the same chapter that "He steadfastly set His face to go" up to the place of suffering and of sacrifice.

Finally came the realisation that He had accomplished what He had set out to do. He had fulfilled the Plan; the Father's business had been done and the "many things" undergone. We read that even on the Cross the Plan still engrossed His attention, and with His final "It is finished,"[25] He passed through the gates of death to a joyful resurrection.

The gradual revelation of the Plan and its service always accompanies the initiation process; the individual learns to subordinate his life to the Will of the Father, and to become —as Christ became—the servant of that Will. The initiation process itself is only a part of the general Plan for the race, and the paths of discipleship and of initiation are but the final stages of the Path of Evolution. The earlier steps on the Path are concerned with human living and experiencing, but the final stages, after the new birth, are concerned with spiritual unfoldment.

What is true of the unfoldment of the individual is true

[23] *St. Luke*, IV, 14, 15.
[24] *St. Luke*, IX, 22, 23.
[25] *St. John*, XIX, 30.

of the race; and all these stages must be worked out in the racial life. Those who see the vision clearly can trace the evidences of this unfolding Plan in the steady growth of several ideas that are now dominant in the world. Without going into detail or entering into lengthy expositions of the subject, the growth of the Plan and of the racial response can be traced quite clearly in the development of the God idea. First, God was a far-away, anthropomorphic Deity, unknown and unloved, but regarded with awe and fear, and worshipped as the Deity expressing Himself through the forces of nature. As time elapsed, this distant God drew a little nearer to His people, taking on a more human colouring until, in the Jewish dispensation, we find Him much like ourselves, but still the wrathful, ethical Ruler, and still obeyed and feared.

He approached still nearer as time went on; and before the advent of Christianity men recognised Him as the beloved Krishna of the Hindu faith, and as the Buddha. Then the Christ came to the West. God Himself was seen incarnate among men. The distant had become the near, and the One Who had been worshipped in awe and wonder could now be known and loved. Today God is coming closer still, and the new age will not only recognise the truth of the past revelations and testify to their validity and their progressive revelation of divinity, but to all this will be added the ultimate revelation of the Presence of God in the human heart, of Christ born in man, and of each human being manifesting, in truth, as a son of God.

In a consideration of the unfoldment of consciousness the same emerging divine Plan appears. Though the race in its infancy was governed by instinct, as time elapsed the intellect began to show itself and is continuing to control human affairs, government and thought. Out of the intellect, rightly used and understood, something fairer and still more revealing is being evolved, and steadily we can trace the growth of this new force, the intuition, in modern intelligent man. This, in its turn, brings illumination, and so man passes from glory to glory until the omniscient cosmic Son of God can be seen, expressing Himself through every son of man.

Again, the same unfoldment can be traced racially in the transition we have made through the various stages from that of the isolated savage to the family and the tribe, then to the unification of the tribes into nations under one central government, until today we live in a world which is beginning to respond to that which is greater than the nation—humanity itself—and to conceive its expression through the development of an international consciousness. No matter by what line we trace the growth of the Plan, we come from a distant, dark and ignorant past to a present point wherein truer values are seen emerging. We begin to see what that Plan is and whither we are going. We are entering steadily into the world of spiritual realities, because "there is a road from every natural group of facts to every spiritual reality in the universe; and the essential nature of mind forces it always in some degree to traverse this road. . . . "[26]

At this "end of the age" man stands before the door of opportunity, and, because he is in process of discovering his own divinity, he will enter into the realm of real values and arrive at a truer knowledge of God. The mystery of the new birth confronts him, and through that experience he must pass.

This divinity in man must be brought to the birth, both in the individual and in the race, and thus can the kingdom of God on earth be brought into being.

3

All of these five initiations have certain basic points in common, resemblances which in themselves are of real significance. There are factors which are germane to all of them. The Way into the kingdom is universal, and man himself is the symbol and the reality. He looks out at all

[26] *The Value and Destiny of the Individual*, by B. Bosanquet, p. 111.

the myths and symbols of the world; he reads and knows the story of the world Saviours; at the same time he himself has to re-enact the same story and make myth a fact in his own personal experience; he must know Christ; he must also follow Christ stage by stage through the great experiences of the initiatory process.

Every initiation is preceded by a journey; each stage and each dramatic happening comes at the end of a period of travel. The symbolism of this is apparent. "The treading of the Path" is a familiar way of describing the approach of a human being to the mysteries. It is interesting to note that today the whole world is on the move. Everybody is travelling and journeying—a process symbolic of an inner condition of search and movement towards a preordained goal. Travel by rail, by steamship and by airplane is today the lot of everyone. Groups of people in many countries are being transferred from place to place as economic conditions make possible and destiny dictates. We are journeying hither and thither. We are on our way, widening our horizons. We are also preparing for expansions of consciousness which will enable us to live in two realms at once—the life which must be lived on earth and the life which we can live in the kingdom of God. Humanity is on the first stage of its journey towards the mystic Bethlehem where the Christ child will be born, and the first initiation is, at this time, an imminent happening for many.

> "To every man there openeth
>   A way, and ways and a WAY.
>   And the high soul takes the high way
>   And the low soul gropes the low;
>   And in between, on the misty flats,
>   The rest drift to and fro,
>   But to every man there openeth
>   A high way and a low.
>   And every man decideth
>   The way his soul shall go."[27]

[27] John Oxenham.

Again, every initiation is marked by the enunciation of a Word of Power. The initiate hears it, though the rest of the world may not. When Christ passed through these crises, in every case a Voice sounded out, and the sound which went forth "opened anew the gates of life." Door after door is opened on the demand of the initiate and at the response by the Initiator, standing on the other side of the portal. We shall see what each Word signified. The Word always issues forth from the centre. Again and again in the New Testament we are told that "He that hath ears to hear, let him hear,"[28] and a study of the words spoken to the seven Churches in Revelations will bring much light upon the factor of the Word.

Great racial Words have been sounded forth and have brought about needed changes, and have signified a potency of true spiritual value to the sensitive.

The Word or sound for ancient Asia in the past was TAO, or the Way. It stood for that ancient Way which the Initiates of the far East trod and taught. For our race the sound is AUM, which has degenerated in our Occidental vernacular into AMEN. The ancient scriptures of India regard this Word as peculiarly the indication of divinity, of the spirit of life, the breath of God. What the new Word will be which will "come forth from the centre" we do not know, for it will not be heard until the race is ready. But there is a common Word of Power which will be given into the custody of our race if we measure up to our opportunity and, through the new birth, enter into the kingdom of God. It is this Word which will quicken into life the hidden soul of man and galvanise him into a renewed spiritual activity. As the race grows in sensitivity, as the aspirants of the world in all the many religions cultivate the ability (through meditation) to hear the Voice which can tune out all other voices, and as they learn to register the Sound which will obliterate all other sounds, they will, as a group, record the new Word which will issue forth.

[28] *St. Matt.*, XI, 15.

At each initiation of Jesus, as we shall see, a Sign was given; it was a Sign which registered upon the consciousness of those who were not initiate. Each time, a symbol or form was seen which was indicative of the revelation. Christ Himself tells us that at the end of the age the sign of the Son of Man will be seen in the Heavens.[29] Just as the Birth at Bethlehem was ushered in by a Sign, that of the Star, so shall that birth towards which the race is hastening be likewise ushered in by a heavenly Sign. The appeal which goes up from the hearts of all true aspirants to initiation is beautifully embodied in the following prayer:

"There is a peace that passeth understanding; it abides in the hearts of those who live in the Eternal. There is a power which maketh all things new. It lives and moves in those who know the Self as One. May that peace brood over us; that power uplift us, till we stand where the One Initiator is invoked, till we see His star shine forth."

When that Sign is seen and the Word is heard, the next step will be the recording of the Vision. The Plan and the part to be played by the initiate are shown to him, and he knows what he has to do. This Vision is spoken of as "the vision of God," but it is expressed to man in terms of God's will and the completeness of that which God intends. We are intended to be initiate into the mystery of that will. The vision of God is the vision of God's Plan. No man has seen God at any time. The revelation of God comes through the revelation of Christ.

"Philip saith unto him, Lord, shew us the Father, and it sufficeth us.

"Jesus saith unto him, Have I been so long time with you, and yet hast thou not known me, Philip? he that hath seen me hath seen the Father."[30]

Christ revealed in Himself the will of God and gave to humanity a vision of God's Plan for the world, this Plan

[29] *St. Matt.*, XXIV, 30.
[30] *St. John*, XIV, 8, 9.

being the coming of the kingdom. He was God, and the word of God went forth from Him.

Man lives by the incarnation of God in himself. By passing through the gate of the new birth, he can redeem the flesh in which that divinity is encased, and can then help in the redemption of the world. For the race, too, there is the crisis, the initiation and the vision. "Where there is no vision, the people perish."[31] But that vision is never of the whole Plan. It is not of the ultimate experience nor of the unfathomable consummation. For that we are not as yet prepared. Christ Himself did not proclaim the final revelation. He saw and proclaimed the next step for the race. The events immediately ahead are sensed, to be later intelligently considered; there is a moment of prevision, a foretelling of movement and activity, of difficulty and service, and of the next unfolding glory.

Following the vision, as that followed initiation, comes a renewed cycle of test and of difficulty. The truths revealed and the revelation accorded have to be worked out in the experience of daily life. Moments of assimilation and reflection must succeed the periods of exaltation and of vision. Unless there is a practical experience of that which is known, it remains upon the mountain top of revelation.

Finally, every initiation leads to expanded service. Practical spiritual living must follow the moments on the mountain top. Self and its attainment must be forgotten in service to others. From this there is no escape. Every pinnacle of achievement is followed by a cycle of testing. Every new revelation grasped and appropriated has to be adapted to the needs of a consequent and strenuous life of service, and initiation ever calls forth renewed testing and enhanced power to serve.

4

"And so it was, that, while they were there, the days were accomplished that she should be delivered. And she brought forth

[31] *Prov.*, XXIX, 18.

her firstborn son, and wrapped him in swaddling clothes and laid him in a manger; because there was no room for them in the inn."[32]

In these simple words the momentous story begins—a story of such far-reaching consequences that only today are we beginning to register the results. Only today, two thousand years after the event, is the lesson of Christ's life taking formative effect in the imaginations of men; only today is the unique lesson which He came to teach producing the needed changes in the capacity of men to apprehend. Only now are we becoming aware that the historical evidence of His arrival on earth *is history itself,* and that there is in the world the evidence of two great streams of endeavour or of activity—that which is the stream of the common, separative, unfolding consciousness of man, and that which is the steady application of the message of Christ to current affairs, modifying them, changing them and determining—far more than we can realise—the way that we should go. Christ came in the fulness of time, just as humanity was approaching maturity, and showed us, in Himself and through His life, what a man could be and was.

The Son of God is also the Son of Man! This fact has, perhaps, been forgotten in the emphasis laid upon His divinity. That divinity is there, and nothing can touch or hide it; it is radiance and pure white light. But the manhood is there also, a guarantee to us of our opportunity and of our potentialities, an endorsement of our faith. In the magnetic power, breathed out through the words of the Beloved Apostle as he portrayed Christ as the Son of God Who speaks divinely, we have fallen down in love and adoration before that divinity. But His manhood is emphasised by St. Luke and St. Matthew, just as His life as the Great Server was emphasised by St. Mark. We have fought over the divinity of Christ. Had there been no Gospel but the Gospel of St.

[32] *St. Luke,* II, 6, 7.

John, only His divinity would have been known to us. Christ as man, and what He did and was *as man,* is not considered by this writer.

Any modern writer, when responsible for a biography of the Christ, would come under most serious criticism (from the theologians and the orthodox) had he omitted these important points. But evidently, in the opinion of the apostle, they were not of paramount importance. It was the Spirit of Christ that was vital and necessary. The other three apostles supplied the setting and the detail, and apparently did much to bring that detail into conformity with the teaching of the past, as to the environment and lives of the past world-teachers and saviours, for there is a curious identity in events and occurrences.

We have fought over the detail connected with the phenomenal appearing of Christ, and have overlooked the emphasis laid in three of the initiations upon His words and their meaning. We have taken our stand upon the physical happenings of His life and have struggled to prove the authentic historicity of those physical events, and all the time God Himself speaks, "Hear ye Him."

Another point which is frequently forgotten is that, in so coming to earth and taking human incarnation, God testified to His faith in the divinity which is in man. God had sufficient confidence in men and in their reaction to world conditions so that He gave His Son to demonstrate the possibility to man and thus save the world. In this He gave expression to His belief, and His conduct was dictated by that belief. In reverence I would like to say that *man's divinity warranted an expression of divinity.* So God acted. Dean Inge, when writing upon the works of Plotinus, says very appositely that "the conduct of life rests on an act of faith which begins with an experiment and ends with an experience." These words are true of God and of man. God had such faith in man's innate spirituality—and what is spirituality but the expression, in form, of divinity?—that He ventured on a great experiment which has led into the Christian experience. Faith in Christ! Faith in humanity! Faith in man's responsiveness to the experiment! Faith that the vision given will be transmuted or developed into experience! Such was the faith of God in humanity. The Christian faith, in spite of dogma and doctrine, and in spite of the distortions of the academic theologian and the impositions of a few unintelligent churchmen, has brought together God and man, blended in the Christ, and so presented the truth that each human being can also have faith to venture the experiment and undergo the experience. This vital, dramatic, mystically pictured yet living truth, when grasped by the mind and understood by the heart, will enable each aspirant to the Christian Mysteries to pass through the gateway of the new Birth into light, and walk thenceforth increasingly in that light, for "the path of the just is as the shining light, that shineth more and more unto the perfect day."[33] This truth is still a living truth and enriches and colours all our faith.

In this continuity (which is the basis of our faith in the love of God) there have been, as we have seen, many Words sent forth from the Centre. Many Sons of God, down the ages, have given to humanity a progressively revealing vision of the "heights of possibility," interpreting God's Plan to the race in terms suited to each age and temperament. The uniformity of their life story, the appearance again and again of the Virgin Mother (whose name is frequently a variation of the name Mary), the similarity in detail of the birth story, all indicate to us the constant re-enactment of a truth, so that from its dramatic quality and its repeated happening, God impresses upon the hearts of men certain great truths which are vital to their salvation.

One of these truths is that the love of God is eternal, and that His love for His people has been steadfast and unalterable. Whenever the time is ripe and the need of the people warrants it, He comes forth for the saving of the souls of men.

[33] *Prov.*, IV, 18.

Krishna in ancient India proclaimed this truth in the majestic words:

"Whenever there is a withering of the law . . . and an uprising of lawlessness on all sides, then I manifest Myself.

"For the salvation of the righteous and the destruction of such as do evil; for the firm establishing of the law I come to birth in age after age.

"He who thus perceives My birth and work as divine, as in truth it is . . . he goes to Me, Arjuna."[34]

Again and again such teachers have come forth, manifested as much of the divine nature as the racial development warranted, spoken those words which determined the culture and the civilisation of the peoples, and then passed on their way, leaving the seed sown, to germinate and bear fruit. In the fulness of time Christ came and, if evolution means anything at all and if the race as a whole has developed and unfolded its consciousness, the message He gave and the life He lived must necessarily sum up all the best in the past, completing and fulfilling it, and proclaim a possible future spiritual culture which will greatly transcend all that the past may have given.

The majority of these great Sons of God were, curiously enough, born in a cave and usually of a virgin mother.

"In regard to the Virgin Birth it is significant that there is no reference to it in the Epistles which form the earliest Christian documents; but, on the contrary, St. Paul speaks of Jesus as 'made of the seed of David according to the flesh'[35] that is to say, of the seed of Joseph, David's descendant. The earliest Gospel, that of St. Mark, dating between A.D. 70 and 100, does not mention it; nor does the Gospel of St. John, dating from some time not earlier than A.D. 100. The Book of Revelation, written between A.D. 69 and 93, is silent on the subject, though had the Virgin Birth then been an important tenet of the faith it would undoubtedly have figured in the mystical symbolism of that composition."[36]

[34] *The Bhagavad Gita,* Translation of Charles Johnston, IV, 7, 8.
[35] *Romans,* I, 3.
[36] *The Paganism in Our Christianity,* by Arthur Weigall, p. 42.

Isis was often represented standing on the crescent moon, with twelve stars surrounding her head. In almost every Roman Catholic church on the continent of Europe may be seen pictures and statues of Mary, the "Queen of Heaven," standing on the crescent moon, her head surrounded with twelve stars.

"It would seem more than a chance that so many of the virgin mothers and goddesses of antiquity should have the same name. The mother of *Bacchus* was Myrrha; the mother of Mercury or Hermes was Myrrha or Maia; the mother of the Siamese Saviour —Sommona Cadom was called Maya Maria, i.e. 'the Great Mary'; the mother of Adonis was Myrrha; the mother of Buddha was Maya; now, all these names whether Myrrha, Maia or Maria, are the same as Mary, the name of the mother of the Christian Saviour. The month of May was sacred to these goddesses, so likewise is it sacred to the Virgin Mary at the present day. *She* was also called Myrrha and Maria, as well as Mary. . . ."[37]

In the symbolic language of esotericism, a cave is regarded as the place of initiation. This has always been so, and a very interesting study of the initiatory process and of the new birth could be made if the many references in the ancient writings to these events which have transpired in caves were collected and analysed. The stable in which Jesus was born was in all likelihood a cave, for many stables were, in those days, hollowed out of the ground. This was recognised by the early Church, and we are told that "it is well known that whereas in the Gospels Jesus is said to have been born in an inn stable, early Christian writers, as Justin Martyr and Origen, explicitly say He was born in a cave."[38]

In studying these five initiations of the Gospel story, we find that two of them took place in a cave, two on a mountain top and one on the level between the deeps and the heights. The first and last initiations (the Birth into life and the Resurrection into "life more abundantly"[39]) took place in

[37] *Bible Myths*, by T. W. Doane, p. 332.
[38] *Pagan Christ*, by J. M. Robertson, p. 338.
[39] *St. John*, X, 10.

a cave. The Transfiguration and the Crucifixion were enacted on the summit of a mountain or hill, whilst the second
initiation, after which Christ entered upon His public minis-
try, took place in a river, in the plains around Jordan—symbolic perhaps of Christ's mission to live and work down
amongst men. The Masonic phrase to "meet on the level"
takes on here an added significance. After each mountain
experience, the Christ came down again on to the level of
daily life and there manifested the effects or results of that
high event.

Mithras was born in a cave, and so were many others.
Christ was born in a cave and entered, as did all the others,
upon a life of service and of sacrifice, thus qualifying for the
task of world Saviour. They brought light and revelation
to mankind and were sacrificed, in the majority of cases, to
the hatred of those who did not understand their message,
or who objected to their methods. All of them "descended
into hell and rose again on the third day." There are twenty
or thirty of these stories scattered through the centuries of
human history, and the stories and the missions are ever
identical.

"The Jesus-story, it will now be seen, has a greater number of
correspondences with the stories of former Sungods and with the
actual career of the Sun through the heavens—so many indeed
that they cannot well be attributed to mere coincidence or even to
the blasphemous wiles of the Devil! Let us enumerate some of
these. There are (1) birth from a Virgin mother; (2) the birth
in a stable (cave or underground chamber); and (3) on the 25th
December (just after the winter solstice). There is (4) the Star
in the East (Sirius) and (5) the arrival of the Magi (the 'Three
Kings'); there is (6) the threatened Massacre of the Innocents,
and the consequent flight into a distant country (told also of
Krishna and other Sungods). There are the Church festivals of
(7) Candlemas (2nd February), with processions of candles to
symbolise the growing light; of (8) Lent, or the arrival of Spring;
of (9) Easter Day (normally on 25th March) to celebrate the cross-
ing of the Equator by the Sun; and (10) simultaneously the out-
burst of lights at the Holy Sepulchre at Jerusalem. There is (11)

the Crucifixion and death of the Lamb-God, on Good Friday, three
days before Easter; there are (12) the nailing to a tree, (13) the
empty grave, (14) the glad Resurrection (as in the cases of Osiris,
Attis and others); there are (15) the twelve disciples (the Zodiacal signs); and (16) the betrayal by one of the twelve. Then later
there is (17) Mid-summer Day, the 24th June, dedicated to the
birth of the beloved disciple John, and corresponding to Christmas
Day; there are the festivals of (18) the Assumption of the Virgin
(15th August) and of (19) the Nativity of the Virgin (8th September), corresponding to the movement of the god through Virgo;
there is the conflict of Christ and his disciples with the autumnal
asterisms, (20) the Serpent and the Scorpion; and finally there is
the curious fact that the Church (21) dedicates the very day of
the winter solstice (when any one may very naturally doubt the
re-birth of the Sun) to St. Thomas, who doubted the truth of
the Resurrection!"[40]

Any student of comparative religion can investigate the
truth of these statements, and at the end will stand amazed
at the persistence of God's love and the willingness to sacrifice Themselves which all these Sons of God manifest.

It is therefore wise and timely to remember that:

"These events are reproduced in the lives of the various Solar
Gods, and antiquity teems with illustrations of them. Isis of Egypt,
like Mary of Bethlehem, was our Immaculate Lady, Star of the
Sea, Queen of Heaven, Mother of God. We see her, in pictures,
standing on the crescent moon, star-crowned, she nurses her child
Horus, and the cross appears on the back of the seat in which he
sits on his mother's knee. The Virgo of the zodiac is represented
in ancient drawings as a woman suckling a child—the type of all
future Madonnas with their divine Babes, showing the origin of
the symbol. Devaki is likewise figured with the divine Krishna in
her arms, as is Mylitta, or Istar, of Babylon, also with the recurrent
crown of stars, and with her child Tammuz on her knee. Mercury
and Aesculapius, Bacchus and Hercules, Perseus and the Dioscuri,
Mithras and Zarathustra were all of divine and human birth."[41]

It is apposite to recall that the cathedral of *Notre Dame*

[40] *Pagan and Christian Creeds,* by Edward Carpenter, p. 50.
[41] *Esoteric Christianity,* by Annie Besant, p. 158.

in Paris is built upon the ancient site of a Temple of Isis, and that the early Church very frequently availed itself of a so-called heathen opportunity to determine a Christian rite or a day of sacred remembrance. Even the establishing of Christmas Day on December 25th was so determined. The same writer quoted above tells us that:

"On the fixing of the 25th December as the birthday of Jesus, Williamson has the following: 'All Christians know that the 25th December is *now* the recognised festival of the birth of Jesus, but few are aware that this has not always been so. There have been, it is said, one hundred and thirty-six different dates fixed on by different Christian sects. Lightfoot gives it as September 15th, others as in February or August. Epiphanius mentions two sects, one celebrating in June, the other in July. The matter was finally settled by Pope Julius in 337 A.D., and St. Chrysostom, writing in 390, says: 'On this day (i.e. 25th December) also the birth of Christ was lately fixed at Rome, in order that while the heathen were busy with their ceremonies (the Brumalia, in honour of Bacchus) the Christians might perform their rites undisturbed.' "[42]

The choice of this particular date is cosmic in its implications, and not unwittingly, we can be sure, did the wise men of earlier times make these momentous decisions. Annie Besant tells us that:

"He is always born at the winter solstice, after the shortest day in the year, at the midnight of the 24th December when the sign Virgo is rising above the horizon; born as this Sign is rising, he is born always of a virgin, and she remains a virgin after she has given birth to her Sun-child as the celestial Virgo remains unchanged and unsullied when the Sun comes forth from her in the Heavens. Weak, feeble as an infant is he, born when the days are shortest and the nights are longest. . . ."[43]

It is also interesting to remember that:

"The Venerable Bede,[44] writing in the early part of the Eighth

[42] *Esoteric Christianity,* by Annie Besant, p. 160.
[43] *Ibid.,* p. 157.
[44] Bede, *De Temp. rat.,* xiii.

Century, says that 'the ancient people of the Anglian nation', by which he means the pagan English before their settlement in Britain about A.D. 500, 'began the year on December 25th, when we now celebrate the birthday of our Lord'; and he tells us that the night of December 24th-25th 'which is the very night now so holy to us was called in their tongue *Modranecht,* that is to say "Mother's Night," by reason of the ceremonies which in that night-long vigil they performed.' He does not mention what those ceremonies were, but it is clear that they were connected with the birth of the Sun-god. At the time when the English were converted to Christianity in the Sixth and Seventh Centuries the festival of the Nativity on December 25th had been already long established in Rome as a solemn celebration; but in England its identification with the joyous old pagan Yule—a word apparently meaning a 'jollification'—gave it a merry character which it did not possess in the south. This character has survived, and is in marked contrast to its nature amongst the Latin races, with whom the northern custom of feasting and giving Christmas presents was unknown until recent years."[45]

At the time of the birth of Christ, Sirius, the Star in the East, was on the meridian line, Orion, called "The Three Kings" by oriental astronomers, was in proximity; therefore the constellation Virgo, the Virgin, was rising in the east, and the line of the ecliptic, of the equator and of the horizon all met in that constellation. It is interesting also to note that the brightest and largest star in the constellation Virgo is called Spica; it is to be found in the "ear of corn" (sign of fertility) which the Virgin holds. Bethlehem means the "house of bread," and there is therefore an obvious connection between these two words. This constellation is also composed of three stars in the shape of a cup. This is the true Holy Grail, that which contains the life blood, the repository of the sacred and the holy, and that which conceals divinity. These are astronomical facts. The interpretation of the symbolism attached from ancient days to these constellations is as old as religion itself. Whence came the signs, and how the

[45] *The Paganism in Our Christianity,* by Arthur Weigall, pp. 236, 237.

meanings and symbols associated with them came into being, is lost in the night of time. They have existed in men's minds and thoughts and writings for thousands of years, and are our joint heritage today. The ancient zodiac of Dendera (ante-dating Christianity by several thousand years) is ample proof of this. In the sun's journey around the zodiac, this "Man of the Heavens" eventually arrives at Pisces; this sign is ex-actly opposite the sign Virgo, and is the sign of all world Saviours. We have already seen that the age of Christianity is the Piscean Age, and Christ came to the Holy Land when our sun transitted into that sign. Therefore that which was started and had its being in Virgo (the birth of the Christ Child) is consummated in Pisces when that Christ Child, having attained maturity, comes forth as the world Saviour.

One other astronomical fact is of interest in this connec-tion. Closely associated with the constellation Virgo, and to be found in the same section of the Heavens, are three other constellations, and in these three there is portrayed for us symbolically the story of the Child which shall be born, suffer and die and come again. There is the group of stars called Coma Berenice, the Woman with the Child. There is Cen-taurus, the Centaur, and Boötes, whose name in the Hebrew language means the "Coming One." First, the child born of the woman and that woman a virgin; then the centaur, ever the symbol of humanity in the ancient mythologies, for man is an animal, plus a god, and therefore a human being. Then He Who shall come looms over them all, overshadow-ing them, pointing to the fulfilment which shall come through birth and human incarnation. Truly the picture-book of the heavens holds eternal truth for those who have eyes to see and the intuition developed rightly to interpret. Prophecy is not confined to the Bible, but has ever been held before men's eyes in the vault of heaven.

Thus as "the heavens declare the glory of God, and the firmament sheweth His handiwork,"[46] we have the prophecy

[46] *Psalm* XIX, 1.

of that world event which took place when Christ was born in Bethlehem, the "house of bread," and Virgo rose above the horizon, whilst the Star in the East shone forth.

Christ came, then, to His Own flesh and blood because the world of men drew Him and the love of the Father impelled Him. He came to give to life a purpose and fulfilment, and to indicate to us the Way: He came to give us an example, so that we could be galvanised by the hope that "maketh not ashamed"[47] to "press toward the mark for the prize of our high calling."[48]

It should be noted here that the journey, preceding the birth, is also a part of the life-story of other teachers sent from God. For instance, we read:

"Among the thirty-two signs which were to be fulfilled by the mother of the expected Messiah (Buddha), the fifth sign was recorded to be, *'that she would be on a journey at the time of her child's birth.'* Therefore, 'that it might be fulfilled which was spoken by the prophets' the virgin Maya, in the tenth month after her heavenly conception, was on a journey to her father, when lo, the birth of the Messiah took place under a tree. One account says that 'she had alighted at an inn when Buddha was born.'

"The mother of Lao-tse, the Virgin-born Chinese sage, was away from home when her child was born. She stopped to rest under a tree, and there, like the virgin Maya, gave birth to her son."[49]

We are told in the Gospel story that the Virgin Mary, with her husband Joseph and bearing within herself the Christ Child, went up from Nazareth in Galilee to Bethlehem. Sometimes, through a study of the significances of the names we meet in the Bible and in tradition, we can throw much light on the episode itself and unveil some of its hidden meaning. In the study of the Bible story, I have used only the Bible itself and Cruden's *Concordance*. The interpretation of the names is taken from Cruden's *Concordance*.

[47] *Rom.*, V, 5.
[48] *Phil.*, III, 14.
[49] *Bible Myths*, by T. W. Doane, p. 5.

Therein we find that "Nazareth" means "that which is consecrated" or set apart. "Galilee" means the "turning of the wheel"—that wheel of life and of death which turns continuously, carrying us all with it and keeping us upon the "wheel of existence," as the Buddhists call it, until we have learnt life's lessons and have become "a vessel unto honour, sanctified, and meet for the Master's use."[50]

The long journey of existence lies behind the Christ, and He, with His Mother, journeys the last part of the way. Consecrated from past aeons to this very work of world salvage, He has first of all to submit Himself to the ordinary processes of birth and childhood. Christ came forth from Nazareth, the place of consecration, and went up to Bethlehem, the House of Bread, where in a peculiar way He Himself was to become the "Bread of Life"[51] to a hungry world. He was set apart, or set Himself apart (as do all awakened sons of God) for the work of redemption. He came to feed the hungry, and in this connection two verses in the Bible convey light upon His task and its preparation. Isaiah tells us that "Bread corn is bruised,"[52] and Christ Himself told us that "Except a corn of wheat fall into the ground and die, it abideth alone, but if it die, it bringeth forth much fruit."[53] This was the destiny awaiting Him when He came to the Birth in Bethlehem. Then He entered upon the career which eventually "bruised" Him and led Him to his death.

According to the concordance, the name Mary means "the exalted of the Lord." As one says these words, the famous picture, by Mulillo, of the Virgin, standing on the crescent moon and being gathered up into the clouds of Heaven, comes to mind. Such is the assumption of the Virgin into glory. There is another interesting point in connection with the constellation Virgo, upon which we might touch. Mary, the Virgin, in the symbolism of the ancient wisdom, stands

[50] *II Tim.*, II, 21.
[51] *St. John*, VI, 33, 35, 41, 58.
[52] *Isaiah*, XXVIII, 28.
[53] *St. John*, XII, 24.

for virgin matter, for the substance which nurtures and nourishes and hides within itself the Christ child, the Christ consciousness. In the last analysis, it is through form and matter that God stands revealed. That is the story of the divine incarnation. Matter, overshadowed by the Holy Ghost, the third Person of the Trinity, brings to the birth the second Aspect of the Trinity, in the Person of Christ—cosmic, mythical and individual.

Associated with the story-book of the heavens there are three constellations (besides the constellation Virgo) which are symbolised by women. There is Cassiopeia, the Woman Enthroned. This is the constellation which is the symbol of the stage in human life at which matter and form are dominant and triumphant; when the inner divine life is so deeply hidden that it shows no sign, and only the material nature controls and rules. Then there comes the later stage in the history of the race and of the individual, when we find Coma Berenice symbolically emerging—the Woman bearing the Christ Child is seen. Here matter begins to reveal its true function, which is to bring to the birth the Christ in every form. When the turning of the great wheel of life has played its part, then Mary can come out of Galilee, from Nazareth, and journey to Bethlehem, there to give birth to the Saviour. Finally there is Andromeda, the Woman chained, or matter brought into subservience to the soul. The Soul or the Christ now rules. First, matter dominant, enthroned and triumphant. Then matter, the custodian of hidden divinity, beauty and reality, ready to bring them to the birth. Finally, matter as the servant of that which has been born, the Christ. However, none of this is brought about unless the journey is made from Nazareth, the place of consecration, and from Galilee, the place of the daily round of life; and this is true, whether one is speaking of the cosmic Christ, hidden by the form of a solar system; of the mythic Christ, hidden in humanity down the ages; of the historical Christ, concealed within the form of Jesus; or of the individual Christ, hidden within the ordinary man. For always the routine is the same—the journey, the new birth, the experience of life, the service to be rendered, the death to be endured, and then the resurrection into more extended service.

Joseph's name means "he who shall add"; he was a builder, a carpenter, a worker in the building trade, one who adds stone to stone, or beam to beam. He is the symbol of the building-creative aspect of God the Father. In these three people, Joseph, the infant Jesus, and Mary, we have the divine Triplicity symbolised and represented, God the Father, God the Son and God the Holy Spirit, or Matter informed by Deity, and therefore typified for us in the Virgin Mary.

Today the masses are on a journey. Today the teaching of the Path and of the Way to God is engrossing the attention of the aspirants in the world. We are on the Path of return to the individual and to the racial Bethlehem. We are now on the point of entering the cave wherein the new birth can take place, and therefore one stage of life's long journey is nearly completed. This symbolism is truer, perhaps, than we care to think it is. The world problem today is *bread*, and our anxieties, our bewilderments, our wars and our struggles are based upon the economic problem of how to feed the peoples. Today the whole world is occupied with the Bethlehem idea, with bread. In this subtle implication there surely comes to us a guarantee that as He came before to the House of Bread so will He again fulfil His word and fulfil Himself and return. The cave, a place of darkness and of discomfort, was for Mary the place of pain and weariness. This cave or stable story of the New Testament is perhaps as full of symbolism as any to be found in the Bible. The long and trying journey ended in a dark cave. The long and weary journey of humanity has brought us today to just such a hard and uninviting place. The life of the individual disciple, prior to taking initiation and passing through the experience of the new birth, is ever one of the utmost difficulty and hardness. But in the dark, and through difficulty, Christ is to be found, the Christ life can flower forth, and we can stand face to face before Him as the Initiator. The blind poet,

George Macdonald, sensed this when he wrote the beautiful words which have brought comfort to so many:

"Challenge the darkness, whatsoe'er it be,
Sorrow's thick darkness or strange mystery
Of prayer or providence. Persist intent,
And thou shalt find love's veiled sacrament.
Some secret revelation, sweetness, light,
Waits to waylay the wrestler in the night.
In the thick darkness, at its very heart,
Christ meets, transfigured, souls He calls apart."

In this cave of initiation, all the four kingdoms of nature can be seen unmistakably symbolised for us. In the rocky structure of the cave, the mineral kingdom appears. The fodder and the hay, naturally there, symbolise the vegetable kingdom. The ox and the ass represent the animal nature, but they represent also far more than that. The ox stood for that form of worship which should have been passing off the earth at the time Christ came. There were still many to be found who worshipped the bull, which was the worship prevalent in the age when our sun was passing through the age of Taurus, the Bull, and which was preserved at that time in the mysteries of Mithras and of Egypt. The sign immediately preceding the Christian era was that of Aries, the Ram or Lamb, and this is symbolised for us in the sheepfolds which surrounded Bethlehem.

It is interesting also to bear in mind that asses are definitely associated with the story of Mary and her Child. Two asses are found mentioned in the Gospel story, one coming from the north and bearing Mary to Bethlehem, and the other taking her down into Egypt. These are symbols of the two constellations called the Northern Ass and the Southern Ass, which are in the neighbourhood of the constellation Virgo.

We find the human kingdom represented in Mary and Joseph, with the human unity plus the duality which are so essential to existence itself. In the newborn Babe divinity expresses itself.   Thus, in that little cave, the cosmos is represented.

When Christ was born in Bethlehem, a threefold Word sounded forth.   "Glory to God in the highest, and on earth peace, good will toward men."[54]   A triple Word was then given to us.   It was chanted by angels in the night to the shepherds tending their flocks in the fields surrounding the stable-cave where the infant Child lay.   A unique event had happened in the cosmos, and the hosts of heaven did honour to it.

This question of the earth's uniqueness has often troubled thinking people.   Can so infinitesimal an atom in space as our planet be indeed of such interest to God that He permitted this great experiment to be tried here?   Is the mystery of man and the significance of our purpose of such importance that nowhere else can it be paralleled?

Can anything really happen on this "ball of dust" of such vital import that it can warrant the angels in singing: "Glory to God in the highest, and on earth peace, good will toward men"?   We like to think that it can be so.   We dread the moment when our futility appears as we look upon the stars of heaven, realising that there are thousands of millions of universes and tens of thousands of millions of constellations! We are such specks in a great immensity.

Perhaps we are of more importance than we had guessed. Perhaps what happens to us in the realm of consciousness really does matter in the cosmic scheme.   We know that it does not much matter what happens to the body.   It is what happens in and through that body which counts.   Perhaps what happens in and through the body, which we call a planet, indwelt likewise by God, *is* of vital moment in the plans of God Himself.   This would give meaning to life; it is only when we apprehend meaning and appreciate it that we can understand the significance of the Word spoken at the birth of Christ.   Let us paraphrase the message of the angels.   It came from a group of beings and was spoken to

[54] *St. Luke,* II, 14.

a group of beings. It is therefore a world message, a message which still awaits response. *When the consciousness which is Christ's has been awakened in all men, then we shall have peace on earth and goodwill among men. When this has taken place, then will God be glorified.* The expression of our divinity will bring to an end the hatred rampant upon earth and break down all the separating walls which divide man from man, group from group, nation from nation, religion from religion. Where there is goodwill there must be peace; there must be organised activity and a recognition of the Plan of God, for that Plan is synthesis; that Plan is fusion; that Plan is unity and at-one-ment. Then Christ will be all in all, and God the Father will be glorified. This must be brought about by a living union with God through Christ —through the historical Christ Who revealed God, and through the individual Christ, hidden in every human heart, Who must be brought to birth. None of the Epistles in the New Testament make this so clear as the *Epistle to the Ephesians,* for there is given the picture of possibility in terms that leave no excuse for misinterpretation. This epistle is:

". . . penetrated through by that idea of a living union with Christ, and indwelling in Him. It is expressed in many metaphors. We are rooted in Him as the tree in the soil, which makes it firm and fruitful. We are built into Him as the strong foundations of the Temple are bedded in the living rock. We live in Him as the limbs in the body. . . . The indwelling, we say, is reciprocal. He is in us and we are in Him. He is in us as the source of our being; we are in Him as filled with His fulness. He is in us all-communicative; we are in Him all-receptive. He is in us as the sunlight in the else darkened chamber; we are in Him as the cold green log cast into the flaming furnace glows through and through with ruddy and transforming heat. He is in us as the sap in the veins of the tree; we are in Him as the branches."[55]

The realisation of this is needed today. Christ in God. God in Christ. Christ in you and Christ in me. This is

[55] *Sermons,* A. MacLaren, 3rd Series, pp. 71, 72.

what will bring into being that one religion which will be the religion of love, of peace on earth, of universal goodwill, of divine understanding, and of the deep recognition of God. Then His impress and His life can be seen everywhere, in everybody and everything. The divine "signature" (as Boehme calls it) will everywhere be recognised. The life of God is today agitating the minds of men and causing them to move towards the birth chamber. From there they will pass into a new world where higher ideals and deeper contacts and richer understandings will characterise humanity.

When Christ came, we read that those of vision who were prepared said, "We have seen his star in the East and are come to worship him."[56] This was the Sign given to the few who were ready, and who had made the necessary journey to Bethlehem. But another sign was seen by the many, and given by the angel of the Lord to the shepherds who were watching in the fields by night. "And this shall be a sign unto you, Ye shall find the babe, wrapped in swaddling clothes, lying in a manger."[57] Here was a sign given to those watching ones, two or three, who were ready to consecrate their all, who perceived the star of initiation flashing forth and hastened to the initiation chamber. The larger number, who were interested and watching, needed a more concrete and more easily interpreted sign and were sent to see the infant with his mother. Their attitude is expressed in the words, "Let us now go even unto Bethlehem and see this thing which is come to pass."[58] But the three who understood came to worship and to give.

When they saw this star shine forth, the three Kings undertook a journey and, laden with gifts, came to Bethlehem. They are symbols of those disciples in the world today who are ready to prepare themselves for the first initiation, to transmute their knowledge into wisdom, and to offer all that they have to the Christ within.

[56] *St. Matt.,* II, 2.
[57] *St. Luke,* II, 12.
[58] *Ibid.,* II, 15.

The gifts they brought teach us the specific type of discipline which must be undergone in order to present to the Christ, at the time of the new birth, gifts which will be symbolic of achievement. These three offered to the infant Jesus three presents—gold, frankincense and myrrh. Let us study for a minute the specific importance of these to the individual would-be initiate. We are told by the esotericists that man is a three-fold person in his human nature, and this truth is endorsed by the psychologists through their investigations and research. He is a physical living body, he is a sum total of emotional reactions, and he is also that mysterious something which we call a mind. These three parts of a man —physical, emotional and mental—have to be offered in sacrifice, worship and as a free gift to the "Christ within" before that Christ can demonstrate through the disciple and initiate as He wishes to do. Gold is a symbol of the material nature, which must be consecrated to the service of God and of man. Frankincense symbolises the emotional nature, with its aspirations, wishes and longing, and this aspiration must rise as incense to the feet of God. Incense is also a symbol of purification, of that burning which removes all dross and leaves only the essence for the blessing of God. Myrrh or bitterness relates to the mind. It is through the mind that we suffer as human beings, and the further the race progresses and the more the mind develops, the greater seems the capacity for suffering. But when suffering is seen in its true light and dedicated to divinity, it can be used as an instrument whereby we approach nearer to God. Then we can offer to God that rare and wonderful gift of a mind made wise through pain, and a heart made kind through distress and through difficulty surmounted.

As we study the meaning of these three gifts brought by the disciples of old to the infant Jesus, and as we see their meaning as it applies to our individual situation, it becomes equally apparent that today humanity, as a race, stands before the infant Jesus, in the House of Bread, at the end of a

long journey, and can now offer, if it so will, the gifts of
material life, of purification through the fires of adversity,
and of the suffering to which it has been subjected.   Humanity can journey from Galilee by way of Nazareth.   Gold, the
thing that today seems to be the very life-blood of the people,
must be consecrated to the Christ.   Frankincense, the dreams
and visions and aspirations of the multitude, so real and deep
that the nations everywhere are struggling for the expression
of these dreams—these too must be dedicated and offered to
the Christ, that He may be all in all.   And the pain and
suffering and agony of humanity, never before so acute as
now, must surely be laid at the feet of Christ.   We have
learnt much.   Let the meaning of it all penetrate into our
hearts and minds, and let the reason of the pain drive us to
offer it up as our ultimate gift to Christ.   Pain is ever the
accompaniment of birth.   Suffering is found within every
birth chamber.   The realisation of this awakens the deepest
and most constructive kind of optimism in the minds of those
who ponder upon world suffering and agony.   May it not indicate the birth pangs which precede the revelation of the
Christ?   When it is realised, then we can say with St Paul:

"For His sake I have suffered the loss of everything, and reckon
it all as mere refuse, in order that I may win Christ, and be
found in Him, not having a righteousness of my own, derived from
the Law, but that which arises from faith in Christ—the righteousness which comes from God through faith. . . . I do not say that
I have already gained this knowledge or already reached perfection. But I press on, striving to lay hold of that for which I was
also laid hold of by Christ Jesus. . . . But this one thing I do—
forgetting everything which is past and stretching forward to what
lies in front of me, with my eyes fixed on the goal, I push on to
secure the prize of God's heavenward call in Christ Jesus. Therefore let all of us who are mature believers cherish these thoughts;
and if in any respect you think differently, that also God will make
clear to you. But whatever be the point that we have already
reached, let us persevere in the same course."[59]

[59] *Phil.*, III, 8, 9, 12, 16, Weymouth Translation.

5

The account of Christ's childhood as given us in the Gospels is dismissed in a very few words. Only one episode is related, and that is the one in which Jesus, having reached the age of twelve years, was taken up by His Mother to the Temple of the Lord and there, for the first time, gave indication of His vocation, and evidenced the realisation that a mission was pre-ordained for Him. Prior to this, His parents had conformed to all the requirements of the Jewish ritual; they had also sojourned in Egypt. Of His time there, we are told nothing. All that we know is covered by the words:

"They returned into Galilee to their own city Nazareth. And the child grew, and waxed strong in spirit, filled with wisdom, and the grace of God was upon Him."[60]

Students would do well to remember that the number *twelve* is regarded by the esotericists of all faiths as signifying the number of completion; it recurs again and again in the various scriptures of the world. The following comments are of interest in this connection, showing as they do the significance of this number, and its relation to initiation:

"The accomplishment of the age of twelve years signifies a full period of evolution when an initiation was undergone by the Christsoul. This took place in the inner mind (the temple) and corresponded to an awakening of the logical and intuition sides of the soul. These are the father-mother principle, indicated by the presence of the parents."[61]

And again,

"This number (of the twelve disciples) is typified by many things in the Old Testament; by the 12 sons of Jacob, by the 12 princes of the Children of Israel; by the 12 running springs in Helim; by the 12 stones in Aaron's breastplate; by the 12 loaves of the shew-bred; by the 12 spies sent by Moses; by the 12 stones

[60] *St. Luke*, II, 39, 40.
[61] *Dictionary of the Sacred Language of all Scriptures and Myths,* by G. A. Gaskell, p. 773.

of which the altar was made; by the 12 stones taken out of Jordan; by the 12 oxen which bare the brazen sea. Also in the New Testament, by the 12 stars in the bride's crown, by the 12 foundations of Jerusalem which John saw, and her 12 gates."[62]

All these recurrences of twelve probably have their origin in the twelve signs of the zodiac, that imaginary belt in the heavens through which the sun appears to pass on its journey in the course of a year, and during its greater cycle of approximately 25,000 years.

Having completed the preparatory work, by His twelfth year Christ again underwent an intuitive experience, going up from Nazareth (the place of consecration) to the Temple, where that intuition led Him to a new realisation of His work. There is no sign that He knew in detail what that mission was; He went into no explanations to His Mother. He started to do the work that was the nearest duty, and to teach those whom He found in the Temple, astonishing them with His understanding and His answers. His mother, bewildered and distressed, called His attention to herself and to His father, but only received the calm answer, spoken with conviction, and so changing all life for her: "Wist ye not that I must be about my Father's business?"[63] That business, as it developed in His consciousness in the passing of the years, became far broader and wider in its all-embracing love than the average orthodox Church seems willing to admit.

The extent of this mission slowly dawned upon His young mind and He began, as all truly initiate sons of God must perforce do, to function as God's messenger as soon as the Vision was recognised, and in the place where He was. Having thus indicated His grasp of the future work, we read that "He went down with them (His parents), and came to Nazareth (the place of renewed consecration), and was subject unto them. . . . And Jesus increased in wisdom and stature, and in favour with God and man."[64]

[62] Bishop Rabanus Manrus, A.D. 857.
[63] *St. Luke,* II, 49.
[64] *St. Luke,* II, 51, 52.

Frequently in the Gospel story, we find the word "down" occurring. Christ went with His mother "down into Egypt"; He went "down to Nazareth"; and again and again He comes down from the mountain-top or from the place of solitude to do His duty among men. After the hidden experience in Egypt (for no account of this is given to us in the Bible), and after the revelation in the Temple and the acceptance of the task to be accomplished, Christ returns to the place of duty. In this case, and after the Birth initiation, for a period of thirty years, we are told, He functioned as a man in the daily life of the carpenter's shop and in the home with His parents. This home life constituted the test to which He was subjected, and its importance cannot be overrated. Does it sound blasphemous to say that had He failed in this immediate duty, the rest of His work would have been abortive? If He had not succeeded in demonstrating divinity in the home circle and in the little town where His lot was cast, is it not possible that He would never have functioned as the world Saviour? He came to reveal to us our humanity as it could be, and will be, when we have finished with the long journey to Bethlehem. This constituted the uniqueness of His mission.

Christ lived quietly in His home with His parents, undergoing that most difficult experience of home life, with its monotony, with its unvarying usualness, with its needed subordination to the group will and need, with its lessons of sacrifice, of understanding and of service. This is ever the first lesson which every disciple must learn. Until he has learnt it, he can make no further progress. Until divinity has been expressed in the home, and among those who know us well and are our familiar friends, it cannot be expected to express itself elsewhere. We must live as sons of God in the setting—uninteresting, drab and sometimes sordid—in which destiny places us; there is nowhere else at this stage that is possible. The place where we are is the place from which our journey begins, and not the place from which we escape. If we cannot make good as disciples where we are,

and in the place where we discover ourselves, no other opportunity will be offered us until we do. Here lies our test,
and here lies our field of service. Many true and earnest
aspirants feel that they could indeed make an impression on
their surroundings and manifest divinely, if they had a different kind of home, a different environment or setting. Had
they married differently, or had they more money or more
leisure, could they meet with more sympathy from their
friends, or had they better physical health, there is no saying
what they might not accomplish. A test is something which
tries our strength to see of what sort it is; it calls forth the
utmost that is in us, and reveals to us where we are weak
and where we fail. The need today is for dependable disciples and for those who have been so tested that they will
not break or crack when difficulties come and dark places in
life are encountered. We have, if we could but realise it,
exactly those circumstances and that environment in which
this lesson of obedience to the highest which is in us can be
learnt. We have exactly the type of body and physical conditions through which the divinity in us can be expressed. We
have those contacts in the world and the kind of work which
are required in order to enable us to take the next step forward upon the path of discipleship, the next step to God.
Until aspirants grasp this essential fact and happily settle
down to a life of service and of giving lovingly in their own
homes, they can make no progress. Until the path of life is
trodden, happily, silently and with no self-pity in the home
circle, no other lesson or opportunity will be given. Many
very well-meaning aspirants need also to understand that they
themselves are responsible for many of the difficulties which
they encounter. Puzzled as to why they seem to evoke so
much antagonism from those around them, they complain of
meeting with no sympathetic response as they attempt to lead
the spiritual life, to study, read and think. The reason can
usually be found in the fact of their spiritual selfishness. They
talk too much about their aspirations, and about themselves.
Because they fail in their first responsibility, they find no

understanding reaction to their demand for time to meditate. It must be recognised that they are meditating. The house must be quiet; they must not be disturbed; no one must break in on them. None of these difficulties would arise if aspirants would remember two things: First, that meditation is a process carried on secretly, silently and regularly in the secret temple of a man's own mind. Secondly, that much can be done if people would not talk so much about what they are doing. We need to walk silently with God, to keep ourselves, as personalities, in the background; to organise our lives in such a way that we can live as souls, giving due time to the culture of our souls, yet at the same time preserving a sense of proportion, retaining the affection of those around us, and fulfilling perfectly our responsibilities and obligations. Self-pity and too much talk are the rocks on which many an aspirant temporarily founders.

Through love and loving practice we prove ourselves initiate in the mysteries. Born into the world of love at Bethlehem, the keynote of our lives from then on must be obedience to the highest that is in us, love to all beings, and complete confidence in the power of the indwelling Christ to demonstrate (through the outer form of our personalities) the life of love. The life of Christ is a life to be lived today, eventually by all. It is a life of joy and happiness, of test and of problems, but its essence is love and its method is love. It leaves us an example that we should follow His steps, and carry on the work which He initiated.

As we have traveled with Christ from Bethlehem towards the time when the second initiation draws near, what is the lesson we have learnt? How can we sum up the significance of that episode in terms of practical individual application? Has this episode any personal significance? What are the requirements and the possibilities which confront us? If a study of these five developments in the life of Christ are of no profit to us, and if they concern an unfoldment which can have no possible human interpretation, then all that has been written and taught, down the centuries, proves futile and unavailing. The ordinary theological applications no longer make an appeal to the developed intelligence of man. Christ Himself is ever powerful to attract human interest, and to draw to Himself those who have the vision to see truth as it is and to hear the Gospel message in terms which each new age demands. It is a waste of time to go on elaborating this ancient story of the living Christ if it contains for us no specific message, if all that is required of us is the attitude of the onlooker and of the man who simply says: "This is so." This believing yet negative attitude has been held too long. Looking on at Christ from too great a distance, we have been so preoccupied with a realisation of His achievement that our own individual part to be played eventually and inevitably has been forgotten. We have allowed Him to do all the work. We have tried to copy Him, and He does not want to be copied. He seeks to have us prove to Him, to ourselves, and to the world, that the divinity which is in Him is in us also. We need to discover that we can be as He is, because we have seen Him. He has had boundless faith in us and in the fact that "we are all the children of God," because "one is our Father," and His call goes out for us to tread the Path of holiness, and to achieve that perfection to which His life challenges us and for which He Himself tells us to work.

One wonders sometimes how right it has been for men to have accepted the ideas of St. Paul as given through translation down the centuries. The thought of sin is very little dwelt upon by Christ. It was emphasised by St. Paul, and the slant which he gave to Christianity is perhaps largely responsible for the dominant inferiority complex of the average Christian—an inferiority which Christ in no way taught. He calls us to holiness of life and admonishes us to follow in His steps, and not to follow in the steps, or to accept the interpretation of His words, which any disciple of His may advocate, no matter how highly esteemed or valuable.

What is this holiness to which He calls us, when we take the first step toward the new birth? What is a holy man? Wholeness, unity, at-one-ment, completeness—this is the hall mark of a perfect man. Having once seen and with open eyes beheld the vision of divinity, what can we do? In this question our problem is voiced. What is the next step, the immediate duty of the man who knows that, in himself, the new birth has not yet taken place, but who feels in himself a readiness to go up to Bethlehem, from Galilee, via Nazareth?

It entails, in the first place, effort. It means initiative, the expenditure of energy, the overcoming of inertia, and the will to exert oneself so that the initial journey can be taken. It means listening for and obeying the insistent demand of the soul for a nearer approach to God and a fuller expression of divinity; and yet "every individual is at some point torn between the splendid urge to go on towards understanding, and the craving to go back to safety."[65]

For there *is* difficulty and danger in the outlined way to the centre. Much is to be overcome and faced. The lower nature (the Mary aspect) draws back from the issue, and prefers inertia and stability to the needed activity and to consequent relative and temporary uncertainty.

This new birth is no mystical dream; neither is it a lovely vision of something that is possible but not probable; it is not simply a symbolic expression of some ultimate goal—lying ahead of us in some dim future, or in some other form of existence and some eventual heaven which we can attain if we fall back upon unthinking faith and blind acceptance of all that theology can tell us. Relatively easy to believe, this is the line of least resistance to the majority. It is difficult to fight one's way to that stage of experience where the divine programme for man becomes clear, and the possibilities which Christ dramatised for us become something permitting us no rest until we have transmuted it into personal experience, through the experiment of initiation. The new birth is as much a natural event and as much a result of the evolutionary process as is the birth of a child into the world of physical life. Eternally, down the ages, men have made and will continue to make the great transition, proving the fact

[65] *Psychology and the Promethean Will,* by W. H. Sheldon, p. 47.

of this experience. It is something which all must face at some time or other.

Two recognitions must emerge into the thought-world of the aspirant of today. First, the presence of the soul, a living entity which can and must be known through the process of bringing it to the birth upon the plane of daily living; and, secondly, the determination to achieve the re-orientation of the entire nature so that a closer identification with that soul may become possible, until a complete unity has been achieved. We begin to see what must be done, we begin to assume the right attitude which will make it possible. The halves of our essential duality—soul and body, Christ and Mary, over-shadowed by the Holy Ghost, the material and the spiritual—face each other and approach nearer and nearer until complete union is achieved and the Christ is born through the instrumentality of the Mother. But the acceptance of this divine idea and the orientation of the life in order to make the idea a fact are the first and immediate steps.

This, Christ taught, and for this He prayed the Father.

"Neither pray I for these alone (His disciples), but for them also which shall believe on me through their word; that they all may be one; as thou, Father, art in me, and I in thee, that they all may be one in us: that the world may believe that thou hast sent me. . . . I in them, and thou in me, that they may be made perfect in one."[66]

This is the doctrine of the At-one-ment; God, immanent in the universe—the cosmic Christ. God, immanent in humanity, revealed through the historical Christ. God, immanent in the individual, the indwelling Christ, the soul.

How can this truth of the soul and the new birth be experienced, so simply and so practically that its meaning can appear, thus enabling us to do that which is needed? Perhaps from the following statements:

1. Hidden in every human being is the "Word incarnate,"

[66] *St. John*, XVII, 20-23.

the Son of God made flesh. This is "Christ in us, the hope of Glory," but as yet only a hope for the mass of men. Christ is not yet made manifest. He is hidden and veiled by the form. Mary is seen, not the Christ.

2. As the wheel of life (the Galilee experience) carries us from one lesson to another, we approach nearer and nearer to the indwelling reality and the hidden deity. But the Christ Child is still hidden in the womb of the form.

3. In due time, the personality—physical, emotional and mental—is fused into one living whole. The Virgin Mary is ready to give birth to her Son.

4. The long journey draws to a close, and the hidden Christ Child is born at the first initiation.

This truth Dr. Inge touches upon in these words:

"Macarius, following Methodius, teaches that the very idea of the Incarnation includes the union of the Logos with pious souls, in whom He is well-pleased. In each of them a Christ is born. Thus besides the ideas of Ransom and Sacrifice of Christ for us, these theologians placed the ideas of sanctification and inner transformation of Christ in us, and they considered the latter as real and as integral a part of our redemption as the former. But the doctrine of Divine Immanence in the human heart never became quite the central truth of theology till the time of the mediaeval mystics. It is Eckhart who says: 'The Father speaks the Word into the soul, and when the Son is born, every soul becomes Mary.' "[67]

We are summoned to the new birth. Our personalities are now alive with potentiality. The hour is upon us.

The human soul must hear the challenge of the Christ soul, and realise that "Mary is blessed, not because she bore Christ bodily, but because she bore Him spiritually, and in this everyone can become like her." (Eckhart.)

[67] *The Paddock Lectures,* by W. R. Inge, p. 66.

CHAPTER THREE

The Second Initiation . . . The Baptism in Jordan

KEY THOUGHT

"It is a propitious moment to put the Christian life into serious practice . . . At a time of catastrophe, a process of ascetic purification takes place, in the absence of which there can be no spiritual life, whether for society or for the individual . . ."

Freedom of the Spirit, by Nicholas Berdyaev, p. 46.

The Second Initiation . . . The Baptism in Jordan

1

"Wherever a thing is both perceived and felt, there is the experience of the soul; and whenever a thought and a feeling become indistinguishable, there is the soul. Soul means oneness, unity, union between the inner wish and outer reality. As man moves toward acceptance of the universe, toward compatibility between what he feels as a wish from within, and what he perceives as the arrangement without, and as both elements expand, *the soul moves towards greatness.*"[1] (Italics are mine. A.A.B.)

THE first initiation has taken place. Christ has been born in Bethlehem. The soul has come into outer expression, and now this soul—Christ (as the historical representative of all a soul can be), the individual initiate—moves on towards greatness. The mission of the Saviour definitely starts at this time, but for the sake of those who will follow after, He must sound the note of purification and conform to the ritual requirements and the general trend of thought of His time. The initiate who has taken the first step must lay emphasis upon the purification of the lower nature which it is essential should preface the second initiation. The baptism of John was the symbol of this purification. Christ submitted Himself to the baptism, setting aside the protests of the Evangelist with His: "Suffer it to be so now; for thus it becometh us to fulfil all righteousness."[2]

Christ had reached maturity. Tradition tells us that He

[1] *Psychology and the Promethean Will,* by W. H. Sheldon, p. 130.
[2] *St. Matt.,* III, 15.

was thirty years old when He was baptised and started on His brief and spectacular public career. How true this may be historically, who can say? It is of no real importance. Christ was, is, and ever shall be. Speaking symbolically, it was necessary that He should be thirty years old, for there is significance in that number, where humanity is concerned. Thirty signifies the perfecting of the three aspects of the personality—the physical body, the emotional nature, and the mind. These three compose the form side of man, and veil or hide the soul. They are in reality his mechanism of contact with the outer world, the equipment whereby his consciousness unfolds and awakens. In their totality they constitute his "response apparatus," as the psychologists call it. We know that man is a physical animal as well as an emotional, sentient being and a thinking entity. When these three parts of man's lower nature are functioning smoothly, and together form a unit for the use of the inner man, an integrated personality, or an efficient lower self, is the result. To this the number thirty testifies. Ten is the number of perfection, and thirty testifies to perfection in all three parts of the equipment of the soul.

It is interesting to bear in mind that through these three aspects (or reflections of the divine being) man is brought en rapport with the existing universe, and therefore with God, immanent in nature. The physical body enables us to touch the tangible, visible world. The emotional, feeling nature enables us to say, "I lift up my heart unto the Lord." Most people live in their heart nature and in the feeling body, and it is through the heart that we find our way to the Heart of God. Only through love can Love be revealed. When through right use and understanding the mind is definitely directed and properly oriented, it is brought en rapport with the Mind of God, the Universal Mind, the Purpose, the Plan and the Will of God. Through the illumined mind of man, the Mind of Deity stands revealed. Thus man is seen as "made in the image of God."[3]

[3] *Gen.*, I, 26.

At the second initiation Christ stood before God, the Initiator, with all these aspects purified and matured; His mechanism was adjusted and ready for the task, and thus enabled to give proof of that purification and tension in attitude which would enable Him to carry through His mission to a satisfactory conclusion. This He had to prove to God and man through the purification which the baptism could give, and through the subsequent temptations in the wilderness. Ready for His work, He possessed what Dr. Sheldon calls "the three cardinal elements of a great mind, namely, *enthusiasm, intuitive insight,* and *systematized factual equipment,*" and it is further pointed out that the first two "are the more vital two, for they cannot be acquired if a person has reached adult life without them."[4]

Christ stood thus equipped.

It may be of value if we study here for a few minutes the purpose for which He stood thus equipped. We saw in our last chapter that this planet we call the Earth, is regarded by many modern scientists of eminence as probably unique in its constitution and its purpose. It apparently provides a conditioning of life to be found on no other planet. This may or may not be so, and only the unfoldment of man's consciousness can verify or negate this theory of uniqueness. Today, as we look out upon our planetary life, in all kingdoms the vision is discouraging. In all kingdoms we find death and disease, and in the animal and human kingdoms not only these, but also violence of many kinds. In the human family particularly the vision is saddening, so little have we learnt to understand that for which Christ stood, and so little have we gained from the purificatory processes of modern living. The will to betterment can be seen working in many fields where individuals are concerned, but the impulse is still weak in humanity as a whole. However, it can be aroused and we shall thus awaken to our environing responsibilities when we study anew the message of love which Christ gave.

[4] *Psychology and the Promethean Will,* by W. H. Sheldon, p. 135.

It is probably true that Christ came to us with a wider and deeper message than any previous Messenger from the Centre, but this in no way detracts from the status and work of Those Who preceded Him. He came at a crucial time, and in a period of world crisis, and embodied in Himself a cosmic principle—the principle of Love, which is the outstanding quality of God. Other aspects, qualities and purposes of the divine nature had been revealed by earlier incarnations of God, and appeared as the race reached the point in its development where a right reaction was possible. Zarathustra, to mention one such Messenger, had called the attention of mankind to the fact of the two basic principles to be found in the world—those of good and of evil—thus emphasising the basic dualities of existence. Moses revealed the Law, calling men to recognise God as the principle of justice, even if it may seem an unloving justice to those of us who live after the revelation which Christ gave. Buddha embodied in Himself the principle of divine wisdom and, with clear insight into the world of causes, saw mortal existence as it was and pointed the way out. But the principle of Love—the fundamental principle of the universe—had not been revealed before Christ came. God is love, and in the fulness of time this outstanding characteristic of the divine nature had to be revealed and in such a manner that man could grasp it. It is thus that Christ embodied in Himself the greatest of the cosmic principles. This Law of Love can be seen functioning in the universe as the Law of Attraction, with all that is involved in that term—coherency, integration, position, direction and the rhythmic running of our solar system; it can be seen also in the disposition of God towards humanity, as revealed to us through Christ. This unique function of Christ as the custodian and the revealer of a cosmic principle or energy lies behind all He did; it was the basis and the result of His achieved perfection; it was the incentive and the impulsion to His life of service, and it is the principle upon which the kingdom of God is founded.

That paganism knows no goal or purpose is today for many of us a statement which will not bear investigation. All that had transpired in the past had for its goal that which happened when Christ appeared; it prepared humanity for the opportunity then offered, forming the foundation upon which the present is based. Similarly, the imminent revelation of the coming century will constitute the foundation upon which the future will rest, and for this purpose all that is now transpiring is of supreme importance.

Not only did Christ bridge the gap between the East and the West, summing up in Himself all that the East had of worth to contribute, but He gave to our occidental civilisation (at that time unborn) those great ideals and that example of sacrifice and of service which today (two thousand years after He walked among men) are becoming the keynote of the best minds of the age. The story of ideas, how they come and how they make their impact upon the human consciousness, thus changing the course of human affairs, is the story of history; but curiously enough, ideas constitute the one unpredictable element of the future. Some individual of outstanding personality steps out from the rank and file of the race, and thinks through into being some great and dynamic idea based on truth. He formulates it into such terms that his fellowmen can grasp it and eventually live by it. New trends, new incentives and new impulses then emerge, and thus history is made. It might be said with truth that without ideas there would be no history. In the enunciation of a cosmic idea, and in the capacity to make that idea an ideal of dynamic force, Christ stands alone. Through His life, He gave to us an idea which became in time the ideal of service, so that today the attention of many rulers and thinkers throughout the world is engrossed with the well-being of nations and men. That the technique employed and the methods used to enforce the sensed and visioned ideal are frequently wrong and undesirable, producing cruel and separative results, in no way alters the fact that behind all these idealistic experiments of the race lies this great ideal, divinely inspired and summarised for us by Christ in His life and teaching.

Christ gave the greatest of all ideas—that God is Love, and that love could manifest in human form, and, thus manifested, could constitute a possibility for all men. His life was the demonstration of a perfection such as the world had never previously seen.

The soul, which is the hidden Christ in all, mediates between the spirit (the Father) and the human being. Christ emphasised this when He called attention to man's essential divinity, speaking of God as "our Father," as He was the Father of Christ. It was the light which He came to show and which He saw also (hidden and veiled) in all, enjoining upon us that we should let that light shine forth.[5] He challenged us to show, and commanded us to demonstrate the perfection of which He was the embodiment. He proved to us the possible, and called upon us to express it. In this uniqueness of revelation Christ stands alone, because He was the greatest, the highest and the truest that has ever appeared, but not because—dare I say it?—He was the greatest that ever could appear. One dare not so limit God. Under the evolutionary revelation of the nature of divinity it appears that Christ climaxed the past and indicated the future. Is it not possible that there may be aspects and characteristics of the divine Nature of which we cannot as yet have the faintest conception? Is it not probable that our sentient apparatus is still inadequate to grasp the fulness of God? May not our mechanism of perception require further evolutionary unfoldment before still other divine and spiritual characteristics can be safely revealed to us and in us? There may be future revelations of such stupendous wonder and beauty that as yet we can form no faintest idea of their possible outline. Otherwise God would be limited and static, and unable to do more than He has already done. How dare we say that it is possible for us to envisage the limits of the nature of Deity? How can the human intellect arrogantly believe that

5 *St. Matt.*, V, 16.

it can recognise, even through Christ, the ultimate objectives of the divine Will? The history of the unfoldment of the human consciousness proves that truth has been given out progressively, and that the brilliant galaxy of World Teachers gave an ever-widening interpretation of Deity, reaching, as time elapsed, an ever larger number. Christ has given us the highest and the most inclusive revelation to which the human consciousness can respond, up to the present era. But how shall we dare to say that no more is possible to God, when we are ready to receive it? For this we are fast preparing. Even Christ Himself told His disciples that "he that believeth on me, the works that I do shall he do also; and greater works than these shall he do."[6] Either these words express a truth, or the whole structure of our belief falls to the ground. There is more still to be revealed, or else past history loses its point; ancient beliefs lose their significance; and we have reached an impasse which God Himself would seem unable to transcend. This we cannot accept.

The cosmic Christ, the mystic Christ, the historical Christ, and the individual Christ, are to all eternity, and the revelation can therefore be progressive. If we can believe that God is inclusive of all forms and of that which the forms reveal, surely as our equipment develops and our mechanism of contact improves, we shall be able to see more of divinity than at present, and be deemed worthy, at a later date, of a greater revelation. It is only our limitations as human beings which prevent our seeing all that there is to be seen.

The new birth brought us to the point where we became aware of a new world of light and of being. Through the process of that initiation we became citizens of the kingdom of God which Christ came to establish as a fact in the consciousness of men; we pass through the new birth into a world which is governed by a higher series of laws, the spiritual laws, and new objectives open up before us, new aspects of our own hidden spiritual nature emerge, and we begin to discover in ourselves the delineation of a new being, with a

[6] *St. John*, XIV, 12.

different set of wishes, desires, ideals, and methods of world activity.

We speak much of the at-one-ment which Christ made within Himself and for man. We recognise the unity He felt with the Father, and that He has called us to a similar divine unity. But is it not possible that He established a synthesis broader than that of the individual and God—the synthesis of the kingdom of God?

What do these words mean? We have talked of the kingdom of Heaven in terms of separation. We are either in that kingdom or out of it. We are told that we must step out of the kingdom of men (controlled by the world, the flesh and the devil) into another kingdom which is pictured as utterly different. Yet is this so? All aspects of the three sub-human kingdoms—animal, vegetable and mineral—are found in man; and their synthesis, plus another factor, the divine *intellect*, we call the human kingdom. Man unifies in himself the so-called lesser manifestations of deity. In the sub-human kingdoms of nature we find three major types of consciousness: the mineral kingdom, with its subjective discriminating power, its capacity to grow, and its ultimate radio-activity; the vegetable kingdom, with its sensitivity or sentiency, and its developing response apparatus which is sensitive to sunlight, to warmth and cold, and to other environing climatic conditions; the animal kingdom with its greatly increased awareness, its capacity for free movement and for wider contacts through its instinctive nature. The human kingdom embodies all these types of awareness—consciousness, sentiency, instinct—plus that mysterious human faculty which we call "the mind," and we sum up all these inherited qualities in the word "self-conscious."

There comes, however, in the experience of the intelligent human being, a slowly dawning recognition that there is something still greater and of deeper value outside himself. He is sensitised to a subtler range of contacts and to impressions which he calls spiritual or ideal or mystical. Another type of consciousness begins to germinate in him, and at the birth at Bethlehem this awareness becomes manifested and recognisable. Just as the human being synthesises in himself all that has been, plus his own peculiar constitution and qualities, so in him can also begin to emerge and demonstrate qualities which are not human.

Members of the kingdom of God will surely embody the heritage of four kingdoms, as man embodies the heritage of three. This higher citizenship involves the expression of the Christ consciousness, which is the consciousness of the group, of the relation of the part to the whole (something which Christ continuously emphasised) and of the human to the divine. The result of this realisation must surely be, under the evolutionary scheme, the appearance of another kingdom in nature. This constitutes the great task of Christ. Through the power of His *realised* divinity He produced the man who blended in Himself the best of all that had been, and revealed also what could be. He brought together into a functioning unity the higher and the lower, and made out of them "one new man." He founded the kingdom of God on earth, and produced a synthesis of all the kingdoms in nature, thus causing the appearance of a fifth kingdom. We might sum up the at-one-ments which He brought about as follows:

1. He unified in Himself to perfection the physical, emotional and mental aspects of man, and demonstrated therefore the perfect Individual.
2. He unified in Himself soul and body, the higher and the lower aspects, and therefore produced a divine incarnation.
3. He unified in Himself the best of all the kingdoms in nature, mineral, vegetable, animal, which means, in their synthesis, the human with the intellect functioning.
4. Then He blended this synthesis with a higher spiritual factor and brought to the birth another kingdom in nature, the fifth.

Christ, having produced in Himself one unification or at-one-ment after another, for the benefit of humanity, appears before John the Baptist, and passes through the second initiation, that of purification in the waters of Jordan. Through the process of baptism, and through the temptations which followed, He evidenced His maturity, faced His mission, and demonstrated to the world His purity and His power.

The third initiation, that of the Transfiguration, testified to the fact of the at-one-ment which Christ made between soul and body. Integration was complete, and the consequent illumination was made apparent to His disciples. He appeared before them as Son of Man and Son of God, and having proved to them Who He was, He faced the death which lay ahead of Him, and the intervening service.

In the fourth initiation, He demonstrated this integration not only as God-Man, but as the One Who enfolded in His consciousness the entire world of men. He unified Himself with humanity, and portrayed the effectiveness of that divine energy which enabled Him to say in truth, "I, if I be lifted up from the Earth, will draw all men unto Me."[7] He was lifted up between Earth and Heaven, and for two thousand years these words of His have stood unchallenged.

2

"Then cometh Jesus from Galilee to Jordan unto John, to be baptised of him. But John forbade him, saying, I have need to be baptised of Thee, and comest Thou to me?

"And Jesus answering said unto him, Suffer it to be so now, for it becometh us to fulfil all righteousness. Then he suffered Him.

"And Jesus, when He was baptised, went up straightway out of the water: and, lo, the heavens were opened unto Him, and He saw the Spirit of God descending like a dove, and lighting upon Him.

"And lo a voice from heaven, saying, This is my beloved Son, in Whom I am well pleased."[8]

In these simple words we are told the story of this initiation. The keynote is purification, and it closed a period of preparation, of quiet service, and inaugurated a cycle of stren-

[7] *St. John*, XII, 32.
[8] *St. Matt.*, III, 13-17.

uous activity. The purification of the lower nature is a requirement which the Christian Church has ever emphasised, as has also the Hindu faith. Christ held this ideal before His disciples and all men when He said, "Blessed are the pure in heart: for they shall see God."[9]

In an ancient treatise upon meditation, the *Yoga Sutras of Patanjali,* we find the teacher proclaiming, "Through purification comes also a quiet spirit . . . and ability to see the Self."[10] Purification is of many kinds and degrees. There is physical purity and moral purity, and there is also that magnetic purity which makes a man a channel for spiritual force. There is psychic purity, which is a rare thing to find, and mental purity. The word "purity" comes from the Sanskrit word *pur,* which means freedom from alloy, from limitation and from the imprisoning of the spirit in the chains of matter. There can be no achievement without purification; there is no possibility of our seeing and manifesting divinity without passing through the waters that cleanse. In the world today a great cleansing is going on. An "ascetic purification" and an enforced abstinence from much that has hitherto been deemed desirable, is going on in the world, and none of us can escape it. This is due to the breakdown of the economic system and the many other systems which are proving ineffectual in the modern world. Purification is being forced upon us, and as a consequence a truer sense of values must eventuate. A cleansing from wrong ideals, a racial purification from dishonest standards and undesirable objectives, is being powerfully applied at this time. Perhaps this means that many in the race today are going down to Jordan, to enter its purifying waters. A self-applied ascetic purification, and the recognition of its value by the pioneers of the human family, may succeed in leading them to the portal of initiation.

There is also to be found in this episode an interesting analogy to what is happening to the race today, from the

[9] St. Matt., V, 8.
[10] The Yoga Sutras of Patanjali, II, 41.

astrological standpoint. We are entering into the sign Aquarius, the Water Carrier. This sign stands symbolically for group purity and relationship, for the universality of experience and for the waters poured over all. When we began to enter this sign, about two hundred years ago, water became for the first time of general interest and of general use for sanitation and irrigation. The control of water and its utilisation as a means of transportation on a world-wide scale became possible. The use of water in our homes is now so universal that we hardly realise what the world must have been like prior to this use.

Christ, in this great initiation, entered into the stream, and the waters passed over Him. In India this initiation is called that of "entering the stream," and he who undergoes it is regarded as having demonstrated both physical and psychic purity. In considering this initiation we must remember that two kinds of baptism are referred to in the story.

"John answered, saying unto them all, I indeed baptise you with water: but one mightier than I cometh, the latchet of whose shoes I am not worthy to unloose: He shall baptise you with the Holy Ghost and with fire."[11]

There are therefore two kinds of baptism:

1. That of John the Baptist, which is the baptism by water.
2. The baptism of Jesus Christ, which is that of the Holy Ghost and of fire.

In these two symbols much of the story of human development is summed up, and the joint work of John the Baptist and of Jesus produced a synthesis which is indicative of the immediate objective of our racial endeavour. The symbolism is exact, according to the ancient mystery teaching. A close study of this symbolic rendering of a basic truth would greatly profit the seeker in all countries, and an understanding of the significance of the symbols employed would throw much light upon reality.

In the evolution of the race the sentient feeling nature is

[11] *St. Luke*, III, 16.

first developed, and *water* has ever been the symbol of that nature. The fluid nature of the emotions, the constant shifting between sentient pleasure and pain, the storms which arise in the world of feeling, and the peace and calm which can descend upon a man, make of water a most apposite symbol of this interior subtle world of the lower nature in which most of us live, and wherein our consciousness is predominantly focussed. The average man or woman is predominantly a blend of the physical and emotional natures; all early races have this characteristic, and the probability is that, in old Atlantis, civilisation was entirely centred in the feelings and the desires, in the emotions, and—among its most advanced types—in the heart life. John the Baptist therefore gave the baptism of water which testified to the purification of the emotional nature, which must always be a preliminary step to the purification by fire.

The Jordan baptism is symbolic of the purification of the conscience in man, just as Christ and His baptism symbolised for us the divine in man and the purification which follows the activity of that divine spirit in the lower nature. Conscience, with its call to the recognition of the higher values, of the deeper truths, and of the birth unto life, leads to Jordan, and so Christ went there to "fulfil all righteousness." This experience ever precedes the baptism into Christ and through Christ.

The baptism of John was a step upon the way into the centre, and of more general application than is the baptism of Jesus, for few are ready yet for the second initiation. It is preparatory to that final baptism, for the purification of the emotional nature must precede in time the purification of the mental nature, just as in the evolution of the race (and of a child, likewise) the feeling, sentient man is first developed, and then the mind comes into active life. The baptism which Christ gives His followers concerns the purification of the mind by fire. Fire, under the universal symbolism of religion, is ever symbolic of the mind nature. This baptism by fire is the baptism of the Holy Spirit.

Thus Jesus went up from Nazareth and Galilee to take the next step which was indicated in His experience. As the result of life experience and inner consecration, He was ready for the next initiation. This was taken in the river Jordan. Jordan means "that which descends," but also, according to some commentators, that which "divides," as a river divides and separates the land. In the symbolism of esotericism, the word "river" frequently means *discrimination*. We have seen that water symbolises the emotional nature, and that the purification in Jordan, through baptism, typifies the complete cleansing of all feeling, of all wishes and of that desire life which is the determining factor with most people. The first initiation symbolises the dedication of the physical body and the physical plane life to the soul. The second initiation stands for the demonstrated control and consecration to divinity of the desire nature, with its emotional reactions and its potent "wish life."

A new factor now enters in, the discriminating faculty of the mind. By means of it, the disciple can bring the mental life under control and dedicate it to the life of the kingdom of God, which is consummated at the third initiation. Through the correct use of the mind, the disciple is led to make right choice, and to balance (with wisdom) the endless pairs of opposites.

We pass through the Birth initiation somewhat unconsciously. The full significance of what we have undergone does not appear to us; we are "infants in Christ," and as infants we just live and submit to discipline, gradually growing toward maturity. But there comes a time in the life of every initiate when choice must be made, and Christ was faced with this. A clear, clean interior break is to be made with the past before we can face towards a future of service, consciously undertaken, and know that from that time on nothing will be the same.

This initiation marked a tremendous change in the life of Jesus of Nazareth. Up to that time, for thirty years, He had simply been the carpenter of the little town, and the son of His parents. He was a personality doing much good in a small sphere. But after the purification in Jordan, having "fulfilled all righteousness,"[12] He became the Christ, and went about His country, serving the race and speaking those words which have moulded for centuries our Western civilisation. For each of us there must come the same great expansion, and it occurs when we are fitted to take the second initiation. Our desire-life is then confronted with essential choices which only the mind can enable us properly to handle.

We are told in *Cruden's Concordance* that the name *John* means "which God gave," and in the three names which appear together in this episode—John, Jesus and Christ—the whole story of the consecrated aspirant is summed up: John, symbolising the divine aspect deeply hidden in man, which prompts a man towards the needed purity; Jesus, in this case symbolising the consecrated, pledged disciple or initiate, ready for that process which will be the seal of his purification; Christ, the divine indwelling Son of God, able now to manifest in Jesus, because Jesus has submitted to the baptism of John. That submission and completed purification brought its reward.

It was at this initiation that God Himself proclaimed His Son to be the One in Whom He was "well pleased." Every initiation is simply a recognition. It is a false idea, current in many schools of the mysteries and of esotericism, that initiation connotes a mysterious ceremony wherein, through the medium of the initiator and the rod of initiation, conditions are definitely changed in the aspirant, so that for ever after he is altered and different. An initiation takes place whenever a man becomes, through his own self-effort, an initiate. Then having taken "the kingdom of Heaven by violence,"[13] and having "worked out" his "own salvation through fear and trembling,"[14] his spiritual status is immediately recognised by his peers, and he is admitted to initiation.

[12] *St. Matt.,* III, 15.
[13] *St. Matt.,* XI, 12.
[14] *Phil.,* II, 12.

At initiation two things happen: the initiate discovers his fellow initiates, those with whom he can associate, and he finds out also the mission to which he is called. He becomes aware of his divinity in a new and factual sense, not just as a deeply spiritual hope, an intriguing hypothetical possibility and his heart's desire. He knows himself to be a son of God, therefore recognition is accorded to him. This was strikingly the case with Jesus Christ. His task emerged in its dread implications before His eyes, and this must surely have been the reason why He was driven into the wilderness. The urge to solitude, the search for that quiet where reflection and determination can strengthen each other, was the natural outcome of this recognition. He saw what He had to do—to serve, to suffer and to found the kingdom of God. The expansion of consciousness was immediate and deep. Dr. Schweitzer says in this connection:

"About Jesus' earlier development we know nothing. All lies in the dark. Only this is sure: at his baptism the secret of his existence was disclosed to him—namely, that he was the One whom God had destined to be the Messiah. With this revelation he was complete, and underwent no further development. For now he is assured that, until the near coming of the messianic age which was to reveal his glorious dignity, he was to labour for the Kingdom as the unrecognised and hidden Messiah, and must prove and purify himself together with his friends in the final Affliction."[15]

To the man Jesus this was probably a staggering disclosure. Dim anticipations of the path which He might have to tread must at times have entered His mind, but the full implications, and the picture of the way which lay ahead of Him could not have dawned upon His consciousness in their fulness until after the second initiation was undergone, when His purification was complete. He then faced the life of service and the difficulties which attend the path of every conscious son of God. The same writer says:

"In Jesus' messianic consciousness the thought of suffering ac-

[15] *The Mystery of the Kingdom of God,* by Albert Schweitzer, p. 354.

quired now, as applied to himself, a mysterious significance. The Messiahship which he became aware of at his baptism was not a possession, nor a mere object of expectation; but in the eschatological conception, it was implied as a matter of course that through the trial of suffering he must become what God had destined him to be. His messianic consciousness was never without the thought of the Passion. Suffering is the way to the revelation of Messiahship!"[16]

Christ's entire life was one long *via dolorosa,* but it was illumined always by the light of His soul and by the recognition of the Father. Though, as recorded in the New Testament, it was divided into definite periods and cycles, and though obviously the detail of what He had to do was only progressively revealed to Him, His life constituted one great sacrifice, one great experience and one definite purpose. This definiteness of objective, and this consecration of the whole man to an ideal are conditions indicative of the state of initiation. All life's happenings are related to the carrying forward of the life task. Life takes on true significance. This is a lesson which all of us, uninitiate and aspiring, can now learn. We can begin to say, "Life to me, as I look back on it, is not a succession of experiences but one great experience illumined here and there by moments of revelation."[17]

This illumination grows more constant as time goes on. The ancient Hindu teacher, Patanjali, taught that illumination is sevenfold, progressing by successive stages.[18] It is as though he were dealing in thought with the seven illuminations which come to all the sons of God who are in process of awakening to their divine opportunities: the illumination which comes when we decide to tread the Path of probation, and to prepare ourselves for initiation. Then the light is shed on the distant vision, and we catch a fleeting glimpse of our goal. Next the light is shed upon ourselves, and we get a vision of what we are, and what we can be, and enter

[16] *Ibid.,* p. 223.
[17] *A Pilgrim's Quest for the Absolute,* by Lord Conway of Allington, p. 8.
[18] *The Yoga Sutras of Patanjali,* Book II, 27.

upon the Path of discipleship, or—in the terminology of the Bible—we begin the long journey to Bethlehem. Then there are the five initiations which we are studying, each of which marks an increase of light which shines upon our way and develops that inner radiance which enables all God's children to say, with Christ: "I am the Light of the World,"[19] and to obey His command wherein He tells us to "let your light so shine before men that they may see."[20] This light, in its seven stages, reveals God—God in nature, God in Christ, God in man. It is the cause of the mystical vision about which so much has been written and taught, and to which the lives of God's saints in both hemispheres have ever testified.

One wonders about the first man who received the first faint glimpse (with his dim inner light) of the infinite possibility lying ahead. He caught a glimpse of God, and from that minute the light from God waxed more and more intense. There is an ancient legend (and who shall say that it is not based on fact?) that Jesus of Nazareth was the very first of our humanity, in a dim and far distant past, to catch this glimpse, and that He was, through the consistency of His constantly directed effort, the first of our humanity to emerge into the very Light of God Himself. St. Paul perhaps touched this truth when he spoke of Christ as the "Eldest in a vast family of brothers."[21] Whether this legend is true or not, Christ entered into light because He was light; and the history of man has been a gradually growing illumination, until today radiance is everywhere to be found.

In this light, inherent and divine, latent and yet emanating from God, Christ saw the vision, and that vision demonstrated to Him His Sonship, His Messiahship and the path of His suffering. This vision is the heritage and the revelation of each individual disciple. This mystical revelation can be perceived, and once perceived, remains a fact—inexplicable often, but a definitely clear and inescapable reality. It gives

---

[19] *St. John*, VIII, 12.
[20] *St. Matt.*, V, 16.
[21] *Romans*, VIII, 29, Weymouth's Translation.

the initiate the confidence and the power to go forward. It is affective in our experience and is the root of all our future consistency and service; it is also unassailable. Upon this basis we move with courage from the known towards the unknown. It is finally ineffable, for it emphasises our divinity, is founded upon divine quality, and emanates from God. It is a glimpse into the kingdom of God, and a revelation of the path to be trodden on our way there. It is an expansion which enables us to realise that "the Kingdom of God is a state of the soul, coming from the spirit and reflected in the body."[22]

The first step into this kingdom is through the new Birth. The second step is through the baptism of Purification. It is a process of growth in the characteristics of the kingdom, and the gradual attainment of that maturity which marks the citizen of that kingdom. To this, Christ testified through the baptism when He attained maturity, setting us an example, and through His triumphant passing of the tests of the three temptations He demonstrated the needed purity.

The babe in Christ, the little child, the full-grown man, the perfected man! Through the Bethlehem experience the babe is born. The little child grows to maturity and manifests in his purity and power at the Baptism. He demonstrates at the Transfiguration as the full-grown man, and, on the Cross, he stands forth the perfected Son of God. An initiation is that moment in which a man feels and knows through every part of his being that life is reality and reality is life. For a brief moment his consciousness becomes all-enfolding; he not only sees the vision and hears the word of recognition, but knows that the vision is of himself, and that the word is himself made flesh.

This is the essential factor. An initiation is a blaze of illumination thrown upon the river of existence, and it is in the nature of a whole experience. There is no indefiniteness in it, and the initiate is never quite the same again in his consciousness.

[22] *The Religion of Love*, by the Grand Duke Alexander of Russia.

In the river Jordan the light from Heaven streamed upon the Christ, and His Father spoke those words which have sounded down the ages, and have evoked response from all aspirants to the kingdom. The spirit of God descended as a dove upon him. The dove is ever a symbol of *peace*. For two reasons it was the chosen sign at this initiation. Water, as we have seen, is the symbol of the emotional nature, which nature, when purified through initiation, becomes a peaceful limpid pool, capable of reflecting the divine Nature in its purity. Thus, in the form of a dove, the peace of God descended upon Jesus.

Secondly, the essential dualities of existence are typified for us in the Bible. *The Old Testament* stands for the natural lower man, the virgin Mary aspect, carrying within itself the promise of the Messiah, of Him Who shall come. *The New Testament* stands for the spiritual man, for God made flesh, and for the birth of that which the material nature carried and veiled for so long. *The Old Testament* opens with the appearance of the raven at the time of the founding of the ancient world, as we can begin to know it. *The New Testament* opens with the appearance of a dove—one the symbol of the raging waters, the other the symbol of the waters of peace. Through Christ and the unfoldment of the Christ life in each human being will come "the peace which passeth understanding."[23]

Standing there in the waters of Jordan, Christ faced the world as Man. Standing upon the top of the Mount of Transfiguration, He faced the World as God. But in this initiation, He stood on a level with His brethren and demonstrated purity and peace. Let us remember that "from the point of view of others only that man is original who can lead them beyond what they already know, but this he cannot do until he has become their equal in their knowledge."[24] This is a point to be remembered. Christ was purified. But ahead of Him lay the temptations. He had

[23] *Phil.*, IV, 7.
[24] *The Recovery of Truth*, by Hermann Keyserling, p. 216.

to become in His consciousness (either anew or through the recovery of an ancient past of test and trial) our equal in all points—of sin, of weakness and of human frailty, and of human success and achievement. Christ had to demonstrate His moral greatness as well as His divinity and His perfection as man attaining maturity. He had to pass through the tests to which every would-be citizen of the kingdom must be subjected when called upon to prove his fitness for the privileges of that kingdom. Of this kingdom the church is the outer and visible symbol, and though faulty and weak in the interpretation of its essential teachings, it symbolises the form of the kingdom of God. But this is not the kingdom of the theologians. It is not entered through the acceptance of certain formal beliefs. It is entered by those who have passed through the new birth, and gone down to Jordan.

The citizenship of this kingdom was on trial in the Person of Christ, and so He goes down into the wilderness, there to be tempted of the devil.

3

In this intimate episode in the life of Jesus Christ we are given perhaps the first real insight into the processes of His innermost mind. The following words open the story and are significant:

"And lo a voice from heaven, saying, This is my beloved Son, in whom I am well pleased. Then was Jesus led up of the spirit into the wilderness to be tempted of the devil."[25]

This story of the temptation in the wilderness is most controversial. Many questions have been propounded and much agony of soul has been experienced by the serious believer who endeavours to reconcile common sense, Christ's divinity, and the devil. Was it possible that Christ could in reality

[25] *St. Matt.,* III, 17, IV, 1.

be tempted, and if so, could He have fallen into sin? Did He meet these temptations as the omnipotent Son of God, or did He meet them as a man and therefore subject to temptation? What is meant by the devil? And what was the relation of Christ to evil? Had this wilderness story never been told to us, what would have been our attitude to Christ? What really took place in the consciousness of Christ while in the wilderness? For what purpose are we permitted to share with Him this experience?

Many such questions arise in the mind of the intelligent man, and many have been the commentaries written to prove the particular point of each writer. It is not the purpose of this book to deal with the difficult subject of evil, nor to define the times when Christ was functioning as a man, and when He was functioning as the Son of God. Some believe that He was simultaneously both, and was "very God of very God,"[26] and yet essentially and utterly human at the same time. People make these statements, but they are apt to forget the implications. They affirm with decision their point of view, and omit to carry their attitude to a logical conclusion. The inference is that we are allowed to know about the temptation in order to teach us, as human beings, a needed lesson; let us therefore study the story from the angle of Christ's *humanity*, never forgetting that He had learned obedience to the divine spirit, the soul in man, and was in control of His body of manifestation.

He was "in all points tempted like as we are, yet without sin;"[27] He came in a human body, and was subject to human conditions as also we are; He suffered and agonised; He felt irritation, and was conditioned by His body, His environment and the period, as we all are. But because He had learnt to master Himself, and because the wheel of life had done its work with Him, He could face this experience and meet evil face to face, and triumph. He taught us thereby how to meet temptation; what to expect, as disciples prepar-

[26] *Athanasian Creed.*
[27] *Hebrews*, IV, 15.

ing for initiation, and the method whereby evil can be turned into good. He met temptation with no great new technique or revelation. He simply fell back on what He knew, what He had been taught and told. He met temptation each time with "It is written,"[28] and employed no new powers to combat the devil. He simply utilised the knowledge which He had. He used no divine powers to overcome the Evil One. He simply used those which we all possess—acquired knowledge and the age-old rules. He conquered because He had taught Himself to overcome. He was the master of conditions at that time because He had learnt to master Himself.

Such a mastery by the soul may indeed be utterly beyond our immediate attaining, but the command of Christ stands for all time: "Be ye therefore perfect;"[29] and some day we too shall meet the temptations in the wilderness and also come forth as He, unsullied and undefeated. Such experience is inevitable for all, and cannot eventually be escaped. Christ did not escape it, and neither shall we. "It is the possibility of being tempted," says Dr. Selbie, "which shows the real greatness of human nature. Apart from it we should be merely unmoral creatures . . . It is with the capacity to choose between ends, and the actions leading to them, that the possibility of sin emerges."[30] This calls for more than superficial consideration. Humanity itself is at stake, in the wilderness story. The whole world of material things, of desire and of ambition, was arrayed before Christ, and because He reacted as He did, and because none of these aspects of life could affect Him, we too can stand free, assured of our own ultimate victory. Christ as man achieved victory. We too can do the same.

To this triumph of the soul over matter and of reality over the unreal, Christ gave testimony in the wilderness experience, and it is towards the same goal that all who follow in His steps are moving. The triumph which was His will

[28] *St. Matt.,* IV, 4, 7, 10.

[29] *St. Matt.,* V, 48.

[30] *Psychology of Religions,* by Dr. Selbie, p. 228.

be ours when we meet the problem in the spirit in which He met it, turning the light of the soul upon it, and resting back upon past experience.

In the Baptism initiation, Christ's purity and freedom from evil had been demonstrated before men. Now they have to undergo a different test. From the crowd and from the experience He went to the solitary place, and for forty days and nights He was alone with Himself, standing between God and the Evil One. Through what agency could this evil force reach Him? Through the agency of His own human nature, through the medium of loneliness, of hunger and of His own visions. Christ was thrown back upon Himself, and there, in the silence of the desert, alone with His thoughts and desires, He was tested throughout all the parts of His nature which might be vulnerable. "As He is, so are we in this world,"[31] vulnerable in all points. The difficulty with most of us is that we are vulnerable in so many petty ways, and in every trifling situation we are apt to fall. The crux of the situation, as far as Christ was concerned, was that these three temptations were climaxing tests, in which the three aspects of the lower nature were involved. They were synthetic temptations. In them was no petty, trifling, silly tempting, but the gathering up of the forces of the threefold lower man—physical, emotional and mental—into one last effort to control the Son of God. Evil is thus constituted, and we shall all some day have to face this testing—this triple evil, this devil, such as Christ faced. Three times He was tempted, and three times He resisted, and only after this capacity to react to form and to material benefit had been finally put aside was it possible for Christ to pass on to His world service and the Mount of Transfiguration. One of the finest thinkers in the field of Christian interpretation today tells us that "all they who are destined for the Kingdom must win forgiveness for the guilt contracted in the earthly aeon by encountering steadfastly the world-power as it collects itself for a last attack. For through this guilt they were still subject to the power

[31] *I St. John,* IV, 17.

of ungodliness. This guilt constitutes a counterweight which holds back the coming of the Kingdom."[32]

Christ faced this last attack and emerged victorious, thus guaranteeing to us our ultimate victory.

The devil approached Jesus when the forty days of solitary communion were over. We are not told what Christ did in those forty days. No account is given to us of His thought and determinations, His realisation and consecration at that time. Alone, He faced the future, and at the end, encountered the tests which released Him from the power of His human nature.

As we study the life of Jesus this solitariness emerges ever more clearly. The great souls are always lonely souls. They tread uncompanioned the most difficult parts of the long way of return. Christ was ever lonely. His spirit drove Him again and again into isolation. "The great religious conceptions which haunt the imaginations of civilized mankind are scenes of solitariness: Prometheus chained to his rock, Mahomet brooding in the desert, the meditations of the Buddha, the solitary Man on the Cross. It belongs to the depth of the religious spirit to have felt forsaken, even by God."[33]

Christ's life alternated between the crowd whom He loved and the silence of the solitary places. First He is to be found in the daily life of the family experience, where the intimacies of personalities can so sadly imprison the soul; thence He passed into the solitary desert and was alone. He returned, and His public life began, until the publicity and noise and clamour of this were succeeded by the deep and interior silence of the Cross, where, forsaken of all, He went through the deep dark night of the soul—utterly alone. Yet it is in these moments of complete silence, when the soul is thrown back upon itself and there is no one to help, no hand to aid and no voice to strengthen, that those revelations come and that clear insight is developed which enable a Saviour to emerge for the helping of the world.

[32] *The Mystery of the Kingdom of God,* by Albert Schweitzer, p. 235.
[33] *Religion in the Making,* by A. N. Whitehead, p. 9.

Christ was tempted of the devil. Is it necessary in a book such as this to give an interpretation of the devil? Is it not apparent that there are in the world today two dominant concepts, both of them passing out as factors in the consciousness of the young, and therefore determining their later beliefs— the devil and Saint Nicholas, or Father Christmas? These names embody opposing ideas. Each of them symbolises one of the two major problems with which man has, in his daily life, to deal. These are called by Oriental philosophers the "pairs of opposites," and surely it is the manner in which man handles these two aspects of life, and his subjective attitude to them, which determine whether his life reacts to evil or to good. The devil is the symbol of that which is not *humanly* divine, for there are evil things done by man which, when done by an animal, are not so regarded. A man or a fox, for instance, may raid a chicken coop, but in the one case a moral law is broken, and in the other a natural instinct is followed. An animal may kill another animal in rage or in defense of its female, but when a man does the same thing it is called murder, and he is duly punished.

Father Christmas is the embodiment of that which is selfless; he is the symbol of giving and of the Christ spirit; he therefore stands to man as a reminder of God, just as this other figment of the imagination, the devil with horns and tail, is a reminder of that which is not God, that which is not divine.

"The key is supplied by mythology. The myths demand a serious interpretation in correspondence with objective reality, they must not be treated as pure poetry without any solid truth behind them, a mere play of the imagination! The garment which clothes the substance may be as fabulous, as fantastic, as inconsistent and as patchy as you please. But this does not alter the fact that popular mythology tells of an invisible reality, and of mysterious 'figures,' 'figures' remember, not 'forces' at work everywhere. Everything is alive and possesses a soul. The world is full of spirits, of souls. The myths speak of them. Who invented these myths? Nobody. For inventions are arbitrary, are fiction. But these tales are accepted by those who tell them and by their audience as unquestioned truth. The psychology of the primitive compels him to regard things in this way 'magically.' What in our more developed and more individual psychology has become a 'sub-conscious' in which the collective life of our ancestors is still operative, is the normal psychology of the primitive, a state of 'natural somnambulism' with its distinctive forms of sensitiveness, telepathy, and second-sight, a direct apprehension akin to the artist's of the whole in its parts, of the essential in a multiplicity of detail."[34]

To this the symbols of the devil and of Father Christmas bear testimony—embodiments of the primal dualities in the realm of *quality*. Man's entire existence, as man, is spent swinging between these pairs of opposites, until eventually the balance is achieved and, from then on, he moves towards that which is divine. It might profit all of us if we pondered long and deeply at times upon these two extremities of human existence—good and evil, light and dark, life and form, spirit and matter, the self and the not-self, the real and the unreal, truth and falsehood, right and wrong, pleasure and pain, the urge and the drag, the soul and the personality, Christ and the devil. In these last two the problem of the three temptations is summed up. These dualities have also been defined as finiteness and infinity which are the characteristics, one of man and the other of God. That which emphasises our finite nature is of humanity, that which is comprehensive is of God. We shall see, in our study of these three temptations, how clearly the distinctions between the dualities emerge. Christ, in the temptations, could not contradict Himself; and thus identifying Himself with perfection, He gives us a presentation of a human being "in the world, and yet not of the world,"[35] tempted of the devil yet free from wrong reaction to the devil's suggestions. Thus He was a free soul, which is a divine soul, untrammeled by desire and its tests, undefiled by the flesh and its temptations, and liberated from the sins of the mental processes. Such is

[34] *Religions of Mankind,* by Otto Karrer, pp. 121, 122.
[35] *St. John,* XVII, 16.

the will of God for each and all of us, and the writer quoted above says: "There cannot be freedom . . . unless the divine will is genuinely one with that of finite beings in a single personality."[36] Such a Personality was Christ. Good is the contradiction of evil, and Christ's attitude to the devil was one of uncompromising contradiction. In this He clarified the issue and did what all souls can do. Herein, as I have earlier pointed out, lies His uniqueness and His distinction—it consists in the basic fact of His utilising those methods of service, triumph and sacrifice which are available to any of us. Many in the past have died for others; many have faced evil with uncompromising opposition; many have dedicated their lives to service, but none have succeeded with the completeness and the perfection of Christ.

His greatness, it cannot be too often reiterated, lies in His universality. Dr. Bosanquet deals with this question of personality as follows:

"What I am urging is rather that our true personality lies in our concrete best, and that in desiring its development and satisfaction we are desiring an increase of our real individuality, though a diminution of our formal exclusiveness . . . It will be rejoined that true individuality—greatness of range and organization—augments personal distinction as well as comprehensiveness. Undoubtedly, but it decreases exclusiveness. The great world-men are not born simply of their earthly parents. Whole ages and countries are focussed in them . . . In desiring a highly developed perfection we are desiring to be something which can no longer be identified either with or by the incidents of the terrestrial life."[37]

If these words are studied in connection with Christ's temptations, the wonder of what He did emerges, and is encouraging for all of us, His younger brothers, equally sons of God.

Therefore, as a whole man and yet utterly divine, Christ entered into final combat with the devil. As a human being,

---

[36] *The Value and Destiny of the Individual,* by B. Bosanquet, p. 245.

[37] *Ibid.,* pp. 284, 285.

in whom the divine spirit was fully expressing itself, He faced the evil in His own humanity (when viewed apart from God) and emerged victorious. Let us not attempt to divorce these two—God and man—when we think of Christ. Some thinkers emphasise His humanity and ignore His divinity. Therein they are surely in error. Others emphasise His divinity and regard as blasphemous and wrong all those who have placed Him on an equality with other human beings. But if we regard Christ as the flower of the human race, because the divine spirit had full control and showed forth through the medium of the human form, we in no way belittle Him or His achievements. The further men progress upon the Path of Evolution, the more they become conscious of their divinity and of the Fatherhood of God. At the same time, the more deeply they appreciate the Christ, the more convinced are they of His perfected divinity and His mission, and the more humbly do they seek to follow in His steps, knowing Him to be the Master of all the Masters, very God of very God, and the Teacher alike of Angels and of men.

This perfected divinity is now to be tested and approved. He has now to demonstrate to God, to the devil and to humanity the nature of His achievement, and how the powers of the lower nature can be overcome by the powers of the soul. These temptations can be understood very simply by all aspirants and disciples, because they embody universal tests which are applied to the human nature in which we all share, and with which we all wrestle in some form and in some measure. It matters not whether we do so from the promptings of conscience, from the control of the higher nature, or through the clear light of divinity. This, all disciples have ever recognised.

We shall consider these three temptations in the order given by St. Matthew, which is different from that given by St. Luke. St. Mark simply mentions that Christ was tempted of the devil, whilst St. John does not refer to them at all. These three temptations tested out all the three aspects of the lower human nature—the physical, the emotional-desire nature, and the mind or mental nature. We read that:

"When he had fasted forty days and forty nights, he was afterwards anhungered. And when the tempter came to him, he said, If thou be the Son of God command that these stones be made bread. But he answered and said, It is written, Man shall not live by bread alone, but by every word that proceedeth out of the mouth of God."[38]

There are two interesting facts connected with all these temptations. Each of them begins with "If" on the lips of the devil, and each is met by Christ with the words, "It is written." These two phrases link all three episodes and give the clue to the whole process. The ultimate temptation is doubt. The test we have all to face eventually, and which climaxed in Christ's life, until He vanquished it upon the Cross, is the test of our divinity. Are we divine? How must our divine powers express themselves? What can we do, or not do, because we are sons of God? That the details of each difficulty, test and trial may differ is relatively immaterial. That the tests may first be focussed in one aspect of our lower nature or another is equally unimportant. *It is the general lifelong urge to divinity which is on trial.* To the man who is but a little evolved the problem of divinity as a whole does not present itself. He can be preoccupied only with the detail, with the problem in the immediate foreground of his life. This he handles or not, as the case may be, by the light of conscience. For the disciple, the detail assumes less importance, and the general truth of his sonship begins slowly to concern him. He then handles his life conditions from the angle of that theory. For a perfected son of God, such as the Christ, or for the man nearing perfection, the problem must be handled as a whole, and the life problem must be considered from the angle of divinity itself. Such was the issue with Christ, and such the implications hidden in the devil's threefold "If."

[38] *St. Matt.,* IV, 2, 3, 4.

Rightly or wrongly, it seems to me that we have erred in interpreting all truth from the angle of the mediocre. That is what has been done. Truth is capable of interpretation in many ways. Those who are simply physical-emotional beings, with therefore little vision, require the protection of theology, despite its imperfections and dogmatic or untenable assertions. This they need, and the responsibility of those who administer dogmas to the "little ones" of the race is great. Truth must also be given in a wider form, and with a more general connotation to those who are beginning to live consciously as souls, and who can therefore be trusted to see the meaning behind the symbol and the significance behind the outer appearance of theology. Truth, for the perfected sons of God, must be something beyond our dreams, of so deep a significance and of such comprehensiveness that it is futile for us to speculate upon it, for it is something to be experienced and not to be dreamed; something to enter into and not to vision.

Christ's reply each time should be viewed in this triple manner. "It is written," He says, and the unthinking and small-minded regard this as endorsing the verbal inspiration of the Scriptures. But surely, He was not referring back only to the ancient sayings of the Jewish Scriptures, beautiful as they are. The possibilities of error are too great to warrant our unquestioning acceptance of every word in any scripture in the world. When the processes of translation are studied this becomes glaringly apparent. Christ meant something much deeper than "The Bible says." He meant that the signature of God was upon Him; that He was the Word, and that that Word was the expression of truth. It is the Word of the soul (which is the influx of divinity) that determines our attitude in temptation and our response to the problem presented by the devil. If that Word is remote, deep-hidden by the veiling form, only distorted sounds will issue forth, and the Word will not be potent enough to withstand the devil. The Word is written in the flesh, defaced and almost invisible though it may be through the activity of the lower nature; it is upon the mind that the Word sounds forth, carrying illumination and insight, distorted as yet though the vision may be, and the light scarcely seen. But *the Word is there*. Some day each of us can say with power: "It is written," and see that Word expressed in every part of our human nature as individuals and—at some distant date—in humanity itself. This is the "lost Word" of the Masonic tradition.

Oriental philosophy refers frequently to four spheres of life or four problems which all disciples and aspirants have to face, and which constitute in their entirety the world in which we live. There are the world of *Maya,* the world of glamour and the world of illusion. There is also that mysterious "Dweller on the Threshold" to which Bulwer Lytton refers in *Zanoni*. All of these four Christ met and vanquished in the desert-experience.

Maya refers to the world of physical forces in which we dwell, and with this the first temptation concerned itself. Modern science has told us that there is nothing visible or invisible which is not energy, and that every form is simply an aggregate of energy units in constant ceaseless motion, to which we have to adjust ourselves and in which we "live and move and have our being."[39] Such is the outer form of Deity, and we are part of it. *Maya* is vital in character, and we know little of its effect upon the physical plane (with all that that term connotes), and upon the human being.

"Glamour" refers to the world of emotional being and of desire, in which all forms dwell. It is this glamour which colours all our lives and produces false values, wrong desires, needless so-called necessities, our worries, anxieties and cares; but glamour is age-old, and has us in so close a grip that there seems little we can do. The desires of men, down the centuries, have brought about a situation before which we turn back appalled; the rampant nature of our longings and wishes, and their glamourous effect upon the individual, provide psychological laboratories with all their material; the

[39] *Acts,* XVII, 28.

wish life of the race has been wrongly oriented and human desire has been turned outward to the material plane, thus producing the world of glamour in which we all habitually struggle. It is by far the most potent of our delusions or mistaken orientations. But once the clear light of the soul is thrown into it, this miasma of forces is gradually dissipated. This work constitutes the major task of all aspirants to the mysteries.

"Illusion" is more mental in its impact. It concerns the ideas whereby we live, and the thought life which more or less (although mostly less) governs our daily undertakings. We shall see, as we take up the consideration of these three temptations, how in the first temptation Christ was confronted by *maya*, with physical forces of such strength that the devil could take advantage of them in an effort to confound Him. We shall see how in the second temptation He was tempted by glamour, and with the submergence of His vital spiritual life by a misconception and an emotional use of His divine powers. The sin of the mind, which is pride, was called into activity by the devil in the third temptation, and the illusion of temporal power to be used for right ends we may be sure was presented to Him. Thus the possible interior weakness of the three aspects of Christ's nature was tested, and through them the vast sum total of the world *maya*, glamour and illusion was poured in on Him. Thus He was confronted with the Dweller on the Threshold, which is only another name for the personal lower self, regarding it as a unified whole, as is only the case in advanced people, disciples and initiates. In these three words—*maya*, glamour and illusion—we have synonyms for the flesh, the world and the devil, which constitute the threefold test that confronts every son of God on the verge of liberation.

"If thou be the Son of God command that these stones be made bread." Let us use our divine powers for personal physical ends. Let us put the material physical nature first. Let us assuage our hunger, whatever it may be, and do it because we are divine. Let us use our divine powers so as to gain for ourselves perfect health, long desired financial prosperity, popularity for our personality, for which we crave, and those physical surroundings and conditions which we want. We are sons of God and are entitled to all these things. Command that these stones be made bread for the satisfaction of our supposed need. Such were the specious arguments used then, and being used today by many teachers and schools of thought. These are peculiarly the temptations of the aspirants of the world today. Upon this theory many teachers and groups thrive, and curiously enough, they do so quite sincerely and entirely convinced of the rightness of their position. The temptations which come to the advanced souls in the world are most subtle. The use of divine powers for the meeting and satisfaction of purely personal, physical needs can be presented in such a manner that they may seem entirely right. Yet we do not live by bread alone, but by means of the spiritual life which (coming forth from God) pours into, and is the life of, the lower man. This is the first essential for understanding. Upon that soul life and upon that inner contact the emphasis should be laid. The healing of the physical body, when diseased, would be satisfactory to the individual, but living as a soul is of more importance. The emphasis upon a divinity which *must* express itself entirely through the meeting of a physical need, in a monetary manner, most definitely limits divinity to an attribute of itself. When we live as souls, when our inner life is oriented to God, not because of what we can receive but because we have the developed sense of divinity, then the forces of divine life will pour through us and produce what is needed. This may not necessarily bring about complete immunity from disease or produce financial affluence; but it will mean a sweetening of the lower nature, a tendency to self-forgetfulness, and unselfishness which puts others first, a wisdom which concerns itself with the teaching and helping of others, a freedom from hatred and suspicion which will make life pleasanter for those with whom we associate, and a kindness and inclusiveness which leave no time for the separated self. That this type of inner nature will make for a sound body and freedom from physical ills is quite possible, but not inevitably so. In time and space, in a particular life and at a special time, illness has its uses and may be a profoundly desirable blessing. Poverty and financial stringency may re-establish a lost sense of values and enrich the heart with com-passion. Money and perfect health may be disasters to many. But the use of divine power for selfish ends, and the affirming of the divine nature for purposes of individual healing, seem a prostitution of reality, and constitute the temptation which Christ so triumphantly met. We live by the life of God. Let that life flow in "more abundantly" upon us and we shall become, as Christ became, living centres of radiant energy for the service of the world. Probably what may happen will be better physical health, because we shall not be so pre-occu-pied with ourselves. Freedom from self-centredness is one of the first laws of good health.

The question of healing, engrossing the attention of so many thousands at this time, is too broad to be considered here, and far more complicated than the average healer or healing group realises. Two things only would I point out:

One is that the affirmation that all disease is the result of wrong thought does not warrant too hasty acceptance. There is much disease in the other kingdoms of nature; animals, plants and minerals suffer from disease as do human beings, and these kingdoms antedate the appearance of the human family upon Earth. Secondly, the affirmation that one is di-vine and therefore entitled to good health may be ultimately true when divinity is really expressed, but it is not expressed by affirmation, but by conscious intelligent organised soul contact. This results in living as Christ lived, with no thought of self but only concern and interest in others.

Christ met this temptation to use His divine powers for selfish ends by the quiet reiteration of His divinity—a divin-ity which was based on the universality of the Word. It is perhaps apposite here to remind ourselves that upon the Cross He was taunted by the words, "He saved others; Himself He cannot save."[40] The *maya* or delusion of the physical nature could not hold Him; from that He stood free.

Today the World Aspirant, humanity, stands confronted with this temptation. Its problem is economic. It is concerned basically and definitely with bread, just as, symbolically speaking, Christ's problem was the problem of food. The world is faced with a material issue. That there is no evading this issue is true, and that men *must* be fed is equally true. Upon what basis shall the problem be met? Will one be regarded as too idealistic and as an impractical mystic and visionary if one falls back, as Christ did, upon the fundamentals of life, and takes the position that when man is readjusted and re-oriented as a spiritual being his problem will automatically take care of itself? One surely will be so regarded. If one feels, as do many today, that the solution of the problem lies in a revaluation of life and a re-education in the underlying principles of living, is one entirely astray and to be regarded as a fool? Many will so regard one. But the solving of man's problem solely in terms of his physical needs may only succeed in plunging him more deeply in a material marsh. Meeting his demands entirely from the angle of bread and butter may be much needed. It. is. But it should be accompanied with something which will meet the need of the whole man, and not simply that of his body, and its desires. There are things which matter essentially to man, which are of greater moment and value than the things which concern the form, even if he himself does not realize it. Christ gave a little time to the feeding of the multitude. He gave much time to teaching them the rules of the kingdom of God. Men can be trusted to take what they want. They are doing so at this time on every hand. But the things which truly matter must at the same time be emphasied and taught, or the end will be disastrous. When we have cleaned the human house of abuses, as the revolutionaries in every country and land claim to be doing, unless that house is beautiful as a result, and unless its inhabitants have ideas based on divine

[40] *St. Matt.*, XXVII, 42.

essentials, the last state will be worse than the first. Seven devils may enter into the house, according to Christ's parable.[41] Unless God indwells the house, when cleaned, and unless our revaluations and national adjustments lead to that leisure and peace of mind wherein the soul of man can come to flower, we are headed towards still worse disasters. "Man shall not live by bread alone, but by every word that proceedeth out of the mouth of God."

"Then the devil taketh him up into the holy city, and setteth him upon a pinnacle of the temple, and saith unto him, If thou be the Son of God, cast thyself down; for it is written, He shall give His angels charge concerning thee, and in their hands they shall bear thee up, lest at any time thou dash thy foot against a stone. Jesus said unto him, It is written again, Thou shalt not tempt the Lord thy God."[42]

It is essential for the right understanding of this temptation that we remember our earlier distinction that such passages in the Bible are interpreted from the angle of the souls involved. Christ meets the devil on the ground of His divine nature. If thou art the Son of God, take advantage of the Fatherhood of God, and cast thyself down. This temptation is different from the first, though it appears to embody the same type of test. The clue to this is found in Christ's answer, where He takes His stand upon His divinity. This He did not do in the earlier temptation. The devil in this test quotes scripture to his own ends. He also takes Christ into the Holy Place, the battle-ground, and it is upon this that the devil casts doubt. The glamour of doubt descends upon the Christ. Hungry, lonely, and weary of conflict, He is tempted to question the very roots of His being. I do not question the fact that Christ was assailed by doubt. The first traces of that glamour which descended upon Him like a great darkness in the Crucifixion assailed Him now. Was He the Son of God? Had He a mission, after all? Was His attitude one of self-

[41] *St. Matt.*, XII, 45.
[42] *St. Matt.*, IV, 5, 6, 7.

delusion? Was it all worth while? He was attacked where He was the strongest, and in this lies the potency of this temptation.

In an ancient scripture of India, *The Bhagavad Gita,* the disciple Arjuna stands faced with the same issue. He is involved in a great battle between two branches of the same family—really between the higher and the lower self—and he, too, questions what he shall do. Shall he go ahead with the battle and the test, and so triumph as the soul? Shall he assert his divinity and defeat the lower and the non-divine? In a commentary on *The Bhagavad Gita* these words occur:

"There is a spiritual significance to all this and the situation of Arjuna is well chosen to bring out great spiritual truths. He stands for the personal self beginning to grow conscious of the Higher Self; touched and enkindled with the spiritual light of that higher self, yet full of dismay and terror from the realisation of what obedience to the Higher Self must mean. The contests of the brothers is now concentrated within a single nature, the life of a single man. A war must be waged within himself, a war long and arduous for the life of the Soul. Nothing but high courage, joined with faith and aspiration, makes the contest possible, and even then there will be shrinking and dismay."[43]

A greater than Arjuna (who stands as the symbol of the disciple on his way towards perfection) faced a similar issue with courage, faith and aspiration, but the question was the same: Is the life of the soul a reality? Am I divine? Christ faced this issue without dismay, and triumphed by the use of an affirmation of such power (because it stated a truth) that the devil temporarily could not reach Him. He practically said: "I am the Son of God. Thou mayest not tempt me." He took His stand upon His divinity and vanquished the doubt.

It is interesting to realise that humanity today stands in the glamour of doubt. Doubt is on every hand. It is an emotional matter. The clear, cool, analysing and synthesising intellect does not doubt in this sense; it questions and waits.

[43] *The Bhagavad Gita,* Commentary by Charles Johnston, p. 26.

But it is in the Holy Place, with a full knowledge of what is written, and frequently after victory, that doubt descends upon the disciple. Perhaps, after all, that sense of divinity which has hitherto upheld the disciple is itself but glamour and not reality. That there have been experiences of a divine and supernatural nature the disciple cannot doubt. There have been moments when there has been "a sense of Divine access as different from other experiences, as original and inexplicable, as Sex or as the sense of Beauty—as hunger or thirst,"[44] for there is no question that "at the heart of all religion and all religions there is an·experience unique, and not to be accounted for by evolution from other experience."[45] But perhaps that too is simply phenomenal, and not real; something that passes, with no immortal basis; something that is experienced as part of the world glamour, but does not and cannot endure. Perhaps God is just a name for everything that is, and, for the individual conscious soul, there is no definite persistence, no essential divinity, and nothing real—only a momentary flash of an awareness. Let us put this sense of divinity to the test and see if, with the change of physical destruction, something lasts which is spirit and is immortal.

As one studies the way in which Christ met this temptation one is inclined to believe that (having affirmed His belief in His Own Divinity) He simply ignored the temptation. His method was so brief and concise, and remains undeveloped as to detail. The way out, in this particular temptation, is dual: to recognise it for what it is, unreal, simply a glamour which has no true and lasting existence, just a delusion which assails us; and then to rest back upon the experience of God. If for one brief minute we have been in the Presence of God and known it, that is real. If the Presence of God in the human heart has at any moment, for an instant, been a reality, then let us take our stand upon that known and felt experience, refusing to deal with the

[44] *The Divinity in Man,* by J. W. Graham, p. 88.
[45] *Ibid.,* p. 88.

detail of the glamour of doubt, of emotion, of depression or of blindness in which we may temporarily find ourselves.

But the doubt in the world today will be solved only when men bring to bear upon the problems of humanity, of God and of the soul, not only the clear cool light of the intellect, illumined by the intuition, but also the potency of past experience. If the sense of God has persisted in the world for untold ages, and if the testimony of the mystics and saints, the seers and the Saviours of all time is historical and verifiable—as it is—then that testimony, in its wealth and universality, constitutes a fact as scientific as any other. These are days when a scientific fact seems to have some glamourous appeal. Cycles of mysticism, cycles of philosophy, cycles of scientific expression, cycles of rank materialism—such is the cyclic way we walk, and such is our history. But persistent through them all runs the thread of God's Plan. Steadily through them all, the soul of man marches from one unfoldment of consciousness to another, and our concept of divinity constantly gains in richness and reality. That is the fact upon which humanity can stand, the divine soul in man. That is the fact upon which Christ took His stand when the devil tempted Him a second time.

"Again, the devil taketh him up into an exceeding high mountain, and sheweth him all the kingdoms of the world and the glory of them; and saith unto him, All these things will I give thee if thou wilt fall down and worship me. Then saith Jesus unto him, Get thee hence, Satan, for it is written Thou shalt worship the Lord thy God, and him only shalt thou serve."[46]

Christ has been tested in His physical nature and has triumphed. He has been tried in His emotional-desire nature, and we have found that neither the forces of the physical nature nor the glamours which the emotional-feeling nature inevitably bring could cause him to swerve the slightest from the path of spiritual living and expression. All His desires were directed towards God; every activity of His

[46] *St. Matt.,* IV, 8, 9, 10.

nature was rightly adjusted and divinely expressed. This triumph must have been known to Him, and this realisation carried in itself the seeds of the final temptation. He had triumphed over materialism and over doubt. He knew that the form side of life could not attract Him, and He had fought through to a full recognition of His divinity. Therefore He had conquered the extremes of His nature, its highest and lowest aspects. He expressed now the quality of divinity. The divine reality which He sensed and upon which He relied was potent to penetrate the *maya* and dispel the glamour. Pure desire was left—desire for God. He had been tried in two aspects of His nature—the material and the divine—and as God-Man He overcame the evil one. Primarily, both temptations lay in the region of desire. The call is to personal desirelessness.

So with Christ, desire was transmuted into power, though victory achieved led to developments which had in them the possibility of danger. It was in the realm of power that Christ was next tried. A character that has been carried to a high degree of perfection and which has established a unity between the source of power, the soul, and the instrument of power, the personal lower self, produces what we call a personality. That personality can be a definite source of danger to its owner. The sense of power, the knowledge of achievement, the realisation of capacity and the sensed ability to rule others because one rules oneself, have in them the germs of temptation, and it was here that the devil next attempted to ensnare the Christ. People are apt to be astonished when it is pointed out to them that a fine character can itself be a source of difficulty. It is difficulty of a peculiar kind, in that the things done and the words spoken by a highly developed person whose character is outstandingly fine and whose personality is well rounded out can do much harm—even when the motive is right or apparently so. Such persons wield much more power than the average.

Just what is a fine character, and how is it produced? First, of course, it is produced by the wheel of life and the Galilee experience; then by conscious effort and self-initiated discipline; and finally by the processes of integrating the various aspects of the lower nature into a synthetic whole, into a unity for purposive use.

In the case of Christ in the third temptation, His "conscious values or purposes" were being tried. His integrity must be undermined, if possible, and the unity for which He stood must be forced to disintegrate. If this could be done, and if the standard which He set could be upset, His mission was, from the start, destined to fail. If He could be deceived by the illusion of power, if ambition of a personal nature could be developed in His consciousness, the founding of the kingdom of God might be indefinitely delayed. This temptation was an attack at the very root of the personality. The mind, the integrating factor, with its ability to think clearly, to formulate definite purpose and to choose, was under test. Such temptations do not come to the little-developed, and because of the strength of the character involved they are of the fiercest kind and the most difficult to handle. The call of the devil was to Christ's ambition. Ambition is, par excellence, the problem of the developed aspirant and disciple—personal ambition, love of popularity, worldly ambition, intellectual ambition, and the dictatorship of power over others. The subtlety of this temptation consists in the fact that appeal is made to right motive. It would—such is the implication—be good for the world of human affairs if it all belonged to Christ. By simply recognising the power of the devil, the material force in the world, as being supreme, that control over the kingdoms of the world could be given to Christ. He was offered it as the reward of a single recognition—given alone and unseen on the top of a high mountain—to the power which represented, or symbolised, the triple world of external living. If Christ would briefly fall down and worship that great power, the kingdoms of the world and the glory of them would be His; and we know enough about Him to realise that there would have been no selfish motive in this gesture, could He have been induced to make it. What stood between Him and the acceptance of this opportunity? His reply indicates it clearly, but needs understanding. What intervened was His knowledge that God was One and God was All. The devil showed Him a picture of diversity, of many kingdoms, much division, of multiplicity, plurality, separated units. Christ came to unify, to bring together and to unite in one all kingdoms, all races and all men, so that the words of St. Paul could be true in deed and in fact:

"There is one body and one Spirit, even as ye are called in one hope of your calling; one Lord, one faith, one baptism, one God and Father of all, who is above all, and through all, and in you all."[47]

Had Christ succumbed to the enticements of the devil and, from apparent right motive and love of humanity, accepted the proffered gift, these words would never have been fulfilled, as they surely will be at some date, perhaps not so distant as the chaotic present might lead us to think. Christ held His values true and His purpose unchanged. The illusion of power could not touch Him. That which was real had such a grip of His mind that the unreal and the immediate could not delude His consciousness. He saw the picture whole. He saw the vision of a world wherein there could be no duality but only unity, and from His efforts to bring that future world into being He could not be swerved.

Where this vision exists, lesser values and smaller issues cannot hold the ardent heart. Where the whole as a possibility is grasped, the part falls into its rightful place. Where the purpose of God stands clearly revealed to the mind of the seer, the lesser ends or motives, and the tiny wishes and desires for and of the personal self fade out of the picture. At the end of the road of evolution lies the consummation, the kingdom of God, not the kingdoms of the world. They are parts of a future whole, and will be later welded into a spiritual synthesis. But that kingdom, as we shall see in our final chapter, when we sum up the results of initiation, is

[47] *Eph.*, IV, 4, 5, 6.

not brought into being through personal ambition, personal effort and personal desire. It comes through the submergence of the part in the whole and of the individual in the group. But this is brought about willingly and intelligently, with no loss of personal prestige, usefulness or sense of identity. It is not enforced or demanded by the group or state or kingdom, as is so frequently the case today. Dr. van der Leeuw tells us:

"If we would enter the kingdom this attitude must change to that of Christ whose love has become radiating, ever giving out to the surrounding world, whether deserving or not, whose life is centred in the Divine, common to all. In Him there is no remnant even of a separated personality, battling for its own existence or aggrandisement; the cup of His existence is emptied of all that is personal and become filled with the wine of the divine life, shared by all. We, by continuous though possibly unconscious effort, may maintain the centre of separate life which we call our personality; if we would follow Christ, we have to give up the laborious struggle for individual assertion in the desire to be the life of the Whole rather than that of a part. Thus alone can we enter the Kingdom where no separateness can be."[48]

Christ's temptation consisted of a demanded recognition of duality. But to Him, there was only one kingdom and one way into the kingdom, and one God Who was bringing, slowly indeed but surely, that kingdom into being. His mission was to reveal the method whereby unity could be brought about; to proclaim that inclusive love and that technique of at-one-ment which all who would study His life and react to His spirit could follow. He could not therefore fall into the error of diversity. He could not identify Himself with multiplicity when He embraced in His consciousness, as God, the larger synthesis. Pope, in his famous *Essay on Man,* sensed this, and expressed it in words familiar to all of us:

"God loves from whole to parts, but human soul
    Must rise from individual to the whole.

[48] *Dramatic History of Christian Faith,* by Dr. van der Leeuw, p. 19.

Self-love but serves the virtuous mind to wake,
As the small pebble stirs the peaceful lake;
The centre moved, a circle straight succeeds,
Another still, and still another spreads;
Friend, parent, neighbour, first it will embrace;
His country next; and next all human race;
Wide and more wide, th' o'erflowings of the mind
Take every creature in, of every kind;
Earth smiles around, with boundless bounty blest,
And Heaven beholds its image in his breast."

Then the devil leaves Him. He could do no more, and Christ "departed into Galilee,"[49] going back again to the round of daily living. The Galilee experience can never be evaded by any Son of God whilst incarnate in the flesh. He then did three things: first, hearing that John the Baptist had been cast into prison, Christ took up the task laid down by him, and went on with the preaching of repentance. Next, He chose with care those who were to work with Him, and whom He had to train to carry forward the mission of the kingdom, and then He began that increased service which is ever the signal to the world that a man has become more inclusive and has passed through another initiation. Even though the world may not at the time recognise that signal, it is never again just the same world as it was before the initiation is taken and the service rendered. The emergence of an initiate into the field of the world makes that field different.

Christ went about doing good, "teaching in the synagogues, preaching the gospel of the kingdom, and healing all manner of disease among the people."[50] He had registered before God and man, and to Himself, His perfection. He emerged from the wilderness experience tried, tested, and with His divinity completely vindicated. He knew Himself to be God; He had demonstrated to Himself His divine humanity. And yet, as is the way with all the

[49] *St. Matt.,* IV, 12.
[50] *St. Matt.,* IV, 17-24.

liberated sons of God, He could not rest until He had shown us the way. He had to transmit the great energy of the Love of God.

Perfected, serving and with a full knowledge of His mission, Christ now enters into the period of active work which must precede the next initiation, that of the Transfiguration.

The Third Initiation: The Transfiguration on a High Mountain

KEY THOUGHT

Arjuna said:

"The word which Thou hast spoken through love of me, the supreme mystery named the Oversoul—through it my delusion is gone.

"For the birth and the passing of beings have been heard by me at length from Thee, whose eyes are lotus petals; I have heard also of the Great Spirit, which passes not away.

"So I would see that Self as it has been spoken by Thee, Mighty Lord; that divine form of Thine, O best of men!

"If Thou thinkest it can be seen by me, Lord, Master of union, then reveal to me the Self everlasting!"

Bhagavad Gita, XI, 1-4.

The Third Initiation: The Transfiguration on a High Mountain

1

A NOTHER period of service is ended. Christ faced another interior crisis, and this time, according to the story, one which He shared with His three favourite disciples, with the three people closest to Him. His demonstrated self control, and henceforth His immunity from temptation, as we can understand it, had been succeeded by a period of intense activity. He had also laid the foundation of the kingdom of God which it was His mission to found, and whose inner structure and skeleton outline were built upon the twelve apostles, the seventy disciples whom He chose and trained, and the groups of men and women everywhere which responded to His message. So far He was successful. Now He faced another initiation and a further expansion of consciousness. These initiations, to which He subjected Himself on our behalf, and to which we may all in due time aspire, constitute in themselves a living synthesis of revelation which it may profit us to study before we consider the detail of the stupendous revelation which was accorded to the three apostles on the mountain-top. Three of these crises are perhaps of greater significance than has hitherto been grasped by humanity, which is prone to lay the emphasis mainly upon one of them only, the Crucifixion.

One wonders sometimes whether the other tremendous experiences through which Christ passed would have been relatively overlooked in favour of the Crucifixion had the

Epistles never been written and had we only the Gospel story upon which to base our Christian belief. This is a point to consider, and worthy of serious speculation. The bias thrown on Christian theology by St. Paul has perhaps over-balanced the structure of the presentation of Christ as we were meant to get it. The three initiations which, in the last analysis, may mean the most to the seeker after truth, are the birth into the kingdom, that august moment when the entire lower nature is transfigured and one realises the fitness of God's sons to be citizens of that kingdom, and the final crisis wherein the immortality of the soul is demonstrated and recognised. The Baptism and the Crucifixion have other values, emphasising as they do purification and self-sacrifice. This may surprise the reader, in that it seems to belittle the Christ, but it is profoundly necessary for us to see the picture as the Gospels present it, uncoloured by the interpretations of a later son of God, no matter if brilliant and sincere, as was St. Paul. In dealing with the subject of Deity, we have always been told that we know God through His nature, and that nature is Spirit or Life, Soul or conscious love, and Form intelligently motivated. Life, quality, and appearance—these are the three major aspects of divinity, and we know no others; but that does not mean that we shall not contact other aspects when eventually we provide the mechanism of knowledge and the intuition to penetrate deeper into the divine Nature. We do not yet know the Father. Christ revealed Him, but the Father Himself remains as yet behind the scenes, inscrutable, unseen and unknown, except as He is revealed through the life of His sons, and by the revelation given peculiarly to the Occident by Jesus Christ.

As we consider these initiations, the three mentioned above stand out clearly. At the Birth in Bethlehem we have the *appearance* of God, God is made manifest in the flesh. At the Transfiguration we have the *quality of God* revealed in its transcendent beauty, whilst at the Resurrection initiation the *life aspect* of divinity makes its presence felt.

In His earthly life, therefore, Christ did two things:

1. He revealed the triple nature of Deity in the first, third, and fifth initiations.
2. He demonstrated the expansions of consciousness which come when the requirements are duly met—purification and self-sacrifice.

In these five episodes the whole story of initiation is told; birth, subsequent purification in order that right manifestation of Deity may follow, revelation of the nature of God through the medium of a transfigured personality, and finally the goal—life eternal and unending because decentralised and freed from the self-imposed limitations of form.

These three major initiations, the first, the third and the fifth, constitute the three syllables of the Word made flesh; they embody the musical chord of Christ's life, as they will be embodied in the life of all who follow in His steps. Through re-orientation to new modes of living and of being we pass through the necessary stages of adaptation of the vehicles of life, up to that mountain-top where the divine in us is revealed in all its beauty. Then we pass to a "joyful Resurrection," and to that eternal identification with God which is the everlasting experience of all who are perfected. We might depict the process as follows:

1st Initiation	3rd Initiation	5th Initiation
New Birth	Transfiguration	Resurrection
Initiation	Revelation	Completion
Beginning	Transition	Consummation
Appearance	Quality	Life

This is the first of the mountain experiences. We have had the cave experience and the stream initiation. Each of them has done its work, each revealing more and more divinity in the Man, Christ Jesus. The experience of Christ, as we have been seeing, was to pass from one process of at-one-ment to another. One of the prime objectives of His mission was to resolve the dualities in Himself, producing unity and synthesis. What are these dualities which are to be resolved into unity before the spirit in man can shine forth in its radiance? We might list five of them in order to gain an idea of what must be done and in order to understand the magnitude of Christ's achievement. Transfiguration is not possible until these unifications have been made.

First, man and God must be fused and blended into one functioning whole. God, made flesh, must so dominate and control the flesh that it constitutes no hindrance to the full expression of divinity. Such is not the case with the average man. With him divinity may be present, but it is deeply hidden. However, today, through our psychological investigations, much is being discovered as to this higher and lower self, and the nature of that which is called at times the "subliminal self" is emerging through a study of the reaction of the outer active self to the activities of that inner subjective guidance. That man is dual has been recognised everywhere, and this in itself presents a problem with which psychologists are constantly confronted. Personalities seem to function in a "split" manner; people are distraught because of this cleavage. We hear of multiple personalities, and the necessity for integration, for co-ordination of the different aspects of man, and the fusing of his nature in one functioning whole becomes more and more urgent. The recognition of man's reach and the constant pull of the world of transcendental values have produced an acute problem for the world. The primitive and the transcendental; the outer conscious man and the inner subjective subliminal man; the higher and the lower self; the personality and the individuality; the soul and the body—how are these to be reconciled? Of the higher values, man is ceaselessly conscious. Of the man who wills to do good, and of the nature which in opposition causes him to perform evil, all the saints testify.

The entire human family today is split on the rock of duality. Either the personality is dual and therefore unmanageable, or groups and nations are divided into opposing camps, and again duality emerges in intense dynamic difficulty.

It is integration which Christ so fully exemplified, thus resolving the dualities of higher and lower in Himself, making "of twain one new man,"[1] and it was this "new man" which shone forth at the Transfiguration before the startled gaze of the three apostles. It is this basic integration or unification which religion should aim to produce, and it is this co-ordination between two fundamental aspects of human nature—the natural and the divine—which education should effect.

This problem of the two selves, which Christ so strikingly synthesised in Himself, is the strictly human problem. The secondary self, in contradistinction to the divine self, is a fact in nature, however we may try to evade the issue and refuse recognition of its existence. The "natural man" exists, as does the "spiritual man," and in the interaction of the two the human problem is focussed. Man himself makes this clear. In speaking of man, Dr. Bosanquet says that:

". . . his innate self-transcendence, his ineradicable passion for the whole, makes it inevitable that out of the superfluity which he cannot systematise under the good, he will form a secondary and negative self, a disinherited self, hostile to the imperative domination of the good which is, *ex hypothesi*, only partial. And this discord is actually necessary to the good; for it sets it its characteristic problem, the conquest of the bad. And the good is necessary to the evil, for beyond rebellion against the good, the would-be totality of the disinherited self can find no other unity."[2]

Here lies man's problem, and here lie his triumph and the expression of his essential divinity. The higher self exists, and finally and inevitably must gain the victory over the lower self. One of the things that is happening today is the

[1] *Eph.*, II, 15.
[2] *The Value and Destiny of the Individual*, by B. Bosanquet, p. 210.

discovery of the existence of this higher self, and many are the testimonies to its nature and qualities. Through a consideration of the self in every man we are steadily approximating an understanding of divinity.

Behind the manifestation of Jesus Christ lay aeons of experience. God had been expressing Himself through natural processes, through humanity as a whole, and through specific individuals, as the ages slipped away. Then Christ came, and in process of time, as a definite fulfilment of the past and as a guarantee of the future, He synthesised in Himself, in one transcendent Personality, all that had been achieved and all that was immediate in human experience. He was a Personality, as well as a divine Individuality. His life with its quality and its purpose has set its seal upon our civilisation, and His demonstrated synthesis is the inspiration of the present. This consummated Personality, synthesising in Itself all that preceded in human evolution, and expressing all that immediately may be, is God's great gift to man.

Christ, as the Personality that healed the division in human nature, and Christ, as the synthesis of the higher and the lower aspects of divinity, is the glorious heritage of mankind today. This is what was revealed at the Transfiguration.

However, it is useful to remember that only at a certain stage in human development does the expression of the indwelling Christ life and consciousness become possible. The fact of evolution, with its necessary distinctions and differences, is incontrovertible. All men are not the same. They vary in their presentation of divinity. Some are really sub-human as yet. Others are simply human, and still others are beginning to display qualities and characteristics which are super-human. The question might justifiably arise: when does the possibility come to man of transcending the human, and becoming divine? Two factors will at that time control. He will have transcended the emotional and physical natures, and, entering the realm of thought, he should be responding in some way to ideals as they are presented to him by the

thinkers of the world. There must come a time in the progress of each human being when the development of the
triple human nature—physical, emotional and mental—
reaches a point of possible synthesis. He then becomes a
personality. He thinks. He decides. He determines. He
assumes control of his life and becomes not only an originat-
ing centre of activity but an impressive influence in the world.
It is the coming in, with power, of the mind quality, and the
capacity to think, which make this possible.

It is this insistence upon thought, and this determination
to handle life from the angle of mind and not of emotion,
which distinguish a "personality" from the rank and file of
human beings. The man who thinks and who acts upon the
resolutions and incentives which have their origin in duly
considered thought-realities becomes, in time, a "personality," and begins to sway other minds. He exercises a definite influence upon other people. Yet overseeing the personality is the inner spiritual man, which we might call the
"individual." It is here again that Christ achieved success,
and the second duality, which He so significantly resolved, is
that of the personal self and the "individuality." The finite
and the infinite must be brought into a close relation. This,
Christ demonstrated in the Transfiguration, when, through
the medium of a purified and developed personality, He manifested the nature and the quality of God. The finite nature
had been transcended and could no longer control His activities. He had passed in His consciousness to the realm of
inclusive realisation, and the ordinary rules governing the
finite individual, with its petty problems and its small reaction to events and persons, could no longer influence Him
nor determine His conduct. He had achieved contact with
that realm of being in which there is not only understanding,
but peace, through unity.

Rules and fixations and considerations Christ had surmounted, and consequently He functioned as an individual
and not as a human personality. He was governed by the

rules which control in the realm of the spirit, and it was this which the three Apostles recognised at the Transfiguration, and which led to their submission to Him henceforth as the One Who represented to them Divinity. Christ, therefore, at the Transfiguration, unified in Himself God and Man, His developed Personality blending with His Individuality. He stood forth as the perfect expression of the uttermost possibility to which humanity could aspire. The dualities, of which mankind is so distressingly the expression, met in Him, and resulted in a synthesis of such perfection that, for all time, He determined the goal of our race.

There is a still higher synthesis, and this Christ also summarised in Himself—the synthesis of the part with the Whole, of humanity with the ultimate Reality. Man's history has been one of development from the state of mass unconscious reactions to that of a slowly recognised group responsibility. The low-grade human being or the unthinking individual has a collective consciousness. He may regard himself as a person, but he does no clear thinking as to human relations, or as to the place of humanity in the scale of being. He is easily swayed by the mass or collective thought, and is regimented and standardised by mass psychology. He moves in rhythm with the mass of men; he thinks as they think (if he thinks at all) ; he easily feels as the mass feels, and he remains undifferentiated from his kind. Upon this, orators and dictators base their success. Through their golden-tongued oratory or through their magnetic and dominant personalities, they swing the masses to their will because they work with the collective, though undeveloped, consciousness.

From this stage we pass to that of the emerging personality who does his own thinking, makes his own plans and cannot be regimented or beguiled by words. He is a thinking individual, and the collective consciousness and the mass mind cannot hold him in thrall. These are the people who pass on to liberation, and who, from one expansion of awareness to another, gradually become consciously integrated parts of the whole. Eventually, the group and its will (not the mass and its feeling) come to be of supreme importance, because they see the group as God sees it, become custodians of the divine Plan, and conscious, integral, intelligent parts of the whole. They know what they are doing, and why they do it. In Himself Christ blended and fused the part with the whole, and effected an at-one-ment between the will of God, synthetic and comprehensive, and the individual will, which is personal and limited. In a commentary on *The Bhagavad Gita,* that supreme argument for the life of the whole as fused and blended in divinity, Charles Johnston points out that:

"The truth would seem to be that, at a certain point in spiritual life, the ardent disciple, who has sought in all things to bring his soul into unison with the great Soul, who has striven to bring his will to likeness with the Divine Will, passes through a marked spiritual experience, in which the great Soul draws him upward, the Divine Will raises his consciousness to oneness with the Divine Consciousness; for a time he perceives and feels, no longer as the person, but as the Oversoul, gaining a profound vision of the divine ways of life, and feeling with the infinite Power, which works through life and death alike, through sorrow and joy, through union and separation, through creation, destruction and recreation. The awe and mystery which surround that great unveiling have set their seal on all who have passed through it."[3]

This realisation is far from the average man, and still further from the undeveloped.

The divine is the Whole, informed and animated by the life and will of God; and in utter self-surrender and with all the power of His purified nature and His divine understanding and wisdom, Christ blended in Himself the collective consciousness, the human realisation and the divine Totality. Some day we shall understand this more clearly. It is as yet something which we cannot grasp, unless for us the Transfiguration is a reality and not a goal.

[3] *The Bhagavad Gita,* translated by Charles Johnston, p. 128.

It is interesting to have in mind another at-one-ment which Christ made. He unified in Himself the past and the future, as far as humanity is concerned. This is significantly typified in the appearance with Him upon the Mount of Transfiguration of Moses and Elias, the representatives respectively of the Law and of the Prophets. In the one figure we find symbolised the past of man, with its summation in the Law of Moses, setting the limits beyond which man may not go, defining the injunctions which he must set upon his lower nature (the desire-nature), and emphasising the restrictions which the race as a whole must set upon its actions. Careful study will reveal that all these laws concern the government and control of the desire-nature, of the emotional, feeling body, to which we have already had need to refer. Curiously enough, the name "Moses," according to *Cruden's Concordance,* means "taken out of the water." We have already seen that water is the symbol of the fluidic emotional desire-nature in which man habitually dwells. Moses therefore appeared with Christ as typifying man's emotional past, and the technique of its control is to be later superseded when the message of Christ's life is duly understood, pouring through man's consciousness in ever greater fulness. Christ indicated the new synthetic commandment which is "to love one another." This would render needless all the Law and the Prophets, and would relegate the Ten Commandments into the background of life, rendering them superfluous, because the love which will flow out from man to God, and from man to man, will automatically and positively produce that right action which will make the breaking of the commandments impossible. The "shalt not" of God, spoken from Mount Sinai through Moses, with its negative emphasis and its punitive interpretation, will give place to the radiance of love and the understanding of goodwill and light which Christ radiated upon the mount of Transfiguration. The past met in Him and was superseded by a living present.

Elias, whose name means "the strength of the Lord," stood

beside Jesus Christ as the representative of all the schools of the Prophets which had for centuries foretold the coming of the One Who would stand for perfect righteousness and Who, in His Own Person, would embody, as He does today, the future achievement and the goal of the human race. That the future holds reaches of consciousness and standards of achievement as much beyond those of Christ as His expression is beyond ours, is entirely possible. *The nature of the Father remains still to be known;* some of its aspects, such as the love and wisdom of God, have been revealed to us by Christ. For us today, and for our immediate goal, Christ stands as the Eternal Prophet, to whom Elias and all the Prophets bear witness. Therefore, as He stood upon the mountain top, the past and the future of humanity met in Him.

That He at-oned in Himself certain basic human cleavages is thus apparent, and to those above enumerated we can add one already considered, the blending in Himself of two great kingdoms in nature, the human and the divine, making possible the emergence into manifestation of a new kingdom upon earth—the kingdom of God, the fifth kingdom in nature.

When considering the Transfiguration it is necessary to realise that it was not simply a great initiation, in which God revealed Himself in His radiance and glory to man, but that it had a definite relation to the medium of revelation—the material physical nature, which we call the "Mother aspect." We saw, when studying the Birth initiation, that the Virgin Mary (even when recognising, as we do, the historicity of Christ's existence) is the symbol of the form nature, of the material nature of God. She typifies in herself that which preserves the life of God, latent yet with infinite potentialities. Christ revealed the love-nature in the Father. Through His Person, He revealed the purpose and objective of the form-life of man.

In this mountain experience we see the glorification of matter as it reveals and expresses the divine, indwelling Christ. Matter, the Virgin Mary, reveals God. Form, the result of active material processes, must express divinity, and the revelation of this is God's gift to us at the Transfiguration. Christ was "very God of very God," but He was also "flesh of our flesh," and in the interplay and the fusion of the two, God stood revealed in all His magnetic and radiant glory.

When we, as human beings, realise the divine purpose, and come to regard our physical bodies as the means whereby the divine, indwelling Christ can be revealed, we shall gain a new vision of physical living and a renewed incentive for the proper care and treatment of the physical body. We shall cherish these bodies, through which we temporarily function, as the custodians of the divine revelation. We shall, each of us, regard them as the Virgin Mary regarded her body, as the repository of the hidden Christ, and we shall look forward to that momentous day when we, too, shall stand upon the Mount of Transfiguration, revealing the glory of the Lord through the medium of our bodies. Browning sensed this and gave us the thought in the following well-known phrases:

"Truth is within ourselves; it takes no rise
  From outward things, whate'er you may believe.
  There is an inmost centre in us all
  Where truth abides in fulness; and around
  Wall upon wall, the gross flesh hems it in.
  . . . . And, to *know*
  Rather consists in opening out a way
  Whence the imprisoned splendour may escape
  Than in effecting entry for a light
  Supposed to be without."[4]

Thus, for humanity, Christ stood revealed as the expression of God. There is for us no other goal. Yet let us remember with humility and awe that the stupendous words spoken by Krishna, in *The Bhagavad Gita,* remain also true

[4] *Paracelsus,* by Robert Browning, Oxford Edition, p. 444.

as an ultimate statement concerning the transfiguration of the whole world:

"Nor is there any end of My divine form, O consumer of the foe; this I have told thee for thy instruction, as an enumeration of My manifold forms. Whatever being is glorious, gracious or powerful, thou shalt recognize that, as sprung from a fragment of my fire. But what need hast thou of this manifold wisdom, O Arjuna? With one part of My being I stand establishing this whole world."[5]

Under the impact of the evolutionary urge God moves towards fuller recognition. "Purification" is the word generally used to cover the process whereby the medium of divine expression is prepared for use. The Galilee experience, and the daily effort to live and meet the eventualities of human existence (which appear to grow more drastic and disciplinary as the great wheel of life turns, and, turning, carries humanity onward), bring man to the point where this purification is not simply the result of life itself, but is something which is definitely imposed by man upon his own nature. When this process is self-initiated, then the speed with which the work is carried forward is greatly accentuated. This produces a *transformation* of the outer man of great significance. The caterpillar becomes transformed into the butterfly. Deep in man lies this hidden beauty, unrealised, but struggling for release.

The life of the indwelling Christ produces the transformation of the physical body, but deeper still, that life operates upon the emotional-feeling nature, and through the process of *transmutation* converts the desires and feelings, the pains and the pleasures, into their higher correspondences. Transmutation has been defined as "the passage across from one state of being to another, through the agency of fire."[6] It is appropriate in this connection to remember that the threefold lower man, with whom we have been dealing so often in these pages, is a dim reflection of

[5] *The Bhagavad Gita,* Book X, 40, 41, 42.
[6] *A Treatise on Cosmic Fire,* by Alice A. Bailey, p. 476.

Deity Itself. The physical body is related to the third aspect of divinity, the Holy Ghost aspect, and the truth of this can be realised if we study the Christian concept of the Virgin Mary overshadowed by the Holy Ghost. The Holy Ghost is that aspect of divinity which is the active principle in matter, and of this the physical body is a correspondence. The emotional, sentient nature is a dim and distorted reflection of the love-nature of God which the cosmic Christ, the second Person in the Trinity, is engaged in revealing; and this aspect (transmuted through the agency of fire, the will or spirit of God) produces the transformation of the physical body. The mind in its turn is therefore the reflection of the highest aspect of deity, the Father, or Spirit, of Whom it is said that our "God is a consuming fire."[7] The releasing activity of this form of God's spirit eventually produces that radiance (as a result of transformation and transmutation) which was the distinguishing characteristic of the Transfiguration initiation. *"Radiation is transmutation in process of accomplishment."* Transmutation being the liberation of the essence in order that it may seek a new centre, the process may be recognised as 'radio activity' as far as humanity is concerned."[8]

It was these processes, carried on in the form nature, which led eventually to the revelation to the Apostles of the essential nature of the Master they loved and followed, and it is this aspect of Christ—the inner radiant reality—to which the mystics of all times bear testimony, not only in connection with Christ, but in lesser degree *in connection with each other also.* Once the world of the senses has been transcended, and the higher correspondences have become active, revealing the inner world of beauty and truth, there will come to the mystic a realisation of a subjective world whose characteristics are light, radiance, beauty and indescribable wonder. All the mystical writings are attempts to describe this world to which the mystics seem to have access, with

[7] *Deut.*, IV, 24.
[8] *A Treatise on Cosmic Fire*, by Alice A. Bailey, p. 478.

its forms varying according to the period, race and point of development of the seer. We know only that the divine stands revealed, while the outer form which has veiled and hidden it dissolves, or is so transformed that only the inner reality is registered. The temperament and tendencies of the mystic—his own innate quality—have also much to do with his description of what he sees. However, all are agreed on the essentially transcendent nature of the experience, and convinced of the divine nature of the person concerned.

Great indeed was the power and mystery of divinity which Christ revealed to the astonished gaze of His three friends upon the Mount of Transfiguration. In one of the ancient scriptures of India, quoted by Dr. Otto, there is an attempt to express or reveal that divine essential Spirit manifested at the Transfiguration:

> "Finer than the fine yet am I greatest,
> I am the All in its complete fullness,
> I, the most ancient, the spirit, the Lord God.
> The golden-gleaming am I, of form divine.
> Without hand and foot, rich in unthinkable might,
> Sight without eyes, hearing without ears,
> Free from all form, I know. But me
> None knows. For I am Spirit, am Being."[9]

The mass of literature that has been written in an attempt to portray the wonder of the transfiguration and the vision of God, is an outstanding phenomenon of the religious life, and one of the strongest testimonies to the fact of the revelations.

The very simplicity of the story as related in the Gospels has a majesty and a convincing power of its own. The Apostles saw a vision and they participated in an experience wherein Christ Jesus stood before them as perfected Man, because fully divine. They had shared with Him His service; they had left their various vocations in order to be with Him; they had gone with Him from place to place and

[9] *Kaivalya*, II, 9. Quoted in *Mysticism, East and West*, by Rudolph Otto, pp. 98, 99.

helped Him in His work, and now, as a reward for faithfulness and recognition, they were permitted to see the Transfiguration. "When the mind," says St. Augustine, "hath been imbued with the beginning of faith which worketh by love, it goes on by living well to arrive at sight also, wherein is unspeakable beauty known to high and holy hearts, the full vision of which is the highest happiness."[10]

2

"After six days Jesus taketh Peter, James and John his brother, and bringeth them up into a high mountain apart, and was transfigured before them; and his face did shine as the Sun, and his raiment was white as the light.

"And behold, there appeared unto them Moses and Elias talking with him. Then answered Peter, and said unto Jesus, Lord, it is good for us to be here: if thou wilt, let us make here three tabernacles; one for thee, and one for Moses, and one for Elias.

"While he yet spake, behold, a bright cloud overshadowed them: and behold a voice out of the cloud, which said, This is my beloved Son, in whom I am well pleased; hear ye him. And when the disciples heard it, they fell on their face, and were sore afraid. And Jesus came and touched them, and said, Arise, and be not afraid. And when they had lifted up their eyes, they saw no man, save Jesus only."[11]

A consideration of the various unifications which Christ had made in Himself will have prepared us for the stupendous phenomenon of the revelation which forced the three disciples to their faces. Three kneeling kings or magi attended the birth initiation. At this crisis there were three disciples prostrate upon the ground, unable to look upon the glory which had been revealed. They thought that they knew their Master, but the familiar Presence had been transformed, and they stood before The Presence. The sense of awe, of wonder and of humility is ever an outstanding

[10] *Psychology and God,* by L. W. Grensted, p. 75.
[11] *St. Matt.,* XVII, 1-8.

reaction of the mystics of all time to the revelation of light. This episode is the first one in which we contact the radiance and the light which shone from the Saviour, and which enabled Him to say with truth "I am the Light of the world." Contact with God will ever cause a light to shine forth. When Moses came down from Mount Sinai, his countenance was so irradiated that men could not look upon it, and history tells that he had to use a veil to shield that radiance from others. But the light which was in Christ shone forth in fulness from His whole Person. Increasingly, I believe, as the evolutionary process goes forward, we shall come to a deeper understanding of the significance of light in relation to humanity. We talk of the light of knowledge, and towards that light and its furtherance all of our educational processes and institutions are consecrated. We desire profoundly the light of understanding, which expresses itself in wisdom, and characterises the sage and the wise upon earth; this light marks them off from the ordinarily intelligent person, making their words of moment, and giving value to their advice. We have been led to believe that there are in the world the *illuminati,* working quietly and silently behind the scenes in world affairs, shedding the light when needed into the dark places of the world, elucidating problems, and eventually bringing to light that which must be eradicated and that which is needed. We have also learnt to recognise the Light-bearers of all time, and we feel that in Christ the light of the ages is focussed, and the light of God is centred. His disciples came into the radius of this light for the first time on the mountain-top, after six days of work, so the story runs, and could not bear the sight of so much brilliance. Nevertheless, they felt that "it was good for them to be there." Yet in our consideration of the light which was in Christ, and the rapture of the Apostles at its revelation, let us not lose sight of the fact that He Himself tells us that there is in us also a light, and that it too must blaze forth for the helping of the world and the glorification of our Father which is in

Heaven.[12] To this light the mystics testify, and it is this light into which they enter, and which enters into them, revealing the light which is latent and drawing it forth to potency. "In Thy light shall we see light." This is the outstanding fact of scientific mysticism. God is light as well as life. This the mystic has proved, and to this he eternally testifies.

This awareness of the fact of divinity is established in our consciousness first of all through the recognition of the wonder latent in every human being. That man who sees no good in his fellowmen is he who is unaware of his own goodness; that man who sees only evil in those around him is he who is seeing them through the distorted lens of his own warped nature. But those who are awakening to the world of reality are constantly made aware of the divinity in man, through his unselfish acts, his kindness, his spirit of enquiry, his light-heartedness in difficulty, and his basic essential goodness. This awareness deepens as he studies the history of the race and the religious inheritance of the ages, and above all when he is brought face to face with the transcendent goodness and wonder which Christ revealed. From this realisation he passes on to the discovery of the divine in himself, and starts on that long struggle which carries him through the stages of intellectual awareness of possibility, and of intuitive perception of truth, to that illumination which is the prerogative and the gift of all the perfected sons of God. The radiant inner body of light is present both in the individual and in the race, unseen and unrevealed, but slowly and surely emerging. At the present hour a large number of mankind are engaged in the activities of the six days which precede the transfiguration experience.

It is important here to study briefly the place of the disciples in the story of this experience. Down through Biblical history we meet this triplicity. Moses, Aaron and Joshua; Job and his three friends; Shadrach, Meschach and

---

[12] *St. Matt.*, V, 16.

Abednego, the friends of Daniel; the three kings at the cradle in Bethlehem; the three disciples at the Transfiguration; the three Crosses on Calvary! What accounts for this constant recurrence of three? What does it symbolise? Apart from their possible historical appearance, does there lie behind them some peculiar symbology which can, when understood, render clear the circumstances in which they played their part? A study of their names and the interpretation of them as given in the familiar *Cruden's Concordance* may supply a clue. Take, for instance, the meaning of the names of Job's friends. They were Eliphaz the Temanite, Bildad the Shuhite, and Zophar the Naamathite. Eliphaz the Temanite means "my God is gold," and also "the southern quarter," the opposite pole to the north. Gold is the symbol of material welfare, and the opposite pole to spirit is matter, therefore in this name we have symbolised the tangible outer form of man, actuated by desire for material possessions and comfort. Zophar the Naamathite means the "one who talks," and his theme is pleasantness, which is the interpretation given to the word "Naamathite." Here we have the desire body typified, with its longing for pleasantness, for happiness and for pleasure, and an indication of the constant and ceaseless call and voice of the sentient nature, to which we can all testify. Bildad the Shuhite represents the mental nature, the mind, signifying as he does "contrition," which becomes possible only when the mind is beginning to be active (including the conscience). Shuhite means "prostration or helplessness," signifying that alone and unaided the mind can reveal but cannot help. Remorse and sorrow, involving memory, are the result of mental activity. Thus, in Job's three friends the three aspects of his lower nature stand revealed. The same is the case when we study the names of Daniel's three friends. Abednego means the "servant of the sun," the server of the light; in that significance the whole duty and purpose of the physical outer man is summed up. Shadrach's name has a definitely emotional sentient connotation, for it means "rejoicing in the way," and wherever we find reference to the basic dualities of pleasure and pain we are considering the emotional-feeling nature. Meschach means "agile," quick moving, which is in itself a very good description of the mental nature. Arjuna, in *The Bhagavad Gita*,[13] points this out in his words to Krishna: "This union through oneness which is taught by Thee, . . . I perceive not its firm foundation, owing to the wavering of the mind; for the mind wavers, Krishna, turblent, impetuous, forceful; and I think it is as hard to hold as the wind."

Thus in the three friends, and in the various triplicities which we find in the Bible, we discover a symbolism which is vitally illuminating. The three aspects through which the soul must express itself, and through which it must shine, are thus portrayed. It is the same in connection with the three friends of Jesus Christ. I cannot here touch upon the friendships of Jesus Christ. They are very real and very deep, and universal in their inclusiveness. They are timeless and eternal, and the friends of Christ are to be found in every race (Christian or otherwise), in every clime and in both hemispheres. And be it remembered, it is only the friends of Christ who have any right to be dogmatic about Him, or who can speak with any authority of Him and His ideas, because theirs is the authority of love and of understanding.

We find also this basic triplicity in the persons of Peter and James and John, and in their names we find the same essential symbolism working out, thus giving us the clue to the meaning of this wonderful story. Peter, as we well know, means "rock." Here is the foundation, the most concrete aspect, the outer physical form, which, at the Transfiguration, is transformed by the glory of God, so that the outer image disappears, and God Himself shines forth. James, we are told, signifies "illusion," distortion. Here we have reference to the emotional-feeling body, with its power

[13] *The Bhagavad Gita*, VI, 33, 34.

to misrepresent and to deceive, to mislead and to delude. Where emotion enters in, and where the focus of attention is in sensitive and sensuous reaction, that which is not true rapidly appears, and the man becomes the subject of illusion. It is this body of illusion which is eventually transmuted, and so changed and stabilised that it provides a clear medium for the revelation of deity. John means "the Lord hath spoken," and herein is the mind nature typified, because it is only when the mental aspect begins to manifest that we have the appearance of speech and of that thinking, speaking animal which we call "man." So, in the apt symbology of the Scripture, Christ's three friends stood for the three aspects of His human nature, and it was upon this integrated, focussed and consecrated personality that the transfiguration made its impact and produced revelation. Thus again the essential duality of humanity is revealed through Christ, and His threefold personality and His essential divinity are portrayed for us in such a way that the lesson (and the possibility) cannot be evaded. The Apostles recognised God in their Master, taking their stand upon the fact of this divinity, as have the mystics of all time.

They "knew Whom they had believed."[14] They saw the light which shone in the Person of Jesus Christ, and for them He was more than the Person they had known heretofore. Through this experience God became a reality to them.

In the synthesis of the past, the present and the future, Christ and those who were immediately His friends, met with God, and so potent was this combination that it evoked from God Himself an immediate response. When feeling and thought meet in a moment of realisation, there is a simultaneous precipitation of energy, and life is forever after different. That which has been believed is known as fact, and belief is no longer necessary.

[14] *II Tim.*, I, 12.

3

The Transfiguration scene was the meeting-ground of significant factors, and since that moment the life of humanity has been radically changed. It was as potent a moment in racial history as the Crucifixion, of more potency perhaps than even that great and tragic happening. Seldom do such moments come. Usually we see only faint glimpses of possibility, rare flashes of illumination, and fleeting seconds wherein a synthesis appears and leaves us with a sense of fitness, of integration, of purpose and of underlying reality. But such moments are rare indeed. We know God is. We know reality exists. But life, with its emphasis directed on phenomena, its stresses and its strains, so preoccupies us that we have no time, after the six days' labour, to climb the mountain of vision. A certain familiarity with God's nature must surely precede the revelation of Himself which He can and does at times accord. Christ's three friends had been admitted to a degree of intimacy with Him which warranted their being chosen as His companions at the scene of His experience, wherein He staged, for the benefit of humanity, a symbolic event as well as a definite experience for which arrangement had duly to be made, with the participants correctly chosen and trained, so that the symbolism which they embodied might appear, and their intuitive reactions be rightly directed. It was necessary that Christ should have with Him those who could be depended upon to recognise divinity when it appeared, and whose intuitive spiritual perception would be such that— for all time—the inner meaning might be made apparent to those of us who have followed later in His steps. This is a point at times forgotten. Inevitably "we shall be like Him, for we shall see Him as He is."[15]

But to bring about this likeness two things are necessary to the consecrated and dedicated disciple. He must be able

[15] *I St. John*, III, 2.

to see clearly, meanwhile standing in the illumination which radiates from Christ, and his intuition must be active, so that he can rightly interpret what he sees. He loves his Master, and he serves with what faithfulness he can; but more than devotion and service are needed. He must be able to face the illumination, and at the same time he must have that spiritual perception which, reaching out beyond the point to which the intellect can carry him, sees and touches reality. It is love and intellect combined, plus the power to know, which is inherent in the soul, which recognises intuitively that which is holy, universal and real, and yet which is specific and true for all time to all people.

Christ revealed the quality of the divine nature through the medium of matter, of form, and "was transfigured before them."

"The Greek word here used is 'metamorphosed,' the very word used by St. Paul to describe the transmutation of the mortal body into the resurrection body; for on the day of fulfilment, when the perfected disciple has attained masterhood, the 'Robe of Glory' shines forth with such splendour through the garment of the flesh that all the beholders perceive it, and, their eyes and ears attuned to finer subtle vibration, they behold their Master in all His divine humanity."[16]

It is interesting to note that, in spite of their recognition of the significance of the event in which they were participating, the three Apostles, speaking through the mouth of St. Peter, were able to do no more than express their awe and their bewilderment, their recognition and belief. They could not explain or understand what they had seen, nor do we find any record of their ever having done so. The meaning of the Transfiguration is something which has to be wrought out in the life before it can be defined or explained. When humanity as a whole learns to transform the flesh through divine experience, to transmute the feeling nature through divine expression, and to transfer the con-

[16] *The Mystery Teaching in the West,* by Jean Delaire, p. 121.

sciousness away from the world of mundane living into the
world of transcendental realities, the true subjective values
of this initiation will reveal themselves to the minds of men.
Then will come a deeper expression of that which has been
intuited. Dr. Sheldon tells us with truth that *"all of the
finest human thought and feeling is carried for generations,
probably for ages, in intuitional minds, long before it becomes articulate."*[17]   Not yet are we articulate where this
experience is concerned. We sense dimly and distantly its
wonder and its finality. We have not yet, as a race, passed
through the new birth; the Jordan experience is only attained as yet by the few. It is the rare and developed soul
which has climbed the Mountain of Transfiguration, and
there seen and met with God in the glorified Person of
Jesus Christ. We have looked on at this episode through the
eyes of others. Peter and James and John, through another
apostle, Matthew, have told us about it. We remain as onlookers, but it is an experience in which we shall some day
share. This we have forgotten. We have taken to ourselves
the language of the fourth great event in Christ's life, and
many of us have attempted to share and enter into the
meaning of the Crucifixion.   We have looked on at the
Transfiguration, but have not attempted to become actively
transfigured. But that must some day happen to us, and
only after the Transfiguration can we dare to climb Mount
Golgotha. Only when we have achieved expression of divinity in and through the lower personal nature shall we
have attained to that of worth and value which can be permitted, under the divine Plan, to be crucified. This is a
forgotten truth. Yet it iş all part of the evolutionary process
whereby God is revealed through humanity.

The great and natural phenomenon which humanity will
some day—through self-expression and also under the law
—reveal in itself includes the beauty which shone forth
from Christ as He stood transfigured before His three

---

[17] *Psychology and the Promethean Will*, by W. H. Sheldon, p. 116.

friends, was recognised by God His Father, and received the testimony of Moses and Elias, the Law and the Prophets, the past and that which bears witness to the future.

One point might here be brought out. In the Oriental correspondence to these five crises in the life of Jesus Christ, this third episode is called the "hut" initiation, and the words of St. Peter as he suggests that they should make three "huts," one for Christ and one for Moses and one for Elias, link up this Christian happening with its ancient prototype. Always, in these rarely occurring events, God has been glorified by the light, ineffable and effulgent, shining forth through the raiment of flesh, and this mountain experience is not uniquely Christian. But Christ was the first to gather together into one sequential presentation all the possible experiences of divinity made manifest, and portrayed them for our edification and inspiration in His life history, and in the five Gospel episodes. More and more men will pass through the birth chamber, enter the stream and climb the mountain, furthering God's work for humanity; and Christ's example is rapidly bearing fruit and bringing results. Divinity cannot be gainsaid, and man is divine. If he is not, then the Fatherhood of God is but an empty form of words, and Christ and His Apostles were in error when They recognised, as They constantly did, the fact of our sonship. The divinity of man cannot be explained away. It is either a fact or it is not. God can be known in the flesh through the medium of His children or He cannot. All rests back on God, the Father, the Creator, the One in Whom we live and move and have our being. God is immanent in all His creatures, or He is not. God is transcendent and beyond manifestation, or else there is no basic reality, purpose or origin. Probably the growing recognition in men's minds that He is both immanent and transcendent is true, and we can take our stand upon His Fatherhood, knowing ourselves to be divine because Christ and the Church of all ages have borne testimony to it.

This time the Word spoken differs from the previous one. The first part of the pronouncement made by the Initiator Who stands silently behind the scenes as Jesus takes initiation after initiation is practically the same as that at the Baptism initiation, except for one expressed command. He said, "This is my beloved Son, in whom I am well pleased," but added this time, "Hear ye him." At the first great episode, God the Father, of Whom the Initiator is the symbol, did not make His Presence known. The angels spoke the word, embodying Christ's mission on His behalf. At the Baptism He accorded recognition, but that was all. At this Initiation, God commanded humanity to pay attention to this particlar crisis in the life of Christ and to listen to His words. The power and the right to speak is now conferred upon the Christ, and it is interesting to note that the major part of the teaching (as given in St. John's Gospel and in many of the parables) was given by Christ only after He had been through this experience. Again God gave evidence that He recognised Christ's Messiahship, which word is man's interpretation of the recognition. At the Baptism, He recognised Him as His Son, sent into the world, from the bosom of the Father, to carry out the will of God. That which Christ had recognised in the Temple as a child was later endorsed by God. This recognition is repeated, and the endorsement is strengthened, by the command to the world to hear the words of the Saviour, or perhaps from the esoteric and spiritual standpoint, to hear that Word which was God made Flesh.

"There is in fact an inward connection between the Baptism and the Transfiguration. In both cases a condition of ecstasy accompanies the revelation of the secret of Jesus' person. The first time the revelation was for him alone; here the Disciples also shared it. It is not clear to what extent they themselves were transported by the experience. So much is sure, that in a dazed condition, out of which they awake only at the end of the scene (St. Mark IX, 8.) the figure of Jesus appears to them illuminated by a supernatural light and glory, and a voice intimates that he is the Son of God.

The occurrence can be explained only as the outcome of great eschatological excitement."[18]

The same writer goes on to point out:

"We have therefore three revelations of the secret of messiahship, which so hang together that each subsequent one implies the foregoing. On the mountain near Bethsaida was revealed to the Three the secret which was disclosed to Jesus at his baptism. That was after the harvest. A few weeks later it was known to the Twelve, by the fact that Peter at Caesarea Phillippi answered Jesus' question out of the knowledge which he had attained upon the mountain. One of the Twelve betrayed the secret to the High Priest. This last revelation of the secret was fatal, for it brought about the death of Jesus. *He was condemned as messiah although he had never appeared in that role.*"[19]

This evokes in its entirety the question as to the nature of that mission which Christ came to forward, and what constituted the Will of God which He came to fulfil. Three major points of view usually held by the orthodox Christian might be enumerated as follows:

1. He came to die upon the Cross to appease the wrath of an angry God, and make it possible for those who believe in Him to go to Heaven.
2. He came to show us the real nature of perfection and how, in human form, divinity might be manifested.
3. He came to leave us an example that we should follow in His steps.

Christ Himself laid no emphasis upon the death on the Cross as being the apex of His life work. It was the *result* of His life work, but not that for which He came into the world. He came that we might have "life abundantly," and St. John tells us in his Gospel that the new birth is de-

[18] *The Mystery of the Kingdom of God,* by Albert Schweitzer, pp. 181, 182.

[19] *Ibid.,* pp. 217, 218.

pendent upon belief in Christ, when power is given to us
to "become the Sons of God, even to them that believe on
his name, which were born, *not of blood,* nor of the will
of the flesh, nor of the will of man, but of God."[20]

Is it not reasonable for us to gather from these words
that when a man reaches the point of recognising and believing in the cosmic Christ, "the Lamb slain from the
foundation of the world,"[21] then the new birth becomes
possible, for the life of that universal Christ, animating
every form of divine expression, can then consciously and
definitely carry the man forward into a new manifestation
of divinity? The "blood is the life,"[22] and it is the living
Christ that makes it possible for all to become citizens of
that kingdom. It is the life of Christ in each of us which
makes us sons of the Father, not His death which makes us
sons. Nowhere in the Gospel story does an opposite statement find support. Christ, at the communion service, gave
His disciples the cup to drink, saying "This is my blood of
the new testament, which is shed for many for the remission
of sins."[23] But these are His only references to blood in its
remedial aspect, so strongly emphasised in the Epistles, and
He Himself nowhere correlates blood with the Crucifixion.
He speaks in the present tense, and does not relate the blood
to the new birth or to the Crucifixion, or make it a factor
in the exclusiveness which has so deeply coloured the presentation of Christianity in the world.

It is the Christ life in all forms which constitutes the
evolutionary urge. It is the Christ life which makes the
steadily unfolding expression of divinity possible in the natural world. It is deep within the heart of every man. The
Christ life brings him eventually to the point where he
transits out of the human kingdom (when the work of
normal evolution has done its part) and leads him into the

[20] *St. John,* I, 13.
[21] *Rev.,* XIII, 8.
[22] *Gen.,* IX, 4.
[23] *St. Matt.,* XXVI, 28.

kingdom of spirit. The recognition of the Christ life within the form of man makes every human being, at some time, play the part of the Virgin Mary to that indwelling reality. It is the Christ life which, at the new birth, comes to fuller expression, and from crisis to crisis leads on the developing son of God until he stands perfected, having achieved "the measure of the stature of the fulness of Christ."[24]

We shall see later that upon the revelation of the risen Christ must the new world religion take its stand. Christ upon the Cross, as will appear when we study the next great crisis, showed us love and sacrifice carried to their extreme expression; but Christ alive from all time, and vitally alive today, is the keynote of the new age, and upon this truth must the new presentation of religion be built and, later, the new theology be constructed. The true meaning of the Resurrection and the Ascension has not yet been grasped; as a divine subjective reality those truths still await revelation. The glory of the new age will be the unveiling of those two mysteries, and our entrance into a fuller understanding of God as life. The true Church of Christ is the assembly of all who live through the life of Christ, and whose life is one with His. This will be increasingly realised and will bring forth into clearer and more radiant light the wonder and glory which lies, unrevealed as yet, in God the Father.

It is only the man who has understood something of the value of the Transfiguration initiation and the nature of the perfection then revealed who can follow along with Christ, to the vision which was accorded Him as He came down from that high point of achievement, and can later share with Him an understanding of the nature of world service. This world service is rendered perfectly by those whose inner perfection is approximate to Christ's and whose lives are controlled by the same divine impulses and subordinated to the same vision. This stage connotes that complete spiritual freedom which we must eventually reach.

[24] *Eph.*, IV, 13.

Now the time has come for human beings to leave off *believing,* and pass on to true knowledge, through the method of thought, reflection, experiment, experience and revelation. The immediate problem for all who are seeking this new knowledge, and who desire to become conscious knowers instead of faithful believers, is that they should achieve it in the world of every-day. After each expansion of consciousness and each unfoldment of a deepened awareness we return, as Christ did, to the plains of every-day life, and there subject our knowledge to the test, discover its reality and truth, and find out also wherein lies for us our next point of expansion, and what new knowledge must be acquired. The task of the disciple is the understanding and the use of his divinity. The knowledge of God immanent, yet based on a belief in God transcendent, is our endeavour.

This was the experience of the Apostles upon the mountain top. We are told that "when they had lifted up their eyes, they saw no man, save Jesus only."[25] The familiar appeared to them again. It is of real interest to compare a somewhat similar story related in *The Bhagavad Gita,* wherein Arjuna has had revealed to him the glorious form of the Lord. At the close of the revelation God, in the person of Krishna, says to him, with tenderness and understanding, "Let not fear nor confusion overcome thee, beholding My form so terrible! Behold my former shape once more, thy fear gone, thy heart at rest!" and then he goes on to tell him:

"This form of Mine which thou hast seen is hard indeed to see! Even the Gods ever desire a sight of this form! Nor can I be seen thus through Vedas, penances, gifts, sacrifices, in the form which thou hast seen. But I can be known thus through single-hearted love, Arjuna, and seen as I truly am, and entered, O Consumer of the foe!"[26]

The Word of Recognition had gone forth, and the command to hear the Christ had been given. Jesus having re-

[25] *St. Matt.,* XVII, 8.
[26] *The Bhagavad Gita,* Book XI, 49, 52, 53, 54.

turned "to His proper form," the descent from the mountain had to follow. Then occurred what might be regarded as a great, sad, spiritual reaction, inevitable and terrible, expressed by Christ in the following words:

"The Son of Man shall be betrayed into the hands of men, and they shall kill him, and the third day he shall be raised again."[27]

Then comes the simple comment that the disciples "were exceedingly sorry." This vision of Christ's, if we trace it in the records, fell into two parts. First, He had a vision of achievement. The mountain-top achievement, a great spiritual experience, lay behind Him. Now He has a vision of a physical consummation in the form of the triumphal entry into Jerusalem. But this is accompanied by a presentiment or a prevision of the culmination of His life of service upon the Cross. He saw clearly, perhaps for the first time, what lay ahead of Him, and the direction in which His service to the world was leading Him. The *via dolorosa* of a World Saviour stretched out before Him; the destiny of all pioneering souls climaxed in His experience, and He saw Himself rejected, pilloried and killed, as have many lesser sons of God. World rejection always precedes world acceptance. Disillusionment is a stage on the way to reality. The hatred of those who are not yet ready to recognise the world of spiritual values is ever the lot of those who are. This, Christ faced, and yet "He steadfastly set His face to go to Jerusalem."[28]

As we consider these happenings, the particular test which Christ now encountered becomes clear in our minds. It was again a threefold test, as was that after the Baptism initiation; but this time it was of a far subtler nature. He was faced with the test as to whether He could endure and handle worldly success, and pass along the triumphant way of His entry into the Holy City, without deviating from

[27] *St. Matt.,* XVII, 22, 23.
[28] *St. Luke,* IX, 51.

His purpose, without being attracted by material achievement and by being acclaimed King of the Jews. Success
constitutes a far more drastic disciplining, and produces
many more opportunities to forget God and reality than do
failure and neglect. Self-pity, a sense of martyrdom, and
resignation are potent and effective ways of handling one's
failure. But to rise upon the crest of the wave, to be accorded public recognition, and to seem to have achieved the
earthly goal are far more difficult factors to face. These
Christ did face, and He faced them with spiritual poise and
with that far-sighted wisdom which produces a correct sense
of values and a proper sense of proportion.

The second phase of the test lay in His prevision as to
His end. He knew He had to die, and He knew how He
would die, and yet He went forward undeviatingly upon
the course assigned Him, although prevision of disaster
was His. Not only had He to demonstrate the power to
endure success, but He had also to demonstrate the power
to face disaster, balancing the two against each other and
seeing in both of them simply opportunities for divine expression and fields for the demonstration of detachment—
that outstanding characteristic of the man who has been
born again, purified and transfigured. To these tests was
added the one which He had before encountered in the
desert, the test of utter loneliness. The power to endure
success! The power to endure disaster! The power to stand
utterly alone! This, Christ had to show the world, and this
He did. He stood triumphant before the world, at an in-
termediate stage on His way to the Cross. The agony of
loneliness in the Garden of Gethsemane was probably a far
harder moment for Him than the publicity on Mount Golgotha. But in these more subtle tests the quality of God
Himself was revealed, and it is God's *quality* and *meaning*
which save the world—the quality of His life, which is Love
and Wisdom and Value and Reality. It was all of this which
Christ accomplished.

Immediately, on the descent from the mountain-top, Christ

began again to serve. He was met, as well we know, by a
person in distress, and He at once responded to the need.
One of the outstanding characteristics of each initiation is
the increased capacity and ability of the initiate to serve.
Christ demonstrated an entirely new and unique way in
which to speak and to meet the masses, as well as to teach
privately and personally His chosen few. His power to heal
still continued, but His work shifted into a field of new
values, and He spoke those words and enunciated those
truths which have proved the foundation of the belief of
those who have had the insight to penetrate the theological
presentation of Christianity and there find reality. His
service consisted primarily at this time in teaching and
speaking. But such is the wisdom and the beauty of His
presentation of truth, He couched divinity in forms which
the average man could grasp. He bridged the old and the
new, and gave out that new truth and that special revelation
which were needed at the time to unite the ancient wisdom
and the more modern hope. Keyserling has grasped the wonder of what the World-Saviour does, and voices it in words
which I quote:

". . . the great mind is essentially the Awakener. If such a mind
were to utter the entirely new, the unique, this would mean
nothing to other men. His social value depends entirely on his
ability to utter clearly what all feel in their innermost hearts to
be true—for could he otherwise be understood?—and to utter it
in so universal a manner, that is, so much in tune with the objective laws in question, that his ideas become organs for the
others."[29]

Christ gave us a great idea. He gave us the new concept
that God is Love, no matter what might be happening in
the world of immediacy. All great ideas come forth from
the world of divinity through the medium of the great In-
tuitives, and the history of humanity is essentially the history
of ideas—their coming forth through the medium of some
intuitive thinker, their recognition by the few, their growth

[29] *The Recovery of Truth,* by Hermann Keyserling, p. 213.

in popularity, and their eventual integration in the thought world, the pattern world of the thinkers of the race. Then their fate is determined, and eventually the new and unique idea becomes the popularly and publicly accepted model of human conduct. "To the question, then, whether it is personalities or ideas which decide the fate of an age, the answer is that the age get its ideas from personalities."[30] Christ embodied a great idea, the idea that God is Love, and that love is the motivating power of the universe. This constitutes the illumination which Christ as the Light of the World refracted upon all world events. The majesty of this realisation cannot be over-emphasised. We need to realise it far more deeply and potently than we do, for it constitutes the basic, fundamental character and quality of all events, no matter what the outer appearance may be. Christ illumines life. This was one of His most important contributions to life as it is lived today. He said in effect: God loves the world; all that happens is along the line of love. If this is realised as fact and fundamental truth, it illumines all of life and lightens all burdens; cause and effect are brought together, and God's purpose and His method are seen as one. Theologians have often forgotten this as they have struggled over the more technical aspects of Christ's life. What He illumined in His function as the "Light of the World," what He received of divine Light and poured forth for the world, what He refracted, is often overlooked in the struggle to prove such doctrines as the fact that the Virgin Mary was an immaculate virgin, and Christ was therefore born through the medium of an immaculate conception. Today only a few of the younger generation care much about such points of doctrine. Let us state that quite emphatically. But we do care that the love which He expressed should be demonstrated in the world and that the illumination He carried should "lighten our darkness."

Christ sounded with clarity the note which can usher in the new civilisation and the new order, and a close study of

[30] *The Decay and Restoration of Civilisation,* by Albert Schweitzer, p. 82.

the ideals and ideas which today, without exception, under-lie every one of the great experiments undertaken by the various nations, will show that they are based, in essence, upon some definitely Christlike concept. That their method of application and the techniques employed are frequently un-Christlike is sadly true, but the foundational concepts will bear with equanimity the light which Christ can throw upon them. The principal difficulty has been that our in-tellectual grasp of the concepts runs ahead of our own per-sonal development, and therefore colours disastrously our application of them. When these basic ideas are transmuted into world ideals by the consecrated thinkers of the race, and applied in the spirit in which Christ conceived of them, then we shall indeed inaugurate a new world order.

It is of supreme value for us to realise that what Christ really did was to usher in the era of *Service,* even if we are only beginning today (two thousand years after He set us an example) to grasp the implications of that word so widely used. We have been apt to regard salvation in terms of the individual, and to study it from the angle of individual sal-vation. This attitude must end if we are ever to understand the Christ spirit. A great Japanese asks the poignant ques-tion "What is the primary aim of a religion worthy of existence?" and goes on to tell us that it is salvation, but a salvation that "is pregnant with relief and redress of life and of the world."[31] Service is becoming more and more an objective in all human affairs. Even modern business is coming to the recognition that it must be a motivating agency if business, as we understand it in the modern sense, is to survive. Upon what is this general trend based? Surely upon our universal relation to Deity and upon our subjec-tive relationships to each other, which have their root in our relationship to God.

That of course is the basis of service. It must be, as it was in the case of Jesus Christ, a spontaneous outcome of

[31] *Modern Trends in World Religions,* edited by A. E. Haydon, quoting Kishio Satomi, p. 75.

divinity. One of the strongest arguments for the divine unfoldment of man is the emergence on a large scale of this tendency to serve. We are just beginning to get a faint vision of what Christ meant by service. He "carried this actuating motive of service to the extent of saying that when the common good and your personal success or welfare conflicted, *you* must sacrifice and not sacrifice the other man."[32] This idea of service is of course in complete conflict with the usually competitive attitude to life and the selfishness generally shown by the average man. But to the man who seeks to follow Christ, and who aims eventually at climbing the Mount of Transfiguration, service leads inevitably to increased illumination, and illumination in its turn must find its expression in renewed and consecrated service, and thus we find our way—through service to our fellow men—into the Way that Christ trod. Following in His steps, we achieve eventually the power to live as illumined and Christlike men and women in our normal everyday surroundings.

What, therefore, is the gift that each of us can make to the world as we study the life of Christ and travel with Him in our minds from one initiation to another? We can aim at that greatness in action which will redeem our natural mediocrity and reveal progressively the divinity in each of us. Each can stand as a beacon light, pointing the way to the centre from which the Word goes forth; and each can begin to express in his daily living some of the quality of God which Christ so perfectly portrayed and which carried Him in triumph from the Mount of Transfiguration down into the valley of duty and of service, and which enabled Him to go forward with staunch determination to the Cross experience, through the triumphal way of acclamation and the sorrowful ways of desertion and of loneliness.

The impulse is strong to close with some words of Arjuna, spoken to Krishna, long before the Christian era, after the revelation of the unveiled beauty to which he had been admitted. Their relevance is unquestionable. One can almost

[32] *Modern Trends in World Religions*, edited by A. E. Haydon, p. 106.

imagine St. Peter or St. John saying them to Christ when they opened their eyes and "saw Jesus only." Perhaps they may apply to us also as we consider Christ and our relation to Him:

"If thinking Thee my comrade, I addressed Thee brusquely . . . not knowing this greatness of Thine, or carelessly, or through affection, or whatever I have done to make a jest of Thee, unseemly, in journeying, resting, or seated, or at the banquet, whether alone, O, unfallen One! or in presence of these, for all this I ask forgiveness from Thee, Immeasurable One! Thou art the Father of the world, of things moving and unmoving; Thou art worthy of honour, the reverend Teacher of the world. None equal Thee; how could any be greater? even in the three worlds there is none like Thee in might.

"Therefore bowing down, prostrating my body before Thee, I seek Thy grace, O worthy Lord! As the Father his son, the comrade his comrade, the beloved his beloved, so deign Thou, Lord, to pardon me! I exult, beholding what was never seen before, and my heart trembles with fear; show me, Lord, the former form; Lord of Gods, be gracious, upholder of worlds."[33]

[33] *The Bhagavad Gita,* Book XI, 41-45.

The Fourth Initiation . . . The Crucifixion

KEY THOUGHT

A fire-mist and a planet,
A crystal and a cell,
A jelly-fish and a saurian,
And caves where the cave-men dwell;
Then a sense of law and beauty,
And a face turned from the clod—
Some call it Evolution,
And others call it God.

Like tides on a crescent sea-beach
When the moon is new and thin,
Into our hearts high yearnings
Come welling and surging in:
Come from the mystic ocean
Whose rim no foot has trod—
Some of us call it Longing,
And others call it God.

A picket frozen on duty,
A mother starved for her brood,
Socrates drinking the hemlock,
And Jesus on the rood;
And millions who, humble and nameless,
The straight, hard pathway plod—
Some call it Consecration,
And others call it God.

William Herbert Carruth.

CHAPTER FIVE

The Fourth Initiation . . . The Crucifixion

1

WE now come to the central mystery of Christianity, and to the climaxing initiation to which men, as human beings, can aspire. Of the next initiation, the Resurrection, and of the Ascension connected with it, we know practically nothing, beyond the fact that Christ rose from the dead. The Resurrection initiation is veiled in silence. All that is recorded is the reaction of those who knew and loved the Lord, and the after effects upon the history of the Christian Church. But the Crucifixion has always been the outstanding, dramatic episode upon which the entire structure of Christian theology has been founded. Upon this has the emphasis been laid. Millions of words have been written about it, and thousands of books and commentaries have attempted to elucidate its meaning and to explain the significance of its mystery. Down the ages a myriad points of view have been presented for the consideration of men. There has been much misinterpretation, but much also that is divinely real has been expressed. God has been misrepresented many times, and the interpretation of what Christ did has been travestied in terms of men's small views. The wonder of the happening on Mount Calvary has been unveiled through the illumined experiences of the believer and the knower.

A new world order came into being when Christ came to earth, and from that time on we have moved steadily forward towards a new age wherein men inevitably will live as brothers because Christ died, and the true nature of the kingdom of God will find expression on earth. Of this, past progress is the guarantee. The immediacy of this happening is already faintly understood by those who, as Christ has said, have the eyes to see and the ears to hear. Inevitably we are moving forward towards greatness, and Christ emphasised this in His life and work. We have not yet achieved this greatness, but the signs of it can be seen. Already there are indications of the coming of this new era, and the dim outlines of a new and more nearly ideal social structure, based on perfected humanity, are discernible. It is this perfection which is of importance.

One of the first things that it seems essential to recognise is the fact, the definite fact, that Christ's Crucifixion must be lifted out of the realm of its purely individual application, into the realm of the universal and the whole. It may perhaps cause some consternation when we emphasise the necessity of realising that the death of the historical Christ upon the Cross was not primarily concerned with each individual man who claims to profit by it. *It was a great cosmic event.* Its implications and its results concern the masses of humanity, and do not concern specifically the individual. We are so apt to take to ourselves, as a personal affair, the many implications of Christ's sacrifice. The selfishness of the spiritual aspirant is often very real.

It is surely evident, if one approches the subject intelligently, that Christ did not die in order that you and I might go to heaven. He died as the result of the very nature of the service which He rendered, of the note which He struck, and because He inaugurated a new age and told men how to live as sons of God.

In considering the story of Jesus upon the Cross, it is essential, therefore, that we see it in broader and more general terms than is usually the case. Most of the treatises and writings upon the subject are controversial and argumentative, usually defending or attacking the evidence or the theology associated with the theme. Or they may be of a purely mystical or sentimental nature in tone and object, concerning themselves with the relation of the individual to the truth or with his personal salvation in Christ. But ... so doing, it is possible that the real elements of the story and their highest meaning have been lost. Two things emerge, however, from the research and the questionings of the past century. One is that the Gospel story is not unique, but has been paralleled in the lives of other Sons of God; secondly, that Christ *was* unique in His particular Person and mission, and that, from a specific angle, His appearance was unprecedented. No student of comparative religion will question the Christian parallels to earlier events. No man who has truly investigated with an open mind will deny that Christ was an integral part of a great continuity of revelation. God has never "left Himself without witness."[1] And the salvation of mankind has always been close to the heart of the Father. To quote one writer who seeks to prove this continuity:

"At the time of the life or recorded appearance of Jesus of Nazareth and for some centuries before, the Mediterranean and neighbouring world had been the scene of a vast number of pagan creeds and rituals. There were Temples without end dedicated to gods like Apollo or Dionysus among the Greeks, Hercules among the Romans, Mithra among the Persians, Adonis and Arris in Syria and Phrygia, Osiris and Isis and Horus in Egypt, Baal and Astarte among the Babylonians and Carthaginians, and so forth. Societies, large or small, united believers and the devout in the service or ceremonials connected with their respective deities, and in the creeds which they confessed concerning these deities. And an extraordinarily interesting fact, for us, is that, notwithstanding great geographical distances and racial differences in the details of their services, the general outlines of their creeds and ceremonials were—if not identical—so markedly similar as we find them.

"I cannot of course go at length into these different cults, but I may say roughly that of all or nearly all the deities above-mentioned it was said and believed that:

1. They were born on or very near our Christmas Day.
2. They were born of a Virgin-Mother.

[1] *Acts*, XIV, 17.

3. And in a Cave or Underground Chamber.

4. They led a life of toil for Mankind.

5. And were called by the names of Light-bringer, Healer, Mediator, Saviour, Deliverer.

6. They were, however, vanquished by the Powers of Darkness.

7. And descended into Hell or the Underworld.

8. They rose again from the dead, and became the pioneers of mankind to the Heavenly world.

9. They founded Communions of Saints and Churches into which disciples were received by Baptism.

10. And they were commemorated by Eucharistic meals."[2]

These facts can be checked by anyone who cares to do so and who is sufficiently interested to trace the growth of the doctrine of world Saviours in world idealism. Edward Carpenter goes on to say, in the same book:

"The number of pagan deities (mostly virgin-born and done to death in some way or other in their efforts to save mankind) is so great as to be difficult to keep account of. The god *Krishna* in India, the god *Indra* in Nepaul and Thibet spilt their blood for the salvation of men; *Buddha* said, according to Max Müller, 'Let all the sins that were in the world fall on me, that the world may be delivered;' the Chinese *Tien* the Holy One—'one with God and existing with him from all eternity'—died to save the world; The Egyptian *Osiris* was called Saviour, so was *Horus;* so was the Persian *Mithra;* so was the Greek *Hercules* who overcame Death though his body was consumed in the burning garment of mortality, out of which he rose into heaven. So also was the Phrygian *Attis* called Saviour, and the Syrian *Tammuz* or *Adonis* likewise—both of whom, as we have seen, were nailed or tied to a tree, and afterwards rose again from their biers or coffins. *Prometheus,* the greatest and earliest benefactor of the human race, was *nailed by the hands and the feet, and with arms extended,* to the rocks of Mount Caucasus. *Bacchus* or *Dionysus,* born of the virgin Semele to be the Liberator of mankind (Dionysus Eleutherios as he was called) was torn to pieces, not unlike Osiris. Even in far Mexico

[2] *Pagan and Christian Creeds,* by Edward Carpenter, pp. 20, 21.

Quetzalcoatl, the Saviour, was born of a virgin, was tempted, and fasted forty days, was done to death, and his second coming looked for so eagerly that (as is well known) when Cortes appeared, the Mexicans, poor things, greeted *him* as the returning god! In Peru and among the American Indians, North and South of the Equator, similar legends are, or were, to be found."[3]

Into the argument for and against these ideas it is no part of this book to enter. The only question which is of importance for us is what part Christ really played as the World Saviour, and what constituted the uniqueness of His mission. What was this world to which He came; and what is the significance of His death to the average human being today? Are the facts of His life historically true; and was there a period in our racial history wherein He walked and talked and lived an ordinary human life? Did He serve His race and return to the Source whence He came?

The *fact* of Christ constitutes no problem to those who know Him. They realise, past all controversy, that He exists. They know Whom they have believed.[4] For them, His reality cannot be disproved. They may differ among themselves as to the emphasis to be laid upon the various theological interpretations of His life story, but Christ they know, and with Him they tread life's pathway. They may argue about whether He was God or man, or God-Man, or Man-God, but on one point they all agree, and that is that He was God and Man, manifesting in one body. They may struggle to perpetuate the memory of the dead Christ upon the Cross, or they may endeavour to live by the life of the risen Christ, but to the reality of Christ Himself they all bear testimony, and by the multitude of witnesses the fact is surely established. The one who knows cannot doubt.

Christianity is the restatement of a very old doctrine. It is not new. It is so essential to the salvation and to the happiness of the world that God has always proclaimed it.

[3] *Pagan and Christian Creeds,* by Edward Carpenter, pp. 129, 130.
[4] *II Tim.,* I, 12.

The Gospel narratives are dependable and true, just because they are integrated with the spiritual revelation of the past, and are being reinterpreted today in terms of Christ. Therefore, mankind being more evolved and intelligent, that reinterpretation will more readily and adequately meet humanity's need. But it is no new thing, and Christ never proclaimed Himself in such terms. He foretold a new age and a coming kingdom of God. Out of the wide sweep of time and out of the æonian grasp of God's consciousness, mankind is only today beginning to see a world and a humanity ready for the new revelation—a revelation which will be based upon truly Christian ethics and vital Christian truths. That for which Christ stood, the truth which He embodies, is so old that there has never been a time when it was not present as a need in the human consciousness, and yet it is so new that there will never be a time when the story of the birth and the death of the world Saviour will not be of the utmost moment to man. Edward Carpenter points this out, throwing light upon this ceaseless and age-old focussing of the love of God and the desire of man in the person of a son of God. He says:

"If the historicity of Jesus, in any degree, could be proved, it would give us reason for supposing—what I have personally always been inclined to believe—that there was also a historical nucleus for such personages as Osiris, Mithra, Krishna, Hercules, Apollo and the rest. The question, in fact, narrows itself down to this, Have there been in the course of human evolution certain, so to speak, *nodal* points or periods at which the psychologic currents ran together and condensed themselves for a new start, and has each such node or point of condensation been marked by the appearance of an actual and heroic man (or woman) who supplied a necessary impetus for the new departure, and gave his name to the resulting movement? *or* is it sufficient to suppose the automatic formation of such nodes or starting-points without the intervention of any special hero or genius, and to imagine that in each case the myth-making tendency of mankind *created* a legendary and inspiring figure and worshiped the same for a long period afterwards as a god?

"As I have said before, this is a question which, interesting as it is, is not really very important. The main thing being that the prophetic and creative spirit of mankind *has* from time to time evolved those figures as idealisations of its 'heart's desire' and placed a halo round their heads. The long procession of them becomes a *real* piece of History—the history of the evolution of the human heart, and of human consciousness."[5]

The Crucifixion and the Cross of Christ are as old as humanity itself. Both are symbols of the eternal sacrifice of God as He immerses Himself in the form aspect of nature and thus becomes God immanent as well as God transcendent.

We have seen that Christ must be recognised, first of all, in the cosmic sense. The cosmic Christ has existed from all eternity. This cosmic Christ is divinity, or spirit, crucified in space. He personifies the immolation or sacrifice of spirit upon the cross of matter, of form or substance, in order that all divine forms, including the human, may live. This has ever been recognised by the so-called pagan faiths. If the symbolism of the cross is traced far back, it will be found that it antedates Christianity by thousands of years, and that finally, *the four arms* of the cross will be seen to drop away, leaving only the picture of *the living Heavenly Man, with His arms outspread in space.* North, south, east and west stands the cosmic Christ upon what is called "the fixed cross of the heavens." Upon this cross God is eternally crucified.

"The sky is mystically spoken of as the Temple and the eternal consciousness of God. Its altar is the sun, whose four arms or rays typify the four corners or the cardinal cross of the universe, which have become the *four fixed signs of the Zodiac,* and as the four powerful sacred animal signs, are both cosmical and spiritual . . . These four are known as the consecrated animals of the Zodiac, while the signs themselves represent the basic fundamental elements of life, Fire, Earth, Air and Water."[6]

[5] *Pagan and Christian Creeds,* by Edward Carpenter, pp. 217, 218.
[6] *The Celestial Ship of the North,* by E. V. Straiton, Vol. 1, p. 104.

These four signs are Taurus, Leo, Scorpio and Aquarius, and they constitute preëminently the cross of the soul, the cross upon which the second Person of the divine Trinity is crucified. Christ personified in His mission these four aspects, and as the cosmic Christ He exemplified in His Person the qualities for which each sign stood. Even primitive man, unevolved and ignorant, was aware of the significance of the cosmic spirit, immolated in matter and crucified upon the four-armed cross. These four signs are to be found unequivocally in the Bible, and are regarded in our Christian belief as the four sacred animals. The Prophet Ezekiel refers to them in the words:

"As for the likeness of their faces, they four had the face of a man, and the face of a lion, on the right side; and they four had the face of an ox on the left side; they four also had the face of an eagle."[7]

And again in the *Book of Revelations,* we find the same astrological symbology:

"And before the throne there was a sea of glass like unto crystal: and in the midst of the throne, and round about the throne, were four beasts full of eyes, before and behind.

"And the first beast was like a lion, and the second beast was like a calf, and the third beast had a face as a man, and the fourth beast was like a flying eagle."[8]

The "face of the man" is the ancient sign of Aquarius, the sign of the man carrying the water-pot, to which Christ referred when He sent His disciples into the city, saying: "Behold, when ye are entered into the city, there shall a man meet you, bearing a pitcher of water; follow him into the house where he entereth in."[9] This is the zodiacal sign into which we are entering. It might be as well to point out that this is astronomically true and not simply a pronouncement

[7] *Ezekiel,* I, 10.
[8] *Rev.,* IV, 6, 7.
[9] *St. Luke,* XXII, 10.

of the astrologers. The symbol which stands for the zodiacal sign Leo, is the Lion. This sign is the symbol of individuality, and under its influence the race arrives at self-consciousness and men can function as individuals. Christ, in His teaching, emphasised the significance of the individual and in His life demonstrated the supreme value of the individual, his perfecting, his service and his ultimate sacrifice in the interests of the whole. The constellation Aquila is always regarded as interchangeable with the sign Scorpio, the serpent, and it is therefore frequently used in this connection when considering the fixed cross of the cosmic Saviour. Scorpio is the serpent of illusion from which the Christ nature finally frees us, and it is to the illusory wiles of this serpent Scorpio that Adam succumbed in the garden of Eden. The "face of the ox" is the biblical symbol for the sign Taurus, the Bull, which was the religion immediately antedating the Jewish revelation, and which found its exponents in Egypt and in the Mithraic Mysteries. Upon this fixed cross all the world Saviours, not excepting the Christ of the West, have been eternally crucified, as reminders to man of the divine intent based upon the divine sacrifice.

The early Fathers recognised this truth, and realised that the story written in the heavens had a definite relation to humanity and to the evolution of human souls. Clement of Alexandria tells us that "the path of souls to ascension lies through the twelve signs of the zodiac," and the church festivals today are based, not upon historical dates in connection with the outstanding religious figures to which they refer, but upon the times and the seasons. We saw how in the Birth at Bethlehem the date was fixed astronomically nearly four centuries after Christ was born. The combination of Virgo with the Star in the East (Sirius), and the Three Kings (symbolised by Orion's belt) was the determining factor. The Virgin was seen in the east, with the line of the horizon passing through her centre, and this is one of the factors determining the doctrine of the Virgin birth.

Another instance can here be given to illustrate the astronomical background of our Christian festivals. There are two festivals kept in the Roman Catholic and the higher Anglican Churches, called the Assumption of the Virgin and the Birth of the Virgin Mary. One is celebrated on August 15th and the other on September 8th. Each year, the sun can be seen entering the sign Virgo about the time of the Assumption, and the entire constellation is enveloped and lost to sight in the radiant glory of the sun. About September 8th the constellation Virgo can be seen slowly reappearing as it emerges from the rays of the sun. This is spoken of as the birth of the Virgin.

Easter Day is always decided astronomically. These facts warrant the most careful consideration. This information should be in the hands of all Christian people, because then and only then can they arrive at a full and clear understanding of what, in His cosmic nature, Christ came to Earth to do. That event was of far greater importance than simply bringing about the salvation of any individual human being. It signified far more than the basis of the belief of several million people in their heavenly future. Christ's incarnation, apart from its historical value, and apart from the keynote which He sounded, marked the closing of a great cosmic cycle, but it marked also the opening of that door into the kingdom which had opened only occasionally theretofore, in order to permit the entrance of those sons of God who had triumphed over matter. After the advent of Christ, the door stood wide open for all time, and the kingdom of God began to form on Earth. In the long processes of time four great expressions of divine life, four forms of God immanent in nature, have appeared upon our planet. We call them the four kingdoms of nature. They constitute, symbolically, the planetary reflection of the four arms of the zodiacal cross upon which the cosmic Christ can be seen crucified. Down the ages human beings have symbolised the cosmic Christ immolated upon the cross of matter, and thus have perpetuated in the consciousness of the race the knowledge of that event; so in a planetary sense, the four kingdoms of nature do the same, portraying the spirit of God stretched upon a cross of material form, in order eventually to make possible the appearance of the kingdom of God on Earth. This connotes the spiritualisation of matter and form, the assumption of matter into heaven, and the release of God from the cosmic crucifixion. The poet, Joseph Plunkett, makes this beautifully clear in the following verses:

"I see His blood upon the rose
  And in the stars the glory of His eyes,
  His body gleams amid eternal snows,
  His tears fall from the skies.

I see His face in every flower,
  The thunder and the singing of the birds
  Are but His voice—and carven by His power
  Rocks are His written words.

All pathways by His feet are worn,
  His strong heart stirs the ever-beating sea,
  His crown of thorns is twined with every thorn,
  His cross is every tree."[10]

The wonder of Christ's mission lay in the fact that, though He was one of a long continuity of perfected divine men, He had a unique function. He summed up in Himself and brought to a conclusion the symbolic presentation of God's eternal sacrifice upon the fixed cross of the heavens, to which the stars bear testimony and which the history of religion has so successfully veiled, and today refuses to recognise. The Heavenly Man is today pendant in the Heavens, as He has been since the creation of the solar system, and as Christ said, "I, if I be lifted up from the earth, will draw all men unto Me,"[11] and not all men only, but eventually all forms of life in all kingdoms will render up their life, not as an imposed sacrifice, but as a willing offering to the

[10] Quoted in *The Testament of Man*, by Arthur Stanley, p. 498.
[11] *St. John*, XII, 32.

final glory of God. "He that loseth his life for my sake shall find it,"[12] is a fact which is often forgotten and one which has a definite bearing upon the story of the crucifixion in its wider implications. It is, however, through the achievement of the last of the manifesting kingdoms, the human, that the cross and its purpose is completed, and to this the death of Christ bears testimony.

But the important point is not His death, though that was climactic in the evolutionary process, but the subsequent Resurrection, symbolising as it did the formation and the precipitation upon Earth of a new kingdom in which men and all forms would be free from death—a kingdom of which the Man released from the Cross should be the symbol. We thus complete the entire circle, from the Man in space, with arms outspread in the form of a cross, through the sequence of crucified Saviours, telling us again and again what God had done for the universe, until we arrive at the culminating Son of God Who carried the symbolism down on to the physical plane, in all its stages. He then rose from the dead to tell us that the long task of evolution had at last reached its final phase—if we so choose, and if we are ready to do as He did—pay the price, and, passing through the gates of death, attain to a joyful resurrection. St. Paul sought to bring this truth home to us, though his words have been so often distorted through translation and theological misinterpretation:

"I long to know Christ and the power which is in His resurrection, and to *share in His suffering and die even as He died;* in the hope that I may attain to the resurrection from the dead. I do not say that I have already gained this knowledge or already reached perfection, but I press on."[13]

It would not appear from this passage that St. Paul regarded it as sufficient to salvation that one should simply believe that Christ died for one's sins.

[12] *St. Matt.*, X, 39.
[13] *Phil.*, III, 10, 11, Weymouth's Translation.

Let me state here, briefly and succinctly, what it would appear really transpired when Christ died upon the Cross. He rendered up the form aspect and identified Himself as Man with the life aspect of Deity. He thereby liberated us from the form side of life, of religion and of matter, and demonstrated to us the possibility of being in the world and yet not of the world,[14] living as souls, released from the trammels and limitations of the flesh, while yet walking on earth. To the very deeps of its being humanity is tired of death. Its only rest lies in the belief that the ultimate victory is over death, and that some day death will be abolished. This we shall go into more definitely in our next chapter, but in passing, it may be said that the race is so imbued with the thought of death that it has been the line of least resistance for theology to emphasise the death of Christ, and to omit to lay the major emphasis upon the renewal of life to which that death was the prelude. This practice will end because the world today demands a living Christ rather than a dead Saviour. It demands an ideal so universal in its implications—so inclusive of time and space and life—that the constant explanations and the endless attempts to make theology conform to the requirements of a deeply sensed vital truth will no longer be needed. The world has outlived the thought of a wrathful God who demands a blood sacrifice. Intelligent people today must agree that ". . . modern thought does not clash with primitive Christian ideas; but in regard to the propitiation for these evil inclinations the case is different. We can no longer accept the appalling theological doctrine that for some mystic reason a propitiatory sacrifice was necessary. It outrages either our conception of God as almighty or else our conception of Him as all-loving."[15] Humanity will accept the thought of a God who so loved the world that He sent His Son to give us the final expression of the cosmic sacrifice and to say to us, as He did

[14] *St. John*, XVII, 16.
[15] *The Paganism in Our Christianity*, by Arthur Weigall, p. 152.

upon the Cross: "It is finished."[16] We can now "enter into the joy of the Lord."[17] Men are learning to love, and they will, and do, repudiate a theology which makes of God a force of hardness and cruelty in the world, unparalleled by men.

The whole trend of human life tends to repudiate those ancient tenets which were founded in fear, and instead, courageously faces the facts and the responsibilities which are inherent in its spiritual birthright.

2

When the Church lays its emphasis upon the living Christ, and when it recognises that its forms and ceremonies, its festivals and rituals are inherited from a very ancient past, we shall then have the emergence of a new religion which will be as much divorced from form and the past as the kingdom of God is divorced from matter and the body nature. Orthodox religion, as a whole, can be regarded as a cross upon which we have crucified Christ; it has served its purpose as the custodian of the ages and the preserver of ancient forms, but it must enter into new life and pass through the resurrection if it is to meet the need of the deeply spiritual humanity of today. "Nations, like individuals," we are told, "are made, not only by what they acquire but by what they resign, and this is true also of religion at this time."[18] Its form must be sacrificed upon the Cross of Christ in order that it may be resurrected into true and vital life for the meeting of the people's need. Let a living Christ be its theme, and not a dying Saviour. Christ has died. About that let there be no mistake. The Christ of history passed through the gates of death for us. The cosmic

[16] *St. John*, XIX, 30.

[17] *St. Matt.*, XXV, 21.

[18] *The Supreme Spiritual Ideal*, by Sir Radhakrishnan, Hibbert Journal, October, 1936.

Christ is still dying upon the Cross of Matter. There He hangs fixed until the last weary pilgrim shall find his way home.[19] The planetary Christ, the life of the four kingdoms of nature, has been crucified on the four arms of the planetary Cross down the ages. But the end of this period of crucifixion is close upon us. Mankind can descend from the cross as Christ did, and enter into the kingdom of God, a living spirit. The sons of God are ready to be manifested. Today as never before:

"The Spirit Himself bears witness with our own spirits that we are children of God; and if children, then heirs too—heirs of God and co-heirs with Christ; if indeed we share Christ's sufferings, in order to share also His glory . . .

"All creation is yearning, longing to see the manifestation of the sons of God. For the Creation was made subject to futility, not of its own choice, but by the will of Him who so subjected it; yet with the hope that at last the Creation itself would be set free from the thraldom of decay to enjoy the liberty that comes with the glory of the children of God.

"For we know that the whole of Creation is moaning in the pangs of childbirth until this hour. And more than that, we ourselves, though we possess the Spirit as a foretaste of bliss, yet we ourselves moan as we wait for full sonship in the redemption of our bodies."[20]

Towards this glorification of God we are all moving. Some of the sons of men have already achieved, through the realisation of their divinity.

It is of interest to note how the two great branches of orthodox Christianity, the Eastern, as expressed through the Greek Church, and the Western, as expressed through the Roman Catholic and the Protestant Churches, have preserved two great concepts which the spirit of the race needed on its great evolutionary journey away from God and back to God. The Greek Church has always emphasised the

[19] *The Secret Doctrine,* Vol. I, p. 229.

[20] *Romans,* VIII, 16-24, Weymouth's Translation.

risen Christ. The West has emphasised the crucified Saviour.
Eastern Christianity looks to the resurrection as its pivotal
teaching.

The need of a death unto things material, the tendency
of man to sin and to forget God, and the necessity for a
change of heart or of intention have been the contribution
of Western Christianity to the religious beliefs in the world.
But we have been so preoccupied with the subject of sin
that we have forgotten our divinity; and we have been so
intensely individual in our consciousness that we have de-
picted a Saviour Who gave His life for us as individuals, believing that had He never died we could never enter heaven.
On these truths the Eastern Christian has placed little emphasis, stressing the living Christ and the divine nature of
man. Assuredly, only when the best of the two lines of
presented truths are brought together and then reinterpreted
shall we arrive at the basic concept upon which we can take
our stand without questioning, and also with the certainty
that it is inclusive enough to be really divine. Sin exists,
and there is sacrifice involved in the process of adjusting our
sinful natures. There is a death unto life, and a need to
"die daily,"[21] as St. Paul says, in order that we may live. Christ
died to all that had its existence in form, leaving us an example that we should follow His steps. But we in the West
have forgotten the Transfiguration and lost touch with divinity, and we should now stand ready to accept from the
Eastern Christian what he has so long believed.

This gnosis has always been in the world. Long before
Christ came the divinity of man was affirmed and divine incarnations were recognised.

The Gnostics themselves claimed to be the custodians of
a revelation which was not uniquely theirs, but which had
always been present in the world. G. R. S. Mead, an authority on these matters, remarks that: "The claim of these Gnostics was practically that the good news of Christ (the Chris-

[21] *I Cor.*, XV, 31.

tos) was the consummation of the inner doctrine of the Mystery-Institutions of all the nations; the end of them all being the revelation of the Mystery of Man. In Christ the Mystery of Man was unveiled."[22]

In view of the proven fact that there has been a continuity of revelation, and that Christ was one of the long line of manifesting Sons of God, wherein did His Person and His mission differ from that of the others? We can and must agree with Pfleger when he says: "The Incarnation of God in Christ is but a greater and more perfect theophany in a series of other more imperfect theophanies, which prepared the way for it by moulding the human nature which received them . . . the Incarnation is not a miracle in the strict and crude sense of the term, any more than the Resurrection, which is the inner union of matter with spirit, is foreign to the universal order of existence."[23] In what, therefore, did the mission of Christ differ from the others?

The difference lay in the point in evolution which humanity itself had reached. The cycle which Christ inaugurated has been one in which men have become strictly human. Up till that Incarnation there had always been those who, having achieved humanity, had then passed on to demonstrate divinity. But now the whole race is at the point of so doing. Although today men are predominantly animal-emotional, yet through the success of the evolutionary process—leading as it has to our widespread educational systems and the general high level of mental awareness—men have reached the point where the masses themselves, given proper encouragement, can "enter into the kingdom of God." Who can say that it is not this realisation, dim and uncertain as it may be, which prompts the universal unrest and the widespread determination to better conditions? That we interpret the kingdom of God in terms of the material is inevitable at first, but it is a hopeful and spiritual sign that we are today so

[22] *Thrice-Greatest Hermes,* by G. R. S. Mead, Vol. I, p. 141.
[23] *Wrestlers with Christ,* by Karl Pfleger, p. 242.

busy cleaning house, and thus attempting to raise the level of our civilisation. Christ incarnated when, for the first time, humanity was a complete whole, as far as the form side of its nature was concerned, with all the qualities manifesting —physical, psychic and mental—which distinguish the human animal. He brought to us a manifestation of what the perfect man could be who, regarding that form side as the temple of God, but recognising his innate divinity, strives to bring it to the foreground, first of all in his own consciousness and then before the world. This Christ did. The mysteries had always been revealed to the individual who fitted himself to penetrate into a hidden arcanum or temple, but Christ revealed them to humanity as a whole, and enacted the whole drama of the God-Man before the race. This was His major achievement, and this we have forgotten—the living Christ—in the emphasis we have laid upon man himself, on his relation to himself as a sinner, and to God as the One against Whom he has sinned.

Again, every great organisation or group religion or cult of any kind has originated with a person, and from that person the idea has spread out into the world, gathering adherents as time elapsed. Christ in this way precipitated the kingdom of God upon earth. It had always existed in the heavenly places. He caused it to materialise, thus becoming a fact to the consciousness of men.

Preparedness for the Kingdom, and the arrival of the time when men in large numbers could be initiated into the mysteries, required from them a recognition of an unworthiness and a sinfulness which only the development of the mind could give. The age of Christianity has been an age of mental unfoldment. It has been an age also wherein much emphasis has been laid upon sin and evil doing. There is no consciousness of sin in the animals, though there may be indications of a conscience among the domesticated animals, due to their association with man. Mind produces the power to analyse and observe, to differentiate and distinguish; and so with the advent of mental development there has been, for a long time, a growing sense of sinfulness, of contrition, and of an almost abject attitude to the Creator, producing in humanity that strongly marked inferiority complex with which today psychologists have to deal. Against this sense of sin, with its concomitants of propitiation, atonement and the sacrifice of Christ for us, there has been a revolt; and in this really wholesome reaction there is the normal tendency to go too far. Fortunately, we are never able to get too far from divinity; and that, as a race, we shall swing back into a state of greater spirituality than ever before is the sincere belief of all who know. Theology over-reached itself with its "miserable sinner" complex and its emphasis upon the necessity for the purification by blood. This teaching of purification through the blood of bulls and of rams (or lambs) was part of the ancient mysteries, and was inherited by us primarily from the Mysteries of Mithra. These mysteries, in their turn, inherited the teaching, and thus formulated their doctrine, which Christianity absorbed. When the sun was in the zodiacal sign of Taurus the Bull, the sacrifice of the bull was offered as a forecast of that which Christ came later to reveal. When the sun passed (in the precession of the equinoxes) into the next sign, that of Aries the Ram, we find the lamb was sacrificed and the scapegoat sent into the wilderness. Christ was born into the next sign, Pisces the Fishes, and it is for this reason that we eat fish on Good Friday, in commemoration of His coming. Tertullian, one of the early Church Fathers, speaks of Jesus Christ as the "Great Fish," and of us, His followers, as the "little fishes." These facts are well known, as the following extract will indicate:

"The ceremonies of purification by the sprinkling or drenching of the novice with the blood of bulls or rams were widespread, and were to be found in the rites of Mithra. By this purfication a man was 'born again' and the Christian expression 'washed in the blood of the Lamb' is undoubtedly a reflection of this idea, the reference thus being clear in the words of the Epistle to the Hebrews: 'It is not possible that the blood of bulls and of goats should take away sins.' In this passage the writer goes on to say: 'Having boldness to enter into the holiest by the blood of Jesus, by a new and living way which he hath consecrated for us through the veil, that is to say his flesh . . . let us draw near . . . having our hearts sprinkled from an evil conscience, and our bodies washed with pure water.' But when we learn that the Mithraic initiation ceremony consisted in entering boldly into a mysterious underground 'holy of holies' with the eyes veiled, and there being sprinkled with blood, and washed with water, it is clear that the author of the Epistle was thinking of those Mithraic rites with which everybody at that time must have been so familiar."[24]

Christ came to abolish these sacrifices by showing us their true meaning, and in His Person as perfect man He died the death of the Cross to show us (in picture form and through actual demonstration) that divinity can be manifested and can truly express itself only when man, as man, has died in order that the hidden Christ may live. The lower carnal nature (as St. Paul loved to call it) must die in order that the higher divine nature may show forth in all its beauty. The lower self must die in order that the higher self can manifest on earth. Christ had to die in order that once and for all mankind might learn the lesson that by the sacrifice of the human nature the divine aspect might be "saved." Thus Christ summed up in Himself the significance of all the past world sacrifices. That mysterious truth which had been revealed only to the pledged and trained initiate when he was ready for the fourth initiation was *given out by Christ to the world of men*. He died for all so that all might live. But this is not the doctrine of the vicarious atonement which was pre-eminently St. Paul's interpretation of the Crucifixion, but the doctrine which Christ Himself taught—the doctrine of divine immanence (see St. John XVII), and the doctrine of the God-Man.

Christianity inherited many of its interpretations, and the teachers and interpreters of the early Christian times were no more free from the thraldom of ancient beliefs than are we

[24] *The Paganism in Our Christianity*, by Arthur Weigall, pp. 132, 133.

from the interpretations given to Christianity during the past two thousand years. Christ did give us the teaching that we must die in order to live as Gods, and therefore He died. He did sum up in Himself all the traditions of the past for He "not only fulfilled the Judaic Scriptures, but He also fulfilled those of the pagan world, and therein lay the great appeal of early Christianity. In Him a dozen shadowy Gods were condensed into a proximate reality; and in His crucifixion the old stories of their ghastly atoning sufferings and sacrificial deaths were made actual and given a direct meaning."[25] But His death was also the consummating act of a life of sacrifice and service, and the logical outcome of His teaching. Pioneers and those who reveal to men their next step, those who come forth as the interpreters of the divine Plan, inevitably are repudiated, and usually die as the result of their courageous pronouncements. To this rule Christ was no exception. "Advanced Christian thinkers now regard the Crucifixion of our Lord as the supreme sacrifice made by Him for the sake of the principles of His teaching. It was the crowning act of His most heroic life, and it affords such a sublime example to mankind that meditation upon it may be said to produce a condition of at-one-ment with the Fountainhead of all goodness."[26]

How then is it that today we have such an emphasis upon the blood sacrifice of Christ and upon the idea of sin? It would appear that two causes are responsible for this:

1. The inherited idea of blood sacrifice. As Dr. Rashdall tells us:

"The various authors of the canonical books in fact were so accustomed to the pre-Christian ideas of an expiatory sacrifice and atonement that they accepted it without going to the roots of the matter. But this vagueness was not to the liking of the early Christian Fathers. In the Second Century A.D., Irenaeus, and after him other writers, explained the doctrine by what is called the 'Ransom Theory,' which states that the Devil was lawful lord of

[25] *The Paganism in Our Christianity*, by Arthur Weigall, p. 158.
[26] *Ibid.*, p. 166.

mankind owing to Adam's fall, and that God, being unable with justice to take Satan's subjects from him without paying a ransom for them, handed over His own incarnate Son in exchange."[27]

In this thought we have a definite demonstration of the way in which all ideas (intuitively perceived and infallibly right) are distorted. Men's minds and preconceived notions colour them. The idea becomes the ideal, and serves a useful purpose and leads men on (as the idea of sacrifice has always led men nearer to God) until it becomes an idol, and consequently limiting and untrue.

2. The growth of the consciousness of sin in the race, due to its increasing sensitivity to divinity and its consequent recognition of the shortcomings and the relative evil of the lower human nature.

We have seen that one of the factors responsible for the sin-complex of the West has been the development of the mind faculty, with its consequent aftermath of a developed conscience, a capacity to have a sense of values, and (as the result of that) the ability to see the higher and the lower natures in opposition to each other. When the higher self with its values and its range of contacts is *instinctively* contacted, and the lower self, with its lesser values and its more material range of activities is also realised, it necessarily follows that a sense of division and of failure is developed; men realise their lack of achievement; they become aware of God and humanity, of the world, of the flesh and the devil, but at the same time of the kingdom of God. As man develops, his definitions alter, and the crude so-called sins of the unevolved man, and the faults and failings of the average "nice" citizen of modern times involve different attitudes of mind and judgment, and surely different punitive approaches. As our sense of God changes and develops, and as we approach nearer to reality, our entire outlook upon life, ourselves and our fellow men is apt to alter and widen, and become more divine as well as more human. It is a human

[27] *The Idea of Atonement*, by H. Rashdall, p. 248.

characteristic to be conscious of sin, and to realise that when a man has offended he must, in some form or other, pay a price. The germ of mind, even in infant humanity, gives rise to this realisation, but it took nearly two thousand years of Christianity to raise sin to a position of such importance that it occupied (as it still does) a primary place in the thought of the entire race. We have a situation wherein the law and the Church and the educators of the race are almost entirely occupied with sin and how to prevent it. One wonders sometimes what the world would have been like today if the exponents of the Christian faith had occupied themselves with the theme of love and loving service instead of with this constantly reiterated emphasis upon the blood sacrifice and upon the wickedness of man.

The theme of sin runs naturally and normally throughout human history; and the effort to expiate it, in the form of animal sacrifice, has always been present. The belief in an angry deity, who exacted penalties for all that was done by man against a brother, and who demanded a price for all that was given to man as a product of the natural processes of the earth, is as old as man himself. It has passed through many phases. The idea of a God Whose nature is love has battled for centuries with the idea of a God Whose nature is wrath. The outstanding contribution of Christ to world progress was His affirmation, through word and example, of the thought that God is love and not a wrathful deity, inflicting jealous retribution. The battle still rages between this ancient belief and the truth of God's love which Christ expressed, and which Shri Krishna also embodied. But the belief in an angry, jealous God is still strongly entrenched. It is rooted in the consciousness of the race, and only today are we slowly beginning to realise a different expression of divinity. Our interpretation of sin and its penalty has been at fault, but the reality of God's love can now be grasped and can thus offset the disastrous doctrine of an angry God Who sent His Son to be the propitiation for the world evil. Of this belief Calvinism is perhaps the best and purest interpretation, and a brief statement as to that theological doctrine will present the concept in understandable terms.

"Calvinism is built upon the dogma of the absolute sovereignty of God, including omnipotence, omniscience and eternal justice—a common Christian doctrine, but developed by Calvinists with relentless logic to extreme conclusions. Calvinism is often summarised in five points. (1) Every human being as a descendant of Adam (whom all Christians in those times supposed to be an historical character) is guilty from his birth of original sin, in addition to later sins committed in his own lifetime. A man can do nothing to remove his own sin and guilt; that can only be done by the grace of God, mercifully vouchsafed to him through the atonement of Christ, and without any merit whatever on his own part; (2) So only those certain persons can be saved (particular redemption); (3) To whom God gives an effectual calling, strengthening their wills, and enabling them to accept salvation; (4) Who shall, and who shall not be saved is thus a matter of divine election, or predestination; (5) God will never fail those who are his elect: they shall never fall from ultimate salvation (perseverance of the saints). Calvinists insisted with great heat, and endeavoured with much subtility to demonstrate, that their doctrine fully provides for human freedom, and that God is in no way responsible for human sin."[28]

In view, therefore, of this emphasis upon human sinfulness, and as a result of the age-old habit of offering sacrifice to God, the true mission of Christ was long ignored. Instead of His being recognised as embodying in Himself an eternal hope for the race, He was incorporated into the ancient system of sacrifices, and the ancient habits of thought were too strong for the new idea which He came to give. Sin and sacrifice ousted and supplanted the love and service which He sought to bring to our attention through His life and His words. That is also why, from the psychological angle, Christianity has produced such sad, weary, and sin-conscious men. Christ, the sacrifice for sin, and the Cross of Christ as the

[28] *A Student's Philosophy of Religion*, by William K. Wright, p. 178.

instrument of His death, have absorbed men's attention, whilst Christ the perfect man and Christ the Son of God have been less emphasised. The cosmic significance of the cross has been entirely forgotten (or never known) in the West.

Salvation is not primarily connected with sin. Sin is a sympton of a condition, and when a man is "truly saved" that condition is offset, and with it the incidental sinful nature. It was this that Christ came to do—to show us the nature of the "saved" life; to demonstrate to us the quality of the eternal Self which is in every man; this is the lesson of the Crucifixion and the Resurrection: the lower nature must die in order that the higher may be manifested, and the eternal immortal soul in every man must rise from the tomb of matter. It is interesting to trace the idea that men must suffer in this world as the result of sin. In the East, where the doctrines of reincarnation and of karma hold sway, a man suffers for his own deeds and sins and "works out his own salvation, with fear and trembling."[29] In the Jewish teaching a man suffers for the sins of his forebears and of his nation, and thus gives substance to a truth which is only today beginning to be a known fact—the truth of physical inheritance. Under the Christian teaching, Christ, the perfect man, suffers with God, because God so loved the world that, immanent in it as He is, He could not divorce Himself from the consequences of human frailty and ignorance. Thus humanity gives a purpose to pain, and thus evil is eventually defeated.

The thought and idea of sacrifice for the sins of the people was not the original and basic idea. Originally, infant humanity offered sacrifices to God to appease His wrath, displayed in the elements through storms and earthquakes and physical disasters. When, instinctively, men turned on each other, when they offended and hurt one another, and so transgressed a dimly sensed realisation of human relationships and intercourse, sacrifice was offered again to God so that He too would not hurt mankind. Thus little by little

[29] *Phil.*, II, 12.

the idea grew until, at last, the salvation concept might be briefly summarised in the following terms:

1. Men are saved from the wrath of God in natural phenomena through animal sacrifices, preceded in still more ancient times by the sacrifice of the fruits of the earth.

2. Men are saved from God's wrath and from each other by the sacrifice of that which is valued, leading eventually to human sacrifices.

3. Men are saved by the sacrifice of a recognised Son of God, hence the vicarious atonement, for which the many crucified world Saviours prepared the way for Christ.

4. Men are definitely saved from eternal punishment for their sins by the death of Christ upon the Cross, the sinner guilty of an unkind word being as much responsible for the death of Christ as the vilest murderer.

5. Finally, the gradually emerging recognition that we are saved by the living risen Christ—historically presenting to us a goal, and present in each of us as the eternal omniscient soul of man.

Today it is the risen Christ who is emerging into the forefront of men's consciousness, and because of this we are on our way towards a period of greater spirituality and a truer expression of religion than at any other time in the history of man. The religious consciousness is the persistent expression of the indwelling spiritual man, the Christ within; and no outer earthly happenings, and no national situations, no matter how temporarily material they may appear to be in their objectives, can dull or obliterate the Presence of God in us. We are learning that that Presence can be released in us only by the death of the lower nature, and this is what Christ has always proclaimed to us from His Cross. We are realising increasingly that the "fellowship of His sufferings" means that we mount the Cross with Him and share constantly in the Crucifixion experience. We are coming to the knowledge that the determining factor in human life is love, and that "God is love."[30] Christ came to show us that love was the mo-

[30] *I St. John*, IV, 8.

tivating power of the universe. He suffered and died because He loved and cared enough for human beings to demonstrate to them the Way that they must go—from the cave of Birth to the mount of Transfiguration, and on to the agony of the Crucifixion—if they too are to share in the life of humanity and become, in their turn, saviours of their fellowmen.

How then shall we define sin? First let us look at the words which are used in the Bible and in theological works and commentaries dealing with the theme of sin, transgression, iniquity, evil, separation. All of these are expressions of man's relation to God and to his fellowmen and, according to the New Testament, these terms—God and our fellowmen—are interchangeable terms. What do these words mean?

The real meaning of the word *sin* is very obscure. It signifies literally "the one who it is."[31] Literally, therefore, the one who is in existence, just in so far as he sets himself up against the divine aspect hidden in himself, is a sinner. Some words by Dr. Grensted are illuminating in this connection. He says:

" 'Men turned away from God,' says Athanasius, 'when they began to give heed to themselves.' Augustine identifies sin with the love of self. Dr. Williams has argued that the underlying principle from which sin arises is to be found in 'the self-assertion of the individual against the herd, a principle which we can only designate by the inadequate titles of selfishness, lovelessness and hate.' And Dr. Kirk declares that 'sin may be said to begin with self-regard.' "[32]

These thoughts bring us directly to the central problem of sin which is (in the last analysis) the problem of man's essential duality, before he has made the at-one-ment for which Christ stood. When man, before he awakens to his dual nature, does that which is wrong and sinful, we cannot and do not regard him as a sinner—unless we are old-

[31] Webster's *Unabridged Dictionary.*
[32] *Psychology and God,* by L. W. Grensted, p. 136.

fashioned enough to believe in the doctrine that every man is irretrievably lost unless he is "saved" in the orthodox sense of the term. To St. James, sin is acting against knowledge, and he says "To him that knoweth to do good, and doeth it not, to him it is sin."[33] There we have a real definition of sin. It is to act against light and knowledge, and with deliberation to do that which we know is wrong and undesirable. Where there is no such knowledge there can be no sin; therefore animals are regarded as free from sin, and men acting in equal ignorance should likewise be so regarded. But the moment a man becomes aware that he is two persons in one form, that he is God and man, then responsibility steadily increases, sin becomes possible, and it is here that the mystery aspect of sin enters in. It consists in the relation between the "hidden man of the heart"[34] and the outer, tangible man. Each has its own life and its own field of experience. Each therefore remains a mystery to the other. The at-one-ment consists in resolving the relationship between these two, and when the wishes of the "hidden man" are violated, the sin occurs.

When these two aspects of man are united and function together as a unity, and when the spiritual man controls the activities of the carnal man, sin becomes impossible, and man moves on towards greatness.

The word "transgression" signifies the walking across a boundary; it involves the displacing of a landmark, as it is called in Masonry, or the infringement of one of the basic principles of living. There are certain things which are recognised by all as having a controlling relation to man. Such a compilation of principles as the Ten Commandments might be cited as a case in point. They constitute the boundry which ancient custom, ordained right habits, and the social order have imposed upon the race. To step across these boundaries, which man, from experience, has himself instituted, and to which God has accorded divine recognition,

[33] *St. James*, IV, 17.
[34] *I St. Peter*, III, 4.

is to transgress, and for every transgression there is an inevitable penalty. We pay the price of ignorance every time, and thereby learn not to sin; we are penalised when we do not keep the rules, and in time we learn not to transgress them. Instinctively we keep certain rules; probably because we have often paid the price, and certainly because we care too much about our reputations and public opinion to transgress them now. There are boundaries across which the average right-minded citizen does not step. When he does, he joins the large group of sinners. Controlled action in every department of human life is the ideal, and this action must be based on right motive, be actuated by unselfish purpose, and be carried forward in the strength of the inner spiritual man, the "hidden man of the heart."

"Iniquity" is a word with a seemingly innocuous meaning. It signifies simply an unevenness, an inequality. An iniquitous man is therefore technically an unbalanced man, one who tolerates some unevennesses in his daily life. A definition such as this is broadly inclusive, and even if we do not regard ourselves as sinners and transgressors, we surely come under the category of those whose lives show certain inequalities in conduct. We are not always the same. We are fluid in our expression of living. We are some days one thing and some days another, and because of this lack of balance and of equilibrium, we are *iniquitous* people in the true sense of the word. These things are good to remember, for they prevent that dire sin, self-satisfaction.

The question of evil is too large to elucidate at length, but it might be defined simply as adherence to that which we should have outgrown, the grasping of that which we should have left behind. Evil is, for the bulk of us, simply and solely an effort to identify ourselves with the form life when we have a capacity for soul consciousness; and righteousness is the steady turning of the thought and life towards the soul, leading to those activities which are spiritual and harmless and helpful. This sense of evil and this reaction to good is again latent in the relationship between the two halves of man's nature—the spiritual and the strictly human. When we turn the light of our awakened consciousness into the lower nature, and then with deliberation do, "in the light," those things which are determined and vitalised from the lower levels of our existence, we are throwing the weight of our knowledge on the side of evil, and are retrogressing. It is not always expedient from the point of view of the "carnal man" to do, or to reject, certain things, and when we choose the lower, and do it, making a specific choice, then the evil which is in us is dominating.

It is gradually dawning on the human consciousness that a separative attitude has in it the elements of sin and of evil. When we are separative in our attitudes or do anything which produces separation, we are transgressing a fundamental law of God. What we are really doing is breaking the Law of Love, which knows no separation, but sees only unity and synthesis, brotherhood and interrelation everywhere. Herein lies our major problem. Our study in connection with sin and evil will, as Dr. Grensted tells us, serve. . . .

"in the main to reveal the fundamental character of our problem as resulting from a failure of faith and a refusal of love. The psychologists do not escape from this view of sin when they deal with it as moral disease, for their one hope of treating such moral disease successfully rests in an attempt to awaken the latent personal resources of the ego, through processes in themselves personal. Where, as in certain of the major psychoses, this appeal cannot be made, there is no human hope of a cure. The key to psychological healing lies in *the transference* and there is the closest possible parallel between this and the Christian way of forgiveness. Both methods are wholly personal, both depend upon a readjustment of relationships which begins at priest or physician and passes out into every relationship of the social environment."[35] [Italics are mine. A. A. B.]

The sense of responsibility for one's actions grows as one progresses from stage to stage upon the Path of Evolution.

[35] *Psychology and God*, by L. W. Grensted, p. 199.

In the early stages there is little or no responsibility. There is little or no knowledge, no sense of relationship to God, and very little sense of relationship to humanity. It is this sense of separateness, this emphasis upon personal and individual good, which is of the nature of sin. Love is unity, at-one-ment and synthesis. Separateness is hatred, aloneness and division. But man, being divine in nature, has to love, and the trouble has been that he has loved wrongly. In the early stages of his development he places his love in the wrong direction, and turning his back on the love of God, which is of the very nature of his own soul, he loves that which is connected with the form side of life, and not with the life side of form.

Sin is therefore a definite infringement of the Law of Love, as we show it in our relation with God or with our brother, a son of God. It is the doing of those things from purely selfish interest which brings suffering to those we have in our immediate surroundings, or to the group with which we may be affiliated—a family group, a social group, a business group, or just the group of human beings with whom our general destiny casts us.

This brings us to the realisation that, in the last analysis, sin signifies wrong relation to other human beings. It was the sense of this wrong relation which in the early days of man's history gave rise to the sacrifice of worldly goods upon the altar, for primitive man seemed to feel that by making an offering to God he succeeded in making redemption of his character possible with his fellow men.

It is beginning to dawn upon the race today that the only real sin is to hurt another human being. Sin is the misuse of our relationships with each other, and there is no evading these relationships. They exist. We live in a world of men, and our lives are spent in contact with other human beings. The way in which we handle this daily problem demonstrates either our divinity or our erring lower nature. Our task in life is to express divinity. And that divinity manifests itself in the same way that the divinity of Christ expressed itself; in harmless living and ceaseless service to our fellow men; in a careful watchfulness over words and deeds lest in any way we should "offend one of these little ones";[36] in the sharing with Christ of the urgency which He felt to meet the world's need and to act the part of a saviour to men. It is gloriously true that this basic concept of Deity is beginning to grip humanity.

Christ's major task was the establishing of God's kingdom upon earth. He showed us the way in which humanity could enter that kingdom—by subjecting the lower nature to the death of the cross, and rising by the power of the indwelling Christ. Each one of us has to tread the way of the cross alone, and enter God's kingdom by right of achievement. But the way is found in service to our fellow men, and Christ's death, viewed from one angle, was the logical outcome of the service which He had rendered. Service, pain, difficulty and the cross—such are the rewards of the man who puts humanity first and himself second. But having done so, he discovers that the door into the kingdom is flung wide open and that he can enter in. But he has first to suffer. It is the Way.

It is through supreme service and sacrifice that we become followers of Christ and earn the right to enter into His kingdom, because we do not enter alone. This is the subjective element in all religious aspiration, and this all the sons of God have grasped and taught. Man triumphs through death and sacrifice.

That superhuman Spirit, Christ, did this perfectly. In Him was no sin because He had perfectly transcended the ephemeral lower self. His personality was subordinated to His divinity. The laws of transgression touched Him not, because He crossed no boundaries and infringed no principles. He embodied in Himself the principle of love and therefore it was not possible for Him, at the stage in evolu-

[36] *St. Luke*, XVII, 2.

tion which He had reached, to hurt a human being. He was perfectly balanced and had achieved that equilibrium which released Him from all lower impacts and set Him free to ascend to the throne of God. For Him there was no holding on to the lower and to that which was humanly desirable but divinely rejected. Evil therefore passed Him by, and he had no traffic with it. "He was in all points tempted like as we are, yet without sin."[37] He knew no separateness. Rich men, publicans, fishermen, learned professors, harlots and simple folk were all His friends, and the "great heresy of separateness" was completely overcome by His all-inclusive spirit. Thus He fulfilled the law of the past, emphasised the type for the humanity of the future, and entered for us within the veil, leaving us an example that we should follow His steps—an example of sacrifice unto the death, of service rendered ceaselessly, of self-forgetfulness, and of a heroism that led Him from point to point upon the way, and from altitude to altitude, until no bonds could hold Him (not even the barriers of death). He remains the eternal God-Man, the Saviour of the world. In perfection He fulfilled the will of God, and said to us the words which give us a simple rule with a great reward: "If any man will do his will, he shall know of the doctrine, whether it be of God."[38]

The simplicity of this instruction is almost baffling. We are told simply to do God's will and then truth will be revealed to us. There were times in Christ's life, as in the Garden of Gethsemane, when He fought with Himself to do God's will. There were moments when His human flesh quailed before the prospect which opened up before Him. He therefore knew the difficulty of this simple rule.

3

In turning our attention to the story of the Crucifixion it is obvious that there is no need to recount the details of it.

[37] *Heb.,* IV, 15.
[38] *St. John,* VII, 17.

It is so well known and so familiar that the words in which is is couched are apt to mean little. The tale of Christ's triumphant entry into Jerusalem, of His gathering the disciples together into the upper room, and there sharing with them the communion of bread and of wine, and of the desertion of those who supposedly loved Him, with His subsequent agony in the Garden of Gethsemane, is as familiar to us as our own names, and much less arresting. That is the tragedy of Christ. He did so much, and we have recognised so little. It has taken us twenty centuries to begin to understand Him and His mission and career. The Crucifixion itself was only an anticipated and expected consummation of that career. No other end was possible. It was predetermined from the beginning, and really dated from the time when, after the Baptism initiation, He started out to serve humanity, and to teach and preach the good tidings of the kingdom of God. That was His theme, and we have forgotten it and have preached the Personality of Jesus Christ—one theme which He Himself ignored and which seemed to Him of small importance in view of the greater values involved. This again is the tragedy of Christ. He has one set of values and the world has another.

We have made of the Crucifixion a tragedy, whereas the real tragedy was our failure to recognise its true significance. The agony in the Garden of Gethsemane was based upon the fact that He was not understood. Many men have died violent deaths. In this, Christ was in no wise different from thousands of other far-seeing men and reformers, down the ages. Many people have passed through the Gethsemane experience and prayed with the same fervour as Christ that God's will might be done. Many men have been deserted by those who might have been expected to understand and participate in the work and service visioned. In none of these respects was Christ really unique. But His suffering was based upon His unique vision. The lack of comprehension of the people, and the distorted interpretations which future theologians would give to His message must surely have been a part of the pre-vision, as likewise the knowledge that the emphasis accorded to Him as the Saviour of the world would retard for centuries the materialising of the kingdom of God on earth, which it was His mission to found. Christ came that all mankind might have "life . . . more abundantly."[39] We have so interpreted His words that only the "saved" are credited with having taken the necessary steps towards that life. But the abundant life is surely not a life to be lived hereafter, in some distant heaven where those who are believers shall enjoy an exclusive life of happiness, whilst the rest of God's children are left outside. The Cross was intended to indicate the line of demarcation between the kingdom of men and the kingdom of God, between one great kingdom in nature which had reached maturity, and another kingdom in nature which could now enter upon its cycle of activity. The human kingdom had evolved to the point where it had produced the Christ and those other children of God whose lives bore constant testimony to the divine nature.

Christ assumed the ancient symbol and burden of the cross, and, taking His stand beside all the previous crucified Saviours, embodied in Himself the immediate and the cosmic, the past and the future, rearing the Cross on the hill outside Jerusalem (the name of which signifies the "vision of peace"), thus calling attention to the kingdom which He died to establish. The work had been completed, and in that strange little country called the Holy Land, a narrow strip of territory between the two hemispheres, the East and the West, the Orient and the Occident, Christ mounted the Cross and fixed the boundary between the kingdom of God and the kingdoms of the world, between the world of men and the world of Spirit. Thus He brought to a climax the ancient Mysteries, which had prophesied the coming of that kingdom, and instituted the Mysteries of the kingdom of God.

The effort to carry out to perfection the will of God brought to an end the most complete life that had been lived on earth. The attempt to found the kingdom, pre-

[39] *St. John*, X, 10.

ordained for all time, and the antagonism it evoked, brought Christ to the place of crucifixion. The hardness of men's hearts, the weakness of their love, and their failure to see the vision, broke the heart of the Saviour of the world—a Saviour because He opened the door into the kingdom.

It is time that the Church woke up to its true mission, which is to materialise the kingdom of God on earth, today, here and now. The time is past wherein we can emphasise a future and coming kingdom. People are no longer interested in a possible heavenly state or a probable hell. They need to learn that the kingdom is here, and must express itself on earth; it consists of those who do the will of God at any cost, as Christ did, and who can love one another as Christ loved us. The way into that kingdom is the way that Christ trod. It involves the sacrifice of the personal self for the good of the world, and the service of humanity instead of the service of one's own desires. In the course of enunciating these new truths concerning love and service Christ lost his life. Canon Streeter tells us that "the significance and value of the death of Christ springs from its inner quality. It is the expression in external act of a freely chosen self-dedication, ungrudging, and without reserve, to the highest service of God and man. The suffering incidental to such self-offering is morally creative."[40]

Is it not, perhaps, a fact that the Crucifixion of Christ, with its great preceding events—the communion and the Gethsemane experience—is a tragedy which has its basis in the conflict between love and hate? It is not the intention of this book to belittle the world event which took place upon Calvary. But today as one looks back upon that event, a certain truth begins to emerge, and this is that we have interpreted that sacrifice and that death in purely selfish terms. We are concerned with our individual interest in the matter. We have emphasised the importance of our individual salvation and feel it to be of tremendous importance. But the world view and what Christ was destined to

[40] *The Buddha and the Christ*, by B. H. Streeter, p. 215.

do for humanity down the ages, and the attitude of God towards human beings from the earliest times, through the period of Christ's life in Palestine and on until the present time, are subordinated to the factor of our belief or non-belief in the efficacy of the Crucifixion upon Calvary to save our individual souls. Yet in His conversation with the repentant thief Christ admitted him into the kingdom of God on the basis of his recognition of divinity. Christ had not yet died, and the blood sacrifice of Christ had not yet been made. It was almost as if Christ had foreseen the turn which theology would give to His death, and endeavoured to offset it by making the recognition of the dying thief one of the outstanding events at His death. He made no reference to the remission of sins through His blood as the reason for that admission.

The real issue was the issue between love and hate. Only St. John, the beloved Apostle, the one closest to Jesus, really understood; and in his Epistles the emphasis is entirely upon love, and the usual orthodox interpretation is nowhere to be found. Just love and hate; the desire to live as children of God and the inclination to live as ordinary human beings: herein lies the distinction between the citizen of the kingdom of God and a member of the human family. It was love which Christ endeavoured to express, but it is hate and separation and war, culminating in the World War, which have characterised the official rendering of His teaching, down the ages. Christ died in order to bring to our notice that the way into the kingdom of God was the way of love and of service. He served and loved and wrought miracles, and gathered together the poor and the hungry. He fed them, and sought in every possible way to call attention to the principle of love as the major characteristic of divinity, only to find that this life of loving service brought Him trouble and eventually the death of the Cross.

We have fought for the theological doctrine of the Virgin Birth. We have fought over the doctrines whereby men shall be saved. We have fought over the subject of baptism, and over the atonement. We have fought over the fact and the denial of immortality, and what man must do in order to be raised from the dead. We have regarded half the world as lost and only the Christian believer as saved, yet all the time Christ has told us that love is the way into the kingdom, and that the fact of the presence of divinity in each of us makes us eligible for that kingdom. We have omitted to realise that the "vicarious atonement is the harmonising of the disharmony of others by the power of a spiritual presence, which brings about the great transmutation; evil is absorbed and transmuted into good or equilibrised."[41] This constitutes the endeavour of Christ, and the fact of His Presence is the harmonising medium in life. *Men are not saved by belief in the formulation of a theological dogma, but by the fact of His living Presence, of the living immediate Christ.* It is the realisation of the fact of the presence of God in the human heart which is the basis of the mystical vision, while the knowledge that one is a son of God gives one the strength to follow the Saviour's footsteps from Bethlehem to Calvary. That which will eventually reorganise our human life is the presence in the world of those who know Christ as their example, and recognise that they possess the same divine life, just as the affirmation of the basic law of the kingdom of God, the Law of Love, will finally save the world. It is the substitution of the life of Christ for the life of the world, the flesh and the devil, which will inject a meaning and a value into life.

A sense of the failure of love constitutes the outstanding problem in the agony in the Garden; it was this sense of travail with world forces which enabled Christ to join the company of all His brothers. Men had failed Him, just as men fail us. In the moment when He most needed understanding, and all the strength which companionship gives, His nearest and dearest either deserted Him or slept, unaware of His agony of mind. "The Promethean conflict is the

[41] *Some Mystical Adventures,* by G. R. S. Mead, p. 161.

strife which takes place in the human mind between the yearning for understanding, and the nearer more immediate pull of those living affections and desires which are conditioned upon the goodwill and the support of fellow beings; desires for the happiness of loved ones; for the alleviation of pain and disappointment in minds that cannot understand the inner dream; and for the warm reassurance of mundane honours. This conflict is the rock upon which the religious mind founders and is split against itself."[42] Upon this rock Christ did not founder, but He had His moments of intensest agony, finding relief only in the realisation of the Fatherhood of God and its corollary, the brotherhood of man. "Father," He said. It was this sense of unity with God and His fellow men which led Him to institute the Last Supper, to originate that communion service, the symbolism of which has been so disastrously lost in theological practice. The keynote of that communion service was fellowship. "It is only thus that Jesus creates fellowship among us. It is not as a symbol that he does it . . . in so far as we with one another and with him are of one will, to place the Kingdom of God above all, and to serve in behalf of this faith and hope, so far is there fellowship between him and us and the men of all generations who lived and live in the same thought."[43]

4

1. "Father, forgive them; for they know not what they do."[44]
2. "To day thou shalt be with me in paradise."[45]
3. "Woman, behold thy son! Then saith He to the disciple, Behold thy mother!"[46]
4. "My God, my God, why hast thou forsaken me?"[47]

[42] *Psychology and the Promethean Will*, by W. H. Sheldon, pp. 85, 86.
[43] *The Mystery of the Kingdom of God*, by Albert Schweitzer, p. 56.
[44] *St. Luke*, XXIII, 34.
[45] *St. Luke*, XXIII, 43.
[46] *St. John*, XIX, 26.
[47] *St. Matt.*, XXVII, 46.

5. "I thirst."[48]
6. "It is finished."[49]
7. "Father, into thy hands I commend my spirit."[50]

The thought of the kingdom coloured all that He said upon the Cross. The Word of Power which emanated from the Cross was spoken by Jesus Christ Himself and not, this time, by the Father. Christ spoke a sevenfold word, and in that word summed up for us the Word that inaugurated the kingdom of God. Each of His utterances had relation to that kingdom, and not the usual small, individual or selfish relation which we have so often ascribed to them. What were those seven words? Let us consider them, realising while doing so that the causes which gave rise to them produced the manifestation of the kingdom of God on earth.

In every case the seven words have been interpreted as having either an individual application in connection with the person to whom they were supposedly spoken, or as having a personal significance to Christ Himself. We have always read the Bible in this manner, with the personal significance in our minds. But these words of Christ are of too great importance to be thus interpreted. They have a meaning far wider than those usually given. The wonder of all He said (as it is the wonder of all the world scriptures) is that the words are capable of various meanings. The time has come when the meaning that Christ gave should be more generally understood by us in the light of the kingdom of God, and with a wider connotation than the individual one. His words were Words of Power, evoking and invoking, potent and dynamic.

One of the first things which emerge in one's consciousness as one studies the first word from the Cross was the fact that Jesus requested His Father to forgive the people who crucified Him; He evidently, then, did not regard His death upon the Cross as adequate to that need. There was

[48] *St. John*, XIX, 28.
[49] *St. John*, XIX, 30.
[50] *St. Luke*, XXIII, 46.

no remission of sins through the shedding of blood; but there was the need to ask God's pardon for the sin committed. The two facts which come to the fore in this word are the Fatherhood of God, and the fact that ignorance, if productive of wrong-doing, does not make a man guilty and therefore punishable. Sin and ignorance are frequently synonymous terms, but the sin is recognised as such by those who know and who are not ignorant. Where there is ignorance there is no sin. In this word from the Cross Christ tells us two things:

1. That God is our Father, and that we approach Him through Christ. It is the inner hidden man of the heart, the unrealised Christ who can approach the Father. Christ had earned this right because of His proven divinity and because He had passed through the third initiation, the Transfiguration; when we too are transfigured (for only the transfigured Christ can be crucified) then we too can invoke the Father and call on the spirit, which is God, the life of all forms, to adjust relationships, and to bring about that forgiveness which is the very essence of life itself.

2. That forgiveness is the result of life. This is a hard truth for the Western believer to accept. He is so used to resting back upon the activity of the Christ in the distant past. Forgiveness is, however, a result of living processes which bring adjustment, cause restitution, and produce that attitude wherein a man is no longer ignorant and therefore not in need of forgiveness. Life and experience do this for us, and nothing can arrest the process. It is not a theological belief that puts us right with God, but an attitude to life and an attitude to the Christ dwelling in the human heart. We learn through pain and suffering (that is, through experience) not to sin. We pay the price of our sins and mistakes, and cease to make them. We arrive eventually at the point where we no longer make our earlier errors or commit our former sins. For we suffer and agonise, and learn that sin brings retribution and causes suffering. But suffering

has its uses, as Christ knew. In His Person He was not only the historical Jesus Whom we know and love, but He was also the symbol to us of the cosmic Christ, God suffering through the sufferings of His created beings.

Justice can be forgiveness when the facts of the case are rightly understood, and in this demand of the crucified Saviour we have the recognition of the Law of Justice, and not that of Retribution, in an act at which the whole world stands aghast. This work of forgiveness is the age-long work of the soul in matter or form. The Oriental believer calls this *karma*. The Western believer talks of the Law of Cause and Effect. Both, however, are dealing with the working out by a man of his soul's salvation, and the constant paying of the price which the ignorant pay for mistakes made and so-called sins committed. A man who deliberately sins against light and knowledge is rare. Most "sinners" are simply ignorant. "They know not what they do."

Then Christ turned to a sinner, to a man who had been convicted of wrong doing in the eyes of the world—and who himself recognised the correctness of the judgment and of his punishment. He stated that he received the due reward of his sins, but at the same time there was something in the quality of Jesus which arrested his attention and forced from him the admission that this third Malefactor had "done nothing amiss." The factor which accorded him admission into paradise was a two-fold one. He recognised the divinity of Christ. "Lord," he said. And he also had a realisation of what Christ's mission was—to found a kingdom. "Remember me when Thou comest into Thy kingdom." The significance of his words is eternal and universal, for the man who recognises divinity, and who at the same time is sensible of the kingdom, is ready to take advantage of the words, "To day, thou shalt be with me in paradise."

In the first word from the Cross, Jesus considered the ignorance and the feebleness of man. He was as helpless as a litle child, and in His words He testified to the reality of the first initiation and to the time when He was a "babe in

Christ." The parallels between the two episodes are significant. The ignorance, helplessness and consequent maladjustment of human beings evoked from Jesus the demand that forgiveness be accorded. But when life experience has played its part, we have again the "babe in Christ," ignorant of the laws of the spiritual kingdom, yet released from the darkness and ignorance of the human kingdom.

In the second word from the Cross we have the recognition of the Baptism episode, which signified purity and release through the purification of the waters of life. The waters of John's Baptism released from the thralldom of the personality life. But the Baptism to which Christ was subjected through the power of His Own life, and to which we are also subjected through the life of Christ within us, was the Baptism of fire and of suffering, which finds its climax of pain upon the Cross. That climax of suffering, for the man who could endure unto the end, was his entrance to "paradise"— a name connoting bliss. Three words are used to express this power to enjoy—happiness, joy and bliss. *Happiness* has a purely physical connotation, and concerns our physical life and its relationships; *joy* is of the nature of the soul and reflects itself in happiness. But *bliss,* which is of the nature of God Himself, is an expression of divinity and of the spirit. Happiness might be regarded as the reward of the new birth, for it has a physical significance, and we are sure that Christ knew happiness, even though He was a "man of sorrows"; joy, being more especially of the soul, reaches its consummation at the Transfiguration. Though Christ was "acquainted with sorrow," He knew joy in its essence, for the "joy of the Lord is our strength," and it is the soul, the Christ in every human being, which is strength and joy and love. He knew also bliss, for at the Crucifixion the bliss which is the reward of the soul's triumph was His.

Thus in these two Words of power "Father, forgive them for they know not what they do," and "To day thou shalt be with me in paradise," we have the significances of the first two initiations summarised for us.

Now we come to the extraordinary and much debated episode between Christ and His mother, summed up in the words: "Woman, behold thy son," and followed by the words spoken to the beloved apostle: "Behold thy mother." What did these words mean? Below Christ stood the two people who meant the most to Him, and from the agony of the Cross He spoke to them a special message, relating them to each other. Our consideration of the previous initiations may make the meaning clear. John typifies the personality which is reaching perfection and whose nature is becoming irradiated by divine love, the major characteristic of the second Person of the divine Triplicity, the soul, the son of God, whose nature is love. As we have seen, Mary represents the third Person of the Trinity, the material aspect of nature which cherishes and nurtures the son and gives birth to him in Bethlehem. In these words Christ, utilising the symbolism of these two persons, relates them to each other, and practically says: Son, recognise who is to give thee birth at Bethlehem, the one who shelters and guards the Christ life. To His mother, He says: Recognise that in the developed personality there is latent the Christ child. Matter, or the virgin Mary, is glorified through her son. Therefore the words of Christ have a definite reference to the third initiation, that of the Transfiguration.

Thus in His first three Words from the Cross He refers to the first three initiations, and recalls to our minds the synthesis revealed in Himself and the stages which we must cover if we are to follow in His steps. It is possible also that the thought was in the consciousness of the crucified Saviour that matter itself, being divine, was capable of infinite suffering; and in these words there was wrung from Him the recognition that though God suffers in the Person of His Son, He also suffers with similar acute agony in the person of that Son's mother, the material form which has given Him birth. Christ stands midway between the two—the mother and the Father. Therein is His problem, and therein is found the problem of every human being. Christ draws the two together—the matter aspect and the spirit aspect, and the union of these two produces the son. This is humanity's problem and humanity's opportunity.

The fourth Word from the Cross admits us into one of the most intimate moments of Christ's life—a moment that has a definite relation to the kingdom, just as had the three previous Words. One always hesitates to intrude upon this episode in His life, because it is one of the deepest and most secret and perhaps most sacred phases of His life on earth. We read that there was "darkness on the face of the earth" for three hours. This is a most significant interlude. From the Cross, alone and in the dark, He symbolised all that was embodied in this tragic and agonised Word. The number three is, of course, one of the most important and sacred numbers. It stands for divinity, and also for perfected humanity. Christ, the perfect Man, hung upon the Cross for "three hours," and in that time each of the three aspects of His nature was carried to the highest point of its capacity for realisation and for consequent suffering. At the end, this triple personality gave vent to the cry, "My God, my God, why hast thou forsaken me?"

Christ had passed through all the climaxing episodes of adjustment. The Transfiguration experience was only just over. Let us not forget that fact. In that experience God had been near, and the transfigured Christ had seemed in His initiation to link God and man. He had just uttered the Word which had testified to the relation of the body nature, the Mary aspect, and the personality, in the person of St. John—the symbol of a personality carried to a very high state of perfection and realisation. Then for three long hours He wrestled in the dark with the problem of the relation of God and the soul. Spirit and soul had to be fused and blended to one great unity—just as He had already fused and blended the soul and the body, and had testified to that consummation in the Transfiguration. Suddenly He discov-

ered that all the achievement of the past, all that He had
done, was but the prelude to another atonement which He
had to make as a human being; and there on the Cross, in the
full blaze of publicity, He had to renounce that to which He
had hitherto held, His soul, and realise for a brief instant
that in this renunciation everything was at stake. Even the
consciousness that He was the Son of God, the soul incarnate in the flesh (for which He had fought and sacrificed),
had to disappear, and He be left bereft of all contacts. All
sense of feeling and all possible reactions failed to fill the
sensed void. He seemed deserted, not only by humanity, but
by God. That upon which He had relied, the divinity of
which He had felt assured, was found to be related to feeling.
That feeling He must also transcend. All had therefore to be
relinquished.

It was through this experience that Christ blazed the trail
to the very heart of God Himself. Only when the soul has
learnt to stand alone, assured of divinity, and yet with no
outer recognition of that divinity, can the very centre of
spiritual life he recognised as stable and eternal. It was in
this experience that Christ fitted Himself for the Resurrection initiation, and so proved to Himself, and to us, that
God existed, and that the immortality of divinity *is* an
established and unalterable fact. This experience of loneliness, of being bereft of all that protects, all that has hitherto
been regarded as essential to one's very being, is the hall
mark of achievement. Disciples are apt to forget this, and
one wonders for a brief moment, as one listens to Christ
thus veiling His agony, whether He was not again "in all
points tempted like as we are," and whether at this moment
He did not descend into the deepest recesses of the valley
and feel that utter aloneness which is the reward of those
who mount the Cross on Golgotha.

Although each son of God at different stages upon his way
of initiation prepares for this final loneliness by phases of
utter rejection, when the final crisis comes he must experi-

ence moments of loneliness such as he could not previously conceive. He follows in the footsteps of his Master, being crucified before men and deserted both by his fellow men and by the comforting presence of the divine self upon which he has learnt to rely. Yet because Christ entered thus into the place of outer darkness, and felt entirely deserted of all that had hitherto meant so much to Him, both humanly and from the angle of divinity, He has enabled us to gauge the value of the experience, and has shown us that only through this place of outer darkness, which the mystics have justifiably called "the dark night of the soul," can we truly enter into the blessed companionship of the kingdom. Many books have been written about this experience, but it is rare—far rarer than the literature of the mystics would have us believe. It will become more frequent, as more and more men pass through the gates of suffering and of death into the kingdom. Christ hung pendent between heaven and earth, and although He was surrounded by crowds, and although at His feet stood those whom He loved, He was utterly alone. It is the loneliness whilst accompanied, the utter sense of being forsaken whilst surrounded by those who seek to understand and help, which constitutes the darkness. The light of the Transfiguration is suddenly obliterated; and because of the intensity of that light, the night appears more dark. But it is in the dark that we know God.

Four Words of Power had now been uttered by the Christ. He had spoken the Word for the plane of everyday life, the Word of forgiveness, and in it He indicated the principle upon which God works in relation to the evil done by men. Where there is ignorance and no defiance or wrong intent, then forgiveness is assured, for sin consists of definite action in the face of the warning voice of conscience. He had spoken the Word which brought peace to the dying thief, and had told him that he was assured, not only of forgiveness, but of peace and happiness. He had spoken the Word which brought together the two aspects which were being symbolically crucified upon the Cross—matter and soul, the matter of the form and the perfected lower nature. These are the three Words of the physical, the emotional, and the mental planes, whereon man habitually lives. The sacrifice of the entire lower nature had been completed, and there was silence and darkness for three hours. Then was uttered that stupendous Word which indicated that Christ had reached the stage of the final sacrifice, and that even the consciousness of divinity, the consciousness of the soul itself, with its strength and power, its light and understanding, had also to be laid upon the altar. He had to undergo the experience of an utter renunciation of all that had constituted His very being. This brought the cry of protest and of questioning: "My God, my God! Why hast Thou forsaken me?"

Then followed three Words of a different quality altogether. In the words, "I thirst," He expressed the motivating power of every Saviour. This was misinterpreted by the onlookers, who have given it most naturally a physical connotation; but it surely had a deeper meaning, and must have reference to that divine thirst which sweeps through the consciousness of every son of God who has achieved divinity, and which indicates his willingness to undertake the task of Saviour. It is characteristic of all who have attained that they cannot rest satisfied with their achievement which brought them liberation and freedom, but immediately reorient themselves to the world of men and stay with humanity, working for the salvation of human beings until all the sons of God shall have found their way back to the Father's home. This thirst for the souls of men forced Christ to open the door into the kingdom, and to hold it open Himself, so that it might be His hand and His aid which should lift us over the threshold. This is the redemption, and in this redemption we all share, not from the selfish angle of our individual salvation, but from the consciousness that, as we redeem are we redeemed, as we save are we ourselves salvaged, and that as we help others to achieve, we too are admitted as citizens into the kingdom. *But this is the way of Crucifixion.* Only when we can utter the five Words of Power do we really understand the meaning of God and His love. The way of the Saviour becomes then our way. God's life and purpose stand revealed.

It is this thirst which we share with the Saviour, and the world need (of which our own is a part, though relatively incidental) that unite us with Him. It is the "fellowship of His sufferings" to which He calls us, and the demand which we hear as He hears it. This aspect of the Cross and its lesson has been summed up in the following words, which warrant our careful consideration, and our consequent consecration to the service of the Cross, which is the service of humanity.

"When I . . . turned from that world-appealing sight, Christ crucified for us, to look upon life's most perplexed and sorrowful contradictions, I was not met as in intercourse with my fellow-men by the cold platitudes that fall so lightly from the lips of those whose hearts have never known one real pang, nor whose lives one crushing blow. I was not told that all things were ordered for the best, nor assured that the overwhelming disparities of life were but apparent, but I was met from the eyes and brow of Him who was indeed acquainted with grief, by a look of solemn recognition, such as may pass between friends who have endured between them some strange and secret sorrow, and are through it united in a bond that cannot be broken."[51]

Then there burst upon Christ's consciousness the wonder of accomplishment. He had succeeded, so that, with full realisation of the significance of the statement, He could say, "It is finished." He had done what He came into incarnation to do. The gate into the kingdom stood open. The boundary between the world and the kingdom was clearly defined. He had given us an example of service unparalleled in history. He had shown us the way that we should go. He had demonstrated to us the nature of perfection. There was

[51] *Colloquia Crucis,* by Dora Greenwell, p. 14 f.

no more that He could then do, and so we hear the triumphant cry, "It is finished."

Only one more Word of Power came forth from the darkness which shrouded the dying Christ. The moment of His death was prefaced by the words, "Father, into Thy hands I commend my spirit." His first word and His last begin with the appeal: "Father"— for ever we are the children of God, and "If children, then heirs; heirs of God, and joint heirs with Christ; if so be that we suffer with Him, that we may be also glorified together;"[52] joint heirs of glory, but also joint heirs in the suffering which must be ours if the world is to be saved and humanity as a whole is to pass into the kingdom. The kingdom is in existence. Through the work of Christ and His living Presence in all of us there exists today, subjective as yet, but awaiting immediate tangible expression . . .

"One body, and one Spirit, even as ye are called in one hope of your calling; One Lord, one faith, one baptism, One God and Father of all, who is above all, and through all, and in you all."[53]

Furthermore, in words later used by Christ, the psalmist says, "Into thine hand I commit my spirit, for thou hast redeemed me."[54] The implication here is clear. It is the spirit of life in Christ and in us which makes us sons of God, and it is that sonship (with its quality of divinity) which is the guarantee of our final accomplishment and entrance into the kingdom of spirit. The sign given is expressed in the words: "Behold, the veil of the temple was rent in twain from the top to the bottom."[55] Access to God was established, and the inner spiritual forces could pass out without hindrance into manifestation. This was an act of God, a stupendous recognition by the Father of what His

[52] *Romans*, VIII, 17.

[53] *Eph.*, IV, 4, 5, 6.

[54] *Psalm* XXXI, 5.

[55] *St. Matt.*, XXVII, 51.

Son had done. Spirit and matter were now one. All separating barriers were abolished, and man and God could meet and hold intercourse.

In an ancient scripture of India we read these words, spoken thousands of years ago, yet capable of being applied in a most significant manner to this act of Christ, which linked Him up not only with ourselves and all past believers prior to His advent, but with the Cosmic Christ, so unmistakably speaking here:

"Brahma, the self-effulgent meditated. He considered . . . Come, let me sacrifice myself in living things and all living things in Myself . . . He thus acquired greatness, self-effulgence, lordship and mastery."

In concluding this chapter upon the Crucifixion, let us consider what really was the purpose of Christ's sacrifice. Why did He die? We are told why most clearly in St. John's Gospel, and yet very little emphasis has been laid upon the statement. Only today are we beginning to understand the meaning of what He did. Only today is the wonder of His sacrifice beginning to dawn upon the minds of those whose intuition is awakened. He came primarily to do two things, upon both of which we have already touched: first of all, He came to found, or to materialise upon the earth, the kingdom of God; secondly, to show us what the love of God signified and how it expressed itself in service and in the eternal sacrifice of divinity upon the cross of matter. Christ stood as a symbol and also as an example. He revealed to us God's Mind, and showed us the pattern upon which we should mould our lives.

The kingdom and the service! These are the keynotes which today have in them that rallying power which the believers of the world demand. Christ shared with us, as a human being, the path of world experience. He mounted the Cross and showed us in His sacrifice and example what we had to do. He shared with us the way of life, because there was nothing else for Him to do, as He was a human being. But He threw upon this life experience the radiant light of divinity itself, telling us also to "let our light shine."[56] He proclaimed Himself Man, and then told us that we were the children of God. He was with us then, and He is with us now, for He is in us all the time, although very often unrecognised and unapproached.

The outstanding lesson with which we are confronted is the fact that ". . . human nature as we know it can neither attain happiness without suffering, nor perfection without the sacrifice of itself."[57] For us the kingdom constitutes the vision, but for Christ it was a reality. The service of the kingdom is our duty and also our method of release from the thralldom of human experience. We must grasp this; we must realise that we shall find release only in the service of the kingdom. We have been held too long by the dogmas of the past, and there is today a natural revolt against the idea of individual salvation through the blood sacrifice of Christ. This latter is the outer and more obvious teaching—but it is the inner meaning which really concerns us, and this we can sense only when we ourselves come face to face with that which dwells within. As the outer forms lose their power it frequently happens that the true significance emerges. This we have each to prove for himself. Frequently fear prevents us from being truthful and from facing facts. It is essential that today we face the problem of the relation of Christ to the modern world, and dare to see the truth, without any theological bias. Our personal experience of Christ will not suffer in this process. No modern view and no theology can take Christ away from the soul which has once known Him. That is outside the range of possibility. But it is quite possible that we may find the ordinary orthodox theological interpretation at fault. It is quite possible that Christ is far more inclusive than we have been led to believe, and that the heart of God the Father is far kinder

[56] *St. Matt.*, V, 16.
[57] *Mirage and Truth*, by M. B. D'Arcy, S.J., p. 179.

than those who have sought to interpret it. We have preached a God of love and have spread a doctrine of hate. We have taught that Christ died to save the world and have endeavoured to show that only believers could be saved—though millions live and die without ever hearing of Christ. We live in a world of chaos, endeavouring to build a kingdom of God divorced from current daily life and the general economic situation, and at the same time postulate a distant heaven which we may some day attain. But Christ founded a kingdom on earth, wherein all God's children would have equal opportunity of expressing themselves as sons of the Father. This, many Christians find impossible to accept, and some of the best minds of the age have repudiated the idea.

Individual salvation is surely selfish in its interest and its origin. We must serve in order to be saved, and only can we serve intelligently if we believe in the divinity of all men and also in Christ's outstanding service to the race. The kingdom is a kingdom of servers, for every saved soul must without compromise join the ranks of those who ceaselessly serve their fellow men. Dr. Schweitzer, whose vision of the kingdom of God is so rare and real, points out this truth and its gradations of recognition in the following words:

"The descending stages of service correspond to the ascending stages of rule.

1. Whosoever would become great *among you,* shall be *your* servant. Mark X.43.

2. Whosoever of *you* would be first, shall be bondservant of *all* (others). Mark X.44.

3. Therefore the Son of Man expected the post of highest rule because he was not come to be served but to serve, in giving his life as ransom for many. Mark X.45.

"The climax is a double one. The service of the Disciples extended only to their circle: the service of Jesus to an unlimited number, namely, to all such as were to benefit by his suffering and death. In the case of the Disciples it was merely a question of unselfish *subjection*: in the case of Jesus it meant the bitter *suffer-ing of death*. Both count as serving, inasmuch as they establish a claim to a position of rule in the Kingdom."[58]

Love is the beginning, and love the end, and in love we serve and work. The long journey ends thus, in the glory of the renunciation of personal desire, and in the dedication to living service.

[58] *The Mystery of the Kingdom of God*, by Albert Schweitzer, p. 75.

CHAPTER SIX

The Fifth Initiation . . . The Resurrection and Ascension

KEY THOUGHT

"Apart from Christ we know neither what our life nor our death is; we do not know what God is nor what we ourselves are."

Pascal: Pensées

"There is a Soul above the soul of each,
  A mightier soul which yet to each belongs!
  There is a sound made of all human speech,
  And numerous as the concourse of all songs:
  And in that Soul lives each, in each that Soul,
  Tho' all the ages are its lifetime vast;
  Each soul that dies in its most sacred whole
  Receiveth life that shall for ever last."

Richard Watson Dixon

CHAPTER SIX

The Fifth Initiation . . . The Resurrection and Ascension

THIS initiation is divided into two halves, and of neither of them do we know very much. The detail of the Resurrection episode, or crisis, in Christ's life is left untold by the writers of the New Testament. It was not possible for them to know more. After the Crucifixion we are told little of Christ's own life, or what occupied Him between the time He rose again until He left the company of the Apostles, and "ascended into Heaven"—a symbolic phrase which can mean very little to any of us. The crucial initiation for humanity to understand at this time is the fourth. Only when we have mastered the significance of service and sacrifice can the fact of immortality and its true meaning be revealed to us. How Christ rose, what were the processes undergone, in exactly what body He appeared, we cannot tell. We are assured by the Apostles that it resembled the one He had previously employed, but whether it was the same body miraculously resurrected; whether it was His spiritual body, which appeared to be the same to the physical eyes of those who loved Him, or whether He had constructed an entirely new body on the same general lines as the previous one, it is not possible for us to say; neither is it possible for us to be confident that the vision of the disciples was not super-normal or that, through the intensification of His expressed divinity, Christ had so stimulated their inner vision that they saw clairvoyantly, or in another dimension. The important matter was that He did rise again, that He was seen of many, and that the fact of His resurrection was credited in the minds of His friends and for the two or three centuries after His departure.

The psychology of the disciples is the best proof we have of the reality of their conviction that death could not hold the Saviour, and that after death He was present and living among them. It is difficult for us to gain this high achievement in consciousness which they showed. Apparently their world had come to an end upon the Cross. Christ had apparently failed them, and instead of being the divine Son of God, and King of the Jews, He was nothing but an ordinary man, convicted of treason and punished as a common malefactor. What they must have endured during the three days of His absence it is not hard for us to imagine. Hopelessness, despair, the loss of confidence in themselves and of prestige among their friends; the cause for which they had been so ready to dedicate themselves, as they tramped with Christ from place to place in the Holy Land, had ended and collapsed. Their Leader was discredited. Then something happened to alter the whole trend of their thought. All that had been lost of confidence and hope and purpose was restored, and the first few centuries of the Christian history (before theology gave a turn to interpretation, and so altered the Gospel of love into a cult of separation) reveal to us

". . . a company of men and women full of confidence, enthusiasm and courage, ready to face persecution and death, eager missionaries. What has given them this new character? Not long before some of them had fled in dismay at the first threat of personal danger. When Jesus was crucified they had lost the last glimmer of hope that he might prove to be the Christ. When he was placed in the tomb, Christianity was dead and buried too. Now we meet these men and women a few weeks later and they are utterly changed. It is not that there is some faint return of hope among a few of them. All are completely certain that Jesus is indeed the Christ. What has happened to cause this transformation? Their answer is unanimous: on the third day he rose from the dead."[1]

[1] *The Valley and Beyond*, by Anthony C. Deane, p. 72.

"Christ is risen," is their cry, and because He has risen the kingdom of God can go forward upon earth, and His message of love can be widely distributed. They know now, past all controversy, that He has overcome death, and that in the years that lie ahead they will see death vanquished. That they expected an immediate kingdom and that they looked to see the fact of immortality universally recognised is evident from their writings and their enthusiasm. That they were mistaken, nearly two thousand years of Christianity has proved. We are not yet citizens of a divine kingdom definitely manifesting upon earth, the fear of death is as strong as ever, and the fact of immortality is still but a source of speculation to millions. But it was their sense of time that was at fault, and their failure to understand the slow processes of nature. Evolution moves slowly, and it is only today that we are truly on the verge of the demonstration of God's kingdom upon earth. Because this is the end of an age, we know that before long the hold death has on the human being, and the terror which the angel of death inspires, will disappear. They will vanish because we shall regard death as only another step on the way towards light and life, and shall realise that, as the Christ life expresses itself in and through human beings, they will demonstrate to themselves, and in the world, the reality of immortality.

The key to the overcoming of death and to the processes of realising the meaning and nature of eternity and the continuity of life can with safety be revealed only when love holds sway over the human consciousness, and where the good of the whole, and not the selfish good of the individual, comes to be the supreme regard. Only through love (and service as the expression of love) can the real message of Christ be understood and men pass on towards a joyful resurrection. Love makes us humbler, and at the same time wiser. It penetrates to the heart of reality and has a faculty of discovering the truth hidden by a form. The early Christians were simple in this way because they loved one another, because they loved Christ and the Christ within each other. Dr. Grensted points this out in the following words, giving us a fine summation of the attitude of the early Christians and of their approach, in those enthusiastic days, to Christ and to life in the world:

"They spoke in plain terms of God. They did not think of Jesus of Nazareth as a crucial experiment. They knew Him as Friend and Master, and they flung their whole being into the enthusiasm of His friendship and service. Their preaching was the good news about Jesus. They assumed that men already meant something when they spoke of God, and, without challenging the inheritance which they received from Judaism, they set side by side with it the Jesus whom they had known living, and dead, and alive again. They had been through much more than a time of inexplicable miracles, healings, and voices, and a strange mastery over Nature itself, and at the end a conquest of death. If they had told the world, and us, these things alone, they would have been believed. Such stories have always found a hearing. And men would still have known nothing more of the meaning of God. But their experience had been one of such a Friendship as man had never known, of disastrous failure and a forgiveness beyond all believing, and of a new, a free, a creative life. Nothing of all this was of their own achievement. They knew they were men remade, and they knew that the mode of their remaking was love. This was a providence, a deliverance, greater and more significant than anything that the Jew had ever claimed for the Creator-God. Yet they could not think of it as other than His work, since God, as all their national tradition taught, is One. It interpreted for them, as we might put it in our more cautious way, the creative reality to which they, with all men, had looked with uncertainty and even with fear. Henceforth the central hypothesis which men call God was known as love, and everywhere He was made manifest just in so far as love had passed out from Christ to the fellowship of the Christian community."[2]

Christ had risen, and by His Resurrection proved that humanity had in it the seed of life, and that there was no death for the man who could follow in the steps of the Master.

[2] *Psychology and God,* by L. W. Grensted, p. 237.

In the past, being wholly engrossed with consideration of the Crucifixion, we have been apt to forget the fact of the Resurrection. Yet on Easter Day, throughout the world, believers everywhere express their belief in the risen Christ and in the life beyond the grave. They have argued along many lines as to the possibility of His rising, and whether He rose as a human being or as the Son of God. They have been deeply concerned to prove that because He rose again, so shall we rise, provided we believe in Him. In order to meet the theological need of proving that God is love, we have invented a place of discipline, called by many names, such as purgatory, or the various stages of the different faiths on the road of departed spirits to heaven, because so many millions die, or have died, without ever having heard of Christ. Therefore belief in Him as an historical figure is not possible for them. We have evolved such doctrines as conditional immortality, and the atonement through the blood of Jesus, in an endeavour to glorify the personality of Jesus and safeguard Christian believers, and to reconcile human interpretations with the truth in the Gospels. We have taught the doctrine of hell-fire and eternal punishment, and then tried to fit it in to the general belief that God is love.

Yet the truth is that Christ died and rose again because He was divinity immanent in a human body. Through the processes of evolution and initiation He demonstrated to us the meaning and purpose of the divine life present in Him and in us all. Because Christ was human, He rose again. Because He was also divine, He rose again, and in the enacting of the drama of resurrection He revealed to us that great concept of the continuity of unfoldment which it has ever been the task of the Mysteries of all time to reveal.

Again and again we have found that the three episodes related in the Gospel story are not isolated happenings in the life of Jesus of Nazareth, but that they have been repeatedly undergone in the secret places of the Temples of the Mysteries, from the dawn of time. The Saviours of the past were all subjected to the processes of death in some form or other, but they all rose again or were translated to glory. In the initiation ceremonies this burial and resurrection at the end of three days was a familiar ceremonial. History tells us of many of these Sons of God who died and rose again, and finally ascended into Heaven. We find, for instance, that "the Obsequies of Adonis were celebrated in Alexandria (in Egypt) with the utmost display. His image was carried with great solemnity to a tomb, which served the purpose of rendering him the last honours. Before singing his return to life, there were mournful rites celebrated in honour of his suffering and his death. The large wound which he received was shown, just as the wound was shown which was made to Christ by the thrust of the spear. The feast of his resurrection was fixed at the 25th of March."[3] There is the same legend attached to the names of Tammuz, to Zoroaster, to Esculapius. To the latter, Ovid addressed the following words:

> "Hail, Great Physician of the world! All hail!
> Hail, mighty Infant who in years to come
> Shall heal the nations and defraud the tomb.
> Swift be Thy growth, Thy triumphs unconfined
> Make kingdoms thicken and increase mankind.
>
> Thy daring art shall animate the dead,
> And draw the thunder on Thy guilty head;
> Then shalt Thou die, but from the dark abode
> Shalt rise victorious and be twice a God."[4]

These words might have been appropriately addressed to Christ, and they serve to indicate the antiquity of the Mystery Teaching which, with unbroken continuity, has revealed the divinity in Man and shown him the Way of a Saviour. But in ancient times these mysteries were enacted in

[3] *Ovid's Metamorphoses*, as rendered by Addison, Quoted in Taylor's *Diegesis*, p. 148.
[4] *Origin of Religious Belief*, by Dupius, p. 161.

secret, and the rites of initiation were administered only to those who were fitted to pass through the five great experiences from the Birth to the Resurrection. The uniqueness of Christ's work lay in the fact that He was the first to enact the whole of the initiation ceremonial rites and ritual publicly, before the world at large, thus giving to humanity a demonstration of divinity centered in one person, so that all could see, could know, believe and follow in His steps.

The same stories are told of Hercules, of Baldur, of Mithra, of Bacchus, and of Osiris, to mention only a few of a large number. One of the early Church Fathers, Firmicus Maternus, tells us that the mysteries of Osiris bear a close resemblance to the Christian teaching, and that after the resurrection of Osiris his friends rejoice together, saying, "We have found him." Annie Besant points out in an illuminating passage that:

"In the Christian Mysteries—as in the ancient Egyptian, Chaldaean, and others—there was an outer symbolism which expressed the stages through which the man was passing. He was brought into the chamber of Initiation, and was stretched on the ground with his arms extended, sometimes on a cross of wood, sometimes merely on the stone floor, in the posture of a crucified man. He was then touched with the thyrsus on the heart—the 'spear' of the crucifixion—and, leaving the body, he passed into the worlds beyond, the body falling into a deep trance, the death of the crucified. The body was placed in a sarcophagus of stone, and there left, carefully guarded. Meanwhile the man himself was treading first the strange obscure regions called 'the heart of the earth,' and thereafter the heavenly mount, where he put on the perfected bliss body, now fully organised as a vehicle of consciousness. In that he returned to the body of flesh, to re-animate it. The cross bearing that body, or the entranced and rigid body, if no cross had been used, was lifted out of the sarcophagus and placed on a sloping surface, facing the east, ready for the rising of the sun on the third day. At the moment that the rays of the sun touched the face, the Christ, the perfected Initiate or Master, re-entered the body, glorifying it by the bliss body He was wearing, changing the body of flesh by contact with the body of bliss, giving it new properties, new powers, new capacities, transmuting it into His own likeness. That was the Resurrection of the Christ, and thereafter the body of flesh itself was changed, and took on a new nature."[5]

Thus we find that the resurrection story is of very ancient date, and that God has always held before humanity, through the Mysteries and through His illumined Sons, the fact of immortality, as before our Christian world, through the death and resurrection of His beloved Son, Jesus Christ.

This whole problem of death and immortality is engrossing a great deal of public attention at this time. The World War brought the fact of death before the public consciousness in a new and arresting manner. There was scarcely a family in over twenty nations which had not been bereft by death, in some form or other. The world has passed through a process of dying, and at the present time the mystery of the Resurrection is becoming a theme of major importance in men's minds. The thought of the Resurrection is coming closer, and its significance has been the central idea of the Masonic Fraternity down the ages, forming the focal point of the work of the sublime Third Degree. In close relation to this Masonic "raising" can be placed a little-known sermon of the Buddha, in which He teaches His disciples the significance of the "five points of Friendship," and thus links up these five points, the five crises in the life of Christ and the five points in the Masonic legend. All these references serve to show the continuity of revelation of which the Resurrection (with its subsequent Ascension) was the climaxing event for the Occident.

The outstanding need of Christianity today is to emphasise the living, risen Christ. We have argued too long over the death of Christ, seeking to impose a narrow sectarian Christ upon the world. We have fed the fires of separation by our Christian divisions, churches, sects and "isms." "Their name

[5] *Esoteric Christianity*, by Annie Besant, pp. 247, 248, 249.

is legion," and most of them are founded upon some sectarian presentation of the dead Christ, and of the earlier aspects of His story. Let us now unite on the basis of the risen Christ— Christ alive today, Christ the source of inspiration and the founder of the kingdom of God; Christ, the cosmic Christ, eternally on the Cross, yet eternally alive; Christ, the historical Saviour, the founder of Christianity, watching over His Church; Christ, the mystic, mythic Christ, portraying upon the canvas of the Gospels the episodes of unfoldment so that all who live may know and follow; and Christ, alive today in every human heart, the guarantee of, and the urge towards divinity, which humanity so constantly exhibits. Because of the presence of Christ in man, the conviction of divinity and of man's consequent immortality seem to be inherent in the human consciousness. It will inevitably occupy more and more of man's attention until it is demonstrated and proven; meanwhile that something apparently persists beyond physical death has been demonstrated. The fact of immortality has not been proven as yet, though it constitutes a basic belief in the minds of millions, and where such a belief is universally found, there must indubitably be a basis for it.

The entire question of immortality is closely linked with the problem of divinity and of the unseen, subjective world, which seems to underlie the tangible and visible, frequently making its presence felt. Working therefore on the premise of the unseen and invisible, it is probable that we shall eventually penetrate to it and discover that it has always been with us, but that we have been blinded and unable to recognise its presence. Always some have done so, and their note sounds forth, strengthening our belief, endorsing our hope, and guaranteeing to us the eventual experience.

How then shall we recognise truth or reality when we meet it? How shall we know that a doctrine is of God, or not? It is so easy to make mistakes, to believe what we want to believe, and to deceive ourselves in the desire to have our own ideas endorsed by other minds. The words of Dr.

Streeter have here a definite note of encouragement because they indicate requirements that are possible for us to follow:

"Even self-deception, the last stronghold of the enemy, will lose its power in proportion as the individual conforms to certain conditions which (in the view of the biblical writers) must be fulfilled to qualify him for the reception of an authentic message from the Divine—whether at the level of the epoch-creating prophet or of the simple person rightly guided on the path of everyday duty.

"These are mainly four:

"(1) 'I would fain be to the Eternal Goodness what his own right hand is to a man.' Absolute devotion or surrender of the self to the Divine. 'Here am I, send me,' says Isaiah; and when Christ addressed to his earliest followers the words 'Follow Me,' we are told they left all and followed Him.

"(2) Self-knowledge, and the consequent admission of failure. The promise 'I will guide thee with mine eye,' in the Psalm quoted above, is given to the man who has confessed his iniquity and thereby established a right relationship with God. The first response of Isaiah to the divine call was that flash of self-knowledge which brings home to a man a conviction of unworthiness and sin: 'I am a man of unclean lips.' . . .

"(3) 'Tarry ye . . . until ye be clothed with power from on high' (St. Luke XXIV.49). But this life of power, a power instinct with love and joy and peace, can only with difficulty be lived continuously except in a fellowship, within which mutual challenge, mutual encouragement and mutual confession of failure are easy. . . .

"(4) Entrance into such a life and such a fellowship involves some measure of suffering, sacrifice, or humiliation. 'Whosoever doth not bear his *own* cross, and come after me, cannot be my disciple' (Luke XIV.27). It is perhaps not an accident that already in the Old Testament the promise 'Thine eyes shall hear a word behind thee, saying This is the way, walk ye in it,' is preceded by the words 'and though the Lord give you the bread of adversity and the water of affliction.' "[6]

It takes courage to face the fact of death, and to formulate with definiteness one's beliefs upon the subject. It is a statistical fact that about fifty million people die every year.

[6] *The God Who Speaks,* by B. H. Streeter, pp. 175, 176.

Fifty million people are more than the entire population of Great Britain, and constitute a large group of human beings who make the great adventure. If this is so, the establishing of the verity of Christ's Resurrection and the truth of immortality are of far greater importance than the individual may deem. We are too apt to study these problems either from the scientific angle or from a purely selfish individual one. Death is the only event which we can predict with absolute certainty, and yet it is the event about which the majority of human beings refuse to think at all until faced with the imminent and personal issue. People face death in many different ways; some bring to the adventure a feeling of self-pity, and are so occupied with what they have to leave behind, what is about to end for them, and the relinquishing of all they have gathered in life, that the true significance of the inevitable future fails to arrest their attention. Others face it with courage, making the best of what may not be evaded, and look up into the face of death with a gallant gesture because there is nothing else they can do. Their pride helps them to encounter the event. Still others refuse altogether to consider the possibility; they hypnotise themselves into a condition wherein the thought of death is refused all lodgement in their consciousness, and they will not consider its possibility, so that when it comes, it catches them unawares; they are left helpless and unable to do more than simply die. The Christian attitude, as a rule, is more definitely an acceptance of the will of God, with the resolution to regard the happening as therefore the best of happenings, even if it does not seem so from the angle of environment and circumstance. A steadfast belief in God and His predestined purpose for the individual carries them triumphantly through the gate of death, but if one told them that this was simply another form of the fatalism of the Eastern thinker, and a fixed belief in an unalterable destiny, they would regard it as untrue. They hide behind the name of God.

Death can, however, be more than these things, and can be met in a different way. It can be made to hold a definite place in life and thought, and we can prepare for it as something which cannot be evaded, but which is simply the Bringer of Changes. Thus we make the process of death a planned part of our entire life purpose. We can *live* with the consciousness of immortality, and it will give an added colouring and beauty to life; we can foster the awareness of our future transition, and live with the expectation of its wonder. Death thus faced, and regarded as a prelude to further living experience, takes on a different meaning. It becomes a mystical experience, a form of initiation, finding its culminating point in the Crucifixion. All previous lesser renunciations prepare us for the great renunciation; all earlier deaths are but the prelude for the stupendous episode of dying. Death brings us release—temporary perhaps, though eventually permanent—from the body nature, from existence on the physical plane and its visible experience. It is a setting free from limitation; and whether one believes (as many millions do) that death is only an interlude in a life of steadily accumulating experience, or the end of all such experience (as many other millions hold), there is no denying the fact that it marks a definite transition from one state *of consciousness into another*. If one believes in immortality and the soul, this transition may make for an intensification of consciousness; while if the materialistic point of view dominates, it may indicate the end of conscious existence. The crucial question is, therefore: Is that which we call the soul immortal? What is the meaning of immortality?

It is urgent today that we recover some form of faith in the inner subjective world, and in our relation to it. Upon this, the success of the work and message of Christ must rise or fall. These are days wherein everything is being questioned —and the fact of the soul and its immortality perhaps most of all. This is a necessary and valuable stage, provided we go on seeking answers to these questions.

Many may regard these "moral disturbances" as hopeful indications of an emergence from the static condition in all realms of human thought which marked the early part of the last century, and that we are today on the verge of a new era of truer spiritual values. But the newer structures of faith and conduct must have their foundations deep in the best that the past has to give. The ideals which Christ enunciated still remain the highest yet given in the continuity of revelation, and He Himself prepared us for the emergence of those truths which will mark the time of the end and the overcoming of the last enemy, whose name is Death.

This questioning of belief, and this wrestling with an inherent hope must go on until assurance has been gained, belief has become knowledge, and faith, certainty. Man knows incontrovertibly that there is a goal greater than his petty aims, and that a life exists which will embrace his widest reach, enabling him eventually to attain his highest, though dimly sensed, ideal. A consideration of the Resurrection may provide a greater surety, provided we keep in mind the long continuity of revelation given out by God, and realise that we can know little as yet beyond the fact that Sons of God have died and risen again, and that behind that fact lies a cause which is basic.

The Tibetans speak of the process of death as that of "entering into the clear cold light."[7] It is possible that death can be best regarded as the experience which frees us from the illusion of form; and this brings clearly to our minds the realisation that when we speak of death we are referring to a process which concerns the material nature, the body, with its psychical faculties and its mental processes. This therefore can be narrowed down to a query as to whether we are the body and nothing but the body, or whether the ancient scripture of India was right when it pointed out that:

"Certain is the death of what is born, and certain is the birth of what dies; therefore, deign not to grieve in a matter that is inevitable. . . . This lord of the body dwells ever immortal in the body of each."[8]

[7] *The Tibetan Book of the Dead*, by W. Y. Evans-Wentz, p. 29.
[8] *The Bhagavad Gita*, II, 26, 29.

A modern Christian poet has expressed the same idea in the following beautiful words:

> "Death is to life as marble to the sculptor,
> Waits for the touch that lets the soul go free;
> Death is that moment when the swimmer feels
> The swift pain of the plunge into the pool,
> Followed by laughter where the bubbles flow
> From the divided water and the sun
> Turns them to crystal: life and light are one."[9]

It might here be pertinent to enquire what it is that we seek to see endure. An analysis of one's attitude to the whole question of death and immortality can frequently serve to clear one's mind of indefiniteness and vagueness, with their base in fear, in mental inertia, and in confused thinking. The following questions therefore come to one's mind, and warrant consideration.

How do we know that the process of death brings about such definite changes in our consciousness that it proves fatal to us, as sentient beings, and renders futile all previous effort of thought, development and understanding? The wonder of Christ's Resurrection, as far as His Personality was concerned, consisted in the fact that, after having passed through death and risen again, He was essentially the same Person, only with added powers. May it not be the same with ourselves? May not death simply remove limitation in the physical sense, leaving us with enhanced sensibilities and a clearer sense of values? This life has moulded us and wrought us into certain definite expressions in form and quality, and these, rightly or wrongly, constitute that which is the Self, that which is the real man, from the angle of human life. There is something in us that refuses final identification with the physical form, in spite of what science and the inexperienced may tell us. An intuitive, *substantial* inner Self steadily and universally repudiates annihilation, and holds firmly to the belief that the search and the goal, the values

[9] *The Modernists*, by Robert Norwood, p. 57, *Socrates*.

perceived and for which we struggle, must somewhere, some time, in some manner, prove themselves worth while. Any other point of view argues for the utter lack of an intelligent plan in existence, and leads to the despair which St. Paul expressed in the words: "If in this life only we have hope in Christ, we are of all men most miserable."[10] We are surely on our way towards something of value and dynamic worth; otherwise life is a futile process of aimless wanderings; of caring for a body and educating a mind which have no worth of any kind, and are of no value to God or men. This, we know, cannot be the case.

It is the prolongation of value, of that which is worth while, and the continuation of the persistent, inner, divine incentive to progress, to create and to benefit others, that seem, to those who have reached the point where thought is consecutively possible, to hold the clue to the problem of immortality. The entire story of Christ goes to prove this. He had, throughout His life of consecrated service and devotion to His fellow men, proved that He had reached the point in His evolution wherein He had somewhat to contribute to the good of the whole; He had attained altitude on the evolutionary ladder, and His humanity was lost to sight in the divinity which He expressed. He had that which was of worth to offer to God and man, and He offered it upon the Cross. It cost Him His life to make His contribution to the source of the whole body corporate, but He made it. Because of the worth of what He had achieved, and the value of the *livingness* of His contribution, He could demonstrate immortality. It is the immortal value which survives, and where that value exists the soul needs no more the school of human experience.

This thought gives rise to the question: What is it, therefore, that we seek to see survive? What part of ourselves do we regard as desirably immortal? What in each of us *warrants persistence?* Surely none of us seek to see the physical body resurrected, nor are we anxious again to be trammeled

[10] *I Cor.*, XV, 19.

and confined by the present limiting vehicle in which most of us find ourselves. Its value seems inadequate for the experience of resurrection and for the gift of immortality. Nor are we desirous, surely, of seeing the same psychic nature, with its aggregate of moods and feelings and sentient reactions to environing condition, hold sway over us again. Equally surely, none of us are pleased to contemplate the old idea of a sugary heaven wherein we pass our time clothed in white robes, singing and talking upon religious matters. We have outgrown these ideas, and to them Christ Himself is a direct refutation. He rose from the dead and entered upon a life of increased active service. The "other sheep" which He had to gather must be sought and shepherded;[11] His disciples must be trained and taught; His followers must be guided and helped; the kingdom of God must be organised on earth. And still the risen Christ moves among us, often unrecognised, but busy with the task of world salvage and service. There is no heaven of peace and rest and inactivity for Christ whilst we remain unsaved; there is surely none for us who seek to follow in His footsteps.

When a man's life has gained significance, then he is ready to tread the path of purification and probation in preparation for the mysteries; as his significance and influence increase he can pass, stage by stage, through the processes of initiation, and tread the path of holiness. He can be "born in Bethlehem," because the germ of that which is dynamic and living is awakened and is gaining potency and significance, and must therefore make its appearance; he can pass through the waters of purification, and attain the mountain-top of transfiguration where that which is of worth shines forth in all its glory. Having achieved that moment of heightened experience, and that which he has of value being recognised by God as worth while, he is then, and then only, ready to offer his life upon the altar of sacrifice and of service, and can set his face to go up to Jerusalem, there to be crucified. It is the inevitable end to that which is of worth. It is the underlying

[11] *St. John*, X, 16.

purpose of the whole process of perfecting, as there is now something worthy to be offered. But though this may be the end of the physical expression of worth, it is essentially the moment of the triumph of value, and the demonstration of its *immortality*. For that which is of value, the divine and hidden beauty which life-experience and initiation have served to reveal, cannot die. It is essentially immortal, and must live. This is the true resurrection of the body. When the consciousness of value and of worth, and the *recognition* of man's reach, as well as his grasp, are considered, the life of service (leading to death) and of resurrection (leading to full citizenship in the kingdom of God) begin to gain in meaning. The body which we now have is relatively worthless; the sum total of moods and mental reactions to which we now submit is of no value to anyone but ourselves; the environment in which we live and move has in it surely nothing to warrant its endless perpetuation. In short, a continuance of the personal self in some heaven which is the extension of our own individual consciousness, and the concept of an endless eternity lived with oneself, have for most of us no allurement whatsoever. Yet an aspect of oneself longs for immortality and the sense of infinity. The "endless prolongation in time of a self's career" has led to much confusion of thought. Few of us, if asked seriously to consider the problem and seriously to give an answer, would feel that as individuals we warrant arrangements being made for our endless persistence. A sense of truth and justice might lead us honestly to the conclusion that our value to the universe is practically *nil*. And yet we know that there is a value and a reason behind all our life experience, and that the phenomenal world, of which we are indubitably a part, veils or hides something of infinite value, of which we are also a part.

We seek assurance that those whom we love and value are not lost to us. We seek to share with them some state of happiness which will have in it truer values than any we have known on earth; we long to prolong, in time and space, the familiar state which we love and cherish. We desire compensation for what we have endured, and the realisation that everything has had a purpose and has been worth while. It is this longing, this belief, this determination to persist, which lies behind all achievement and which is the incentive and impulse upon which we base all effort. Socrates pointed out this basic argument for immortality when he said that "no-one knows what death is, and whether it is not the greatest of all good things. Nevertheless, it is feared as if it were the supreme evil. . . . When death comes near to man that which is mortal in him is scattered; that which is immortal and incorruptible withdraws intact."

Three thoughts are of importance in considering this problem of value, which is so amazingly evidenced by Christ, and which was the true reason why He rose again. His immortality was based upon His divinity. His divinity expressed itself through human form, and in that form evidenced value, destiny, service and purpose. All of these He demonstrated perfectly, and therefore death could not hold Him, nor could the chains of the grave prevent His liberation.

The first thought is that immortality is the safeguarding of what we really care about. The factor on which we place the emphasis in our daily lives survives and functions on some level of consciousness. We must, and do, eventually attain what we demand. When we care for that which is eternal in value, then eternal life, free from the limitations of the flesh, is ours. Dean Inge tells us that "in so far as we can identify ourselves with the absolute values, we are sure of immortality." What we really care about, then, in our highest moments, when free from the illusions of the emotional nature, determines our immortal life.

The question then arises as to what occurs when the sense of values is distorted or temporarily nonexistent. In an attempt to meet this question millions of people have accepted the Oriental doctrine of rebirth, which states the world to be the "vale of soul-making," as Keats calls it, and which teaches that we return again and again to physical life, until the time comes when our values are properly adjusted, and we can pass through the five initiations into liberation. Much of the teaching given in the occult and esoteric books is distorted and fanciful, but that there is much to be said for the doctrine of rebirth is evident to the unprejudiced student. In the last analysis, if perfection is to be ultimately achieved, the question is merely one of time and location. The Christian may believe in a sudden perfecting through the process of death itself, or in a mental acceptance of the death of Jesus, which he calls "conversion"; he may regard death as the door into a place of discipline and development which he calls "purgatory," where a purificatory process goes on; or he may believe that in heaven itself adjustments are made and expansions of consciousness are undergone which render him a different man from what he was before. The Oriental may believe that the earth provides adequate facilities for the training and developing processes, and that again and again we return, until we have reached perfection. The goal remains one. The objective is identical. The school is in a different place, and the consciousness is unfolded in varying localities. But that is all. Plato held that:

"Confined in the body as in a prison . . . the soul seeks its pristine sphere of pure rationality by pursuing the philosophic life, by thinking the universal, by loving and living according to reason. The bodily life is but an episode in the eternal career of the soul, which precedes birth and proceeds after death. Life in the flesh is a trial and a probation; death, the release and the return to the soul's destiny; to another term of probation, or to the realm of pure reason."

In some place, consciously and willingly, we must learn to enter and work in the world of values, and so fit ourselves for citizenship in the kingdom of God. It was the demonstration of this that Christ gave.

The second thought which should be considered is that man's effort, his struggle to achieve, his sense of God, innate and true, his constant effort to better conditions and to master himself as well as the natural world, must have an objective; else all that we see going on around is void, futile and senseless. It was this command of Himself and of the elements of nature, and the undeviating direction of His purpose, that led Christ from point to point and enabled Him to open the door into the kingdom and to rise from the dead, the "first fruits of them that slept."[12]

Purpose must underlie pain. An objective must be sensed under all human activity. The idealism of the leaders of the race cannot all be hallucination. The realisation of God must have some basis in fact. Human beings are convinced that the apparent injustice of the world provides legitimate assurance of a hereafter wherein the integrity of the divine purpose will be vindicated. There is a basic belief that good and evil are in combat in man's nature, and that good must inevitably triumph. Down the ages, man has asserted this. Humanity has evolved many theories to account for man and his future, for his preparation for the after-life, and for his reason here on earth. With the detail of these theories there is no need, or time, to deal. They are in themselves proof of the fact of immortality and of man's divinity. He has intuited the ultimate possibility, and will not rest until he has achieved it. Whether it is plurality of lives upon our planet, leading to an ultimate perfection, or the Buddhistic theory leading to *Nirvana,* the goal is one. This latter theory is beautifully summarised in a book dealing with the secret doctrines of the Tibetan philosophy:

". . . when the Lords of Compassion shall have spiritually civilised the Earth and made of it a Heaven, there will be revealed to the Pilgrims the Endless Path, which reaches to the Heart of the Universe. Man, then no longer man, will transcend Nature, and impersonally, yet consciously, in at-one-ment with all the Enlight-

[12] *I Cor.,* XV, 20.

ened Ones, help to fulfil the Law of the Higher Evolution, of which *Nirvana* is but the beginning."[13]

Here we have the idea of the kingdom of God appearing on earth because humanity is spiritually civilised, and the attainment of the perfection which Christ inculcated.

There is also the doctrine of eternal recurrence, in which both Nietzsche and Heine believed, with its emphasis upon a ceaseless, recurrent, earthly existence by each unit of force, until a soul has been evolved. The dreary doctrine of our survival as influences perpetuated in the race to which we belong has also been developed, emphasising a selflessness which is admirable, but is also the negation of the individual. The orthodox Christian doctrines are three in number, and consist of the doctrine of eternal retribution, of universal restoration, and of conditional immortality. To these we must add the speculations of the Spiritualists, with their various spheres, corresponding somewhat to the subtle worlds, seven in number, of the Theosophists and the Rosicrucians; and also the extreme theory of annihilation, which does not find much response from the healthy-minded. The value of all these doctrines consists in attracting attention to the eternal interest of man in the hereafter, and his many speculations as to his future and his immortality.

Christ died and rose again. He lives. And some people in the world today do not need to have this fact proven to them. They know He is alive, and that because He lives we shall live also. In us is the same germ of essential life which flowered forth to perfection in Him, overcoming the tendency to death inherent in the natural man. Surely, then, we can say that immortality consists for us in three stages:

First, as that livingness which we call the urge to evolution, the impulse to progress, to push forward, to live, and to know that one lives. This is the incentive behind man's determina-

[13] *Tibetan Yoga and Secret Doctrines,* edited by W. Y. Evans-Wentz, p. 12.

tion to know himself an individual, with his own life cycle, his own innate purpose and his eternal future.

Secondly, as that dynamic spiritual awareness which manifests in the re-orientation to eternity and the eternal values, which is the distinguishing feature of the man who is ready to take the necessary steps to demonstrate his spiritual life and to function as an immortal. Then the resurrection which lies ahead of him, and which Christ expressed, is seen to be something different from what had earlier been supposed. The following definition of the true resurrection, as it begins to dawn on the eyes of the man who is awakening to the glory of the Lord within his own heart and immanent in every form, finds place:

"The resurrection is not the rise of the dead from their tombs but the passage from the death of self-absorption to the life of unselfish love, the transition from the darkness of selfish individualism to the light of universal spirit, from falsehood to truth, from the slavery of the world to the liberty of the eternal. Creation 'groaneth and travaileth in pain' 'to be delivered from the bondage of corruption into the liberty of the glory of the children of God.' "[14]

The third and final thought which must be emphasised is that we are resurrected to life eternal and become of the company of the immortals when we have fitted ourselves to be co-workers with Christ in the kingdom. It is when we lose the consciousness of the separative individual and become divinely aware of the whole of which we are a part that we have learnt life's final lesson and need "no more return." It is the death of the individual which we fear and dread, and the loss of personal consciousness. We do not realise that when the vision of the kingdom is ours, when the whole of creation shines forth before our eyes, it is that Whole which matters to us, and we lose sight of our personal selves.

The resurrection therefore might be defined as the per-

[14] *The Supreme Spiritual Ideal*, by S. Radhakrishnan, Hibbert Journal, October, 1936.

sistence on into the future of that which is the divine aspect, and which is integrated with the life and consciousness of that sum total which we call God. That life and that consciousness flow through all parts of God's manifestation, the natural world. The kingdoms of nature have one by one evolved, and in so doing have expressed some aspect of His life as it informs and animates His creation. One by one, they have steadily progressed from the inert consciousness and slow, heavy rhythm of the mineral kingdom, and have revealed sequentially more and more of the hidden divine nature, until we come to man whose consciousness is of a much higher order and whose divine expression is that of the self-conscious, self-determined Deity. From automatic forms of consciousness, the life of God has carried the forms of life through sentient consciousness to the instinctive consciousness of the animal; then it has progressed on into the human kingdom, wherein self-consciousness holds sway, until the higher members of that kingdom begin to show a disposition towards divinity. The faint, dim signs of a still higher kingdom can now be seen, in which self-consciousness will give place to group-consciousness, and man will know himself to be identified with the Whole, and not to be simply a self-sufficient individual. Then the life of the whole body of God can flow consciously into and through him, and the life of God becomes his life and he is resurrected into life eternal.

Therefore the trend in human affairs at this time towards synthesis, cooperation, fusion and amalgamation is a sign of the advanced stage humanity has reached. It is a portent of promise, and indicates that the resurrection to life, to which all the Sons of God, down the ages, have testified, is now a general possibility. Humanity today, as a whole, faces towards life because its values are real, its integrity is being steadily assured, and the world indications (as manifested through the nations and groups) are oriented towards synthesis and cooperation. The present world turmoil is simply the result of this process of re-orientation, and has its parallel in the process of Christian "conversion" and the adjustments incident to that happening, which usually alter and re-arrange a man's entire life programme. The world pro-gramme is thus being re-adjusted, and the immediate result is chaos. But the new direction is assured, and nothing can arrest the progress of humanity's entrance into life. Hence the world crisis—the readjustments, the tendency to fusion and synthesis. The new race, which is immortal, is coming into being, and yet it is the same race at a new and high point of achievement. The Great Expectation then is that Birth into the Deathless Race may be realised here and now, as it has been realised already by those of humanity who have been made Divine.

The kingdom of God moves on to fulfilment. The pur-pose of Christ's life, death and resurrection is on the verge of achieving consummation. A new kingdom is coming into being; a fifth kingdom in nature is materialising, and already has a nucleus functioning on earth in physical bodies. There-fore let us welcome the striving and struggling of the present time, for it is a sign of resurrection. Let us understand the upheaval and the chaos, as humanity breaks out of the tomb of selfishness and individualism and comes to the place of living light and unity, for it is the resurrection. Let us pene-trate into the darkness with what light we have, and see humanity stirring, the dead bones coming to life, and the wrappings and bands being discarded, as spiritual strength and life pour into the race of men, for this is the resurrection.

We are privileged to be present at a moment of great crisis for the race. We are seeing the birth of a new and deathless race—a race in which the germ of immortality will flower, and in which divinity can express itself through the trans-figuration of mankind. That which is of value is coming to the fore. It has always been there, but today it can be seen, ushering in the consummation of Christ's work, and bringing to realisation His vision.

CHAPTER SEVEN

Our Immediate Goal . . . The Founding of the Kingdom

KEY THOUGHT

"Any given moment of life must choose between two gods, psychologically incompatible. On the one hand, the peace of the hermit, the silence of the forest, the exaltation of sacrifice, the mightiness of simplification and unity, the joy of self-abandonment, the calm of absolute contemplation, the vision of God. On the other hand, the variety and stress of life, the zest of common ends, the mastery of means, the glory of infinite enterprise, the pride of creativity and self-possession. The modern world as a whole has made its choice. But there is a better choice; namely, the choice of both. For the life of each is that it may lose itself, from time to time, in the life of the other. And this, which is obvious in things partial, is true—and even chiefly true—in things total."

The Meaning of God in Human Experience, by W. E. Hocking, p. 427.

Our Immediate Goal . . . The Founding of the Kingdom

1

WE have followed Christ from Bethlehem to Calvary, and through the Resurrection to the episode wherein He disappeared from tangible worldly view and entered the world of subjective values, therein to function as the "Master of all the Masters and the Teacher alike of angels and of men." We approached the subject of the five crises in His life from the angle of their world importance far more than from that of their significance to us as individuals. We have seen that there has been a revolt (and rightly so) from the emphasis laid by past theologians upon the blood sacrifice of Christ; and have arrived at the conclusion that the need of the world today is for the recognition of a risen Saviour. We have noted the fact that the uniqueness of His mission consisted in the fact that in "the fulness of time" He came to found the kingdom of God, to bring into being upon earth another kingdom of nature, and so set up the boundary line between that which is objective and illusory and that which is subjective and real. His coming marked the line of demarcation between the world of forms or symbols and that of values or of meaning. Into the latter world we are entering with great rapidity. Science, religion and philosophy are today occupied with *significance,* and their investigations are carrying them out of the world of appearances; governments and the allied sciences—politics and economics and sociology —are, in their turn, dealing with ideas and ideals. Even in the realm of social disorders and wars—general, sporadic or civil—we see the conflict of differing ideals, and no longer wars of aggression or for the defense of property. These distinctions between the objective and the subjective, between the tangible and the intangible, the visible and the invisible, Christianity has fostered, because it was these differences which the kingdom of God and the kingdom of man presented. Christ came to give to life a meaning and a value, just as the Buddha came to make clear to us the false values upon which our modern world is based.

A study of the teachings earlier given will show that every teaching, and every suffering Son of God who antedated Christ, did two things:

First of all, He prepared the way for Christ, giving out the teaching that His particular age, period and civilisation required; and secondly, He enacted in His life the teaching of the Mysteries, which however, before Christ's time, was confined to the very few who were being prepared for initiation, or who could penetrate by right of initiation into the temples of those Mysteries.

Then the Buddha came and spoke to the multitude, telling them what was the source of their misery and discontent, and giving them, in the Four Noble Truths, a concise statement of the human situation. He outlined to them the Noble Eightfold Path governing right conduct, and gave in reality the rules which should control one upon the Path of Discipleship. Then, having Himself achieved Illumination, He entered into the "Secret Place of the Most High," to come forth once a year, so legend tells us, in order to bless the world. That day of blessing (the day of the full moon of May) is preserved in the East as a general holiday, and in the West many hundreds also keep it as a day of spiritual remembrance.

Then Christ came, and presented to the world, and made public in His life and through its critical points, the great processes of initiation (five in number) which lie ahead of all who keep the rules which His great Brother laid down. He carried the teaching forward the next step, and made it available to the masses. Thus the continuity of revelation was perpetuated. The Buddha taught us the rules for disciples in preparation for the Mysteries of initiation, whilst Christ gave us the next stage, and showed us the process of initiation from the moment of the new birth into the kingdom to that of the final resurrection into life. His work was unique in its time and place, for it marked a consummation of the past, and an entrance into something utterly new, as far as humanity as a whole was concerned.

Humanity had also reached a unique stage in its development. The race had become intelligent, and the personality of man—physical, emotional and mental—had been carried forward to a definite point of integration and coordination. This, on a scale so immense, was unique. There had been isolated personalities. Now, in the Christian era, we live in an age of personalities. So high is the general level of integrated personality life that we are apt to feel we have reached an era where there are no outstanding figures. This is probably due to the fact that the general average of human development is so high that the power to stand out dominantly is much more limited. Because of this development, humanity (regarding it as a kingdom in nature) has reached a point where something new can emerge, as has always happened in analogous circumstances in other kingdoms. We can produce, and as a race give birth to, the next kingdom in nature, which Christ called the kingdom of God; this is the kingdom of souls, the kingdom of spiritual lives, and herein, uniquely, Christ emerges. He is the founder of that kingdom. He proclaimed its existence and He indicated its nature. In Himself He gave us an expression of its qualifications, and showed us the characteristics of the citizen of that kingdom.

Through the example of its Founder, Christianity has also had a unique mission in inaugurating the era of service. World service, world welfare, world interest, world intercommunication and the importance of the general good are all products of the emphasis Christ laid upon human divinity and on the brotherhood of man, based upon the Fatherhood of God. No other religion or era has thus emphasised these points. They still remain in many ways ideals, but are slowly in process of becoming facts.

Christ therefore achieved through His work the following things:

1. He externalised the Mysteries so that they have become known to humanity as a whole, and are not only the secret possession of the Initiates.

2. He enacted the drama of initiation before the world, so that its symbolism could penetrate into the human consciousness.

3. He gave us a demonstration of perfection so that we can no longer question the nature of God, yet at the same time He gave us the guarantee that we too are the children of God, and can likewise achieve divinity if we follow in His steps.

4. He revealed to us the world of meaning, and, in the Person of the historical Christ, showed us the significance of the cosmic Christ, the mythic Christ, and the mystical Christ in the heart of every man. He revealed the nature of God transcendent and of God immanent.

5. The past of humanity culminated in Him; the present finds in Him its solution, and the future is symbolised in His life and death. Therefore all three lines of past, present and future meet in Him, and give Him His unique significance.

6. He founded the kingdom of God in due time when the human kingdom was reaching maturity. He demonstrated the values of that kingdom in His Own life, portraying for us the character of its citizenship, and He opened the door wide for all who could fit themselves (through service and discipline) to pass out of the human kingdom into the spiritual kingdom.

7. He reared His Cross as a boundary, a symbol, and an example of method, between the world of tangible values and the world of spiritual values, and called us to the death of the lower nature in order that the Spirit of God may have full sway.

8. He taught us that death must end, and that the destiny of humanity is the resurrection from among the dead. Immortality must take the place of mortality. For our sakes, therefore, He rose from the dead and proved that the bonds of death cannot hold any human being who can function as a Son of God.

Many sons of God had passed through the Temples of the Mysteries; many had learnt to function divinely and had, in the process of expressing divinity, lived and served and died. But none of them came at the particular period of unfoldment which made possible the universal recognition which Christ has evoked, nor was the intellect of the masses sufficiently developed to profit by their teaching on a large scale until that time. In these respects Christ and His mission were uniquely important. He taught us to work towards unity and to bring to an end isolation and hatred and separation, telling us to love our neighbour as ourselves. He gave a message which was universal in its implications, for the kingdom of God stands wide open to all who love and serve and who purify the lower nature, irrespective of creed and dogma. He taught the unity of the faith, the Fatherhood of God, and the necessity not only to walk with God, but to walk with each other in love and understanding. He emphasised the necessity for cooperation, indicating that if we truly follow the Way, we shall put an end to competition, and substitute for it cooperation. He urged us to live by principles, divine, basic and fundamental, and to lay no emphasis upon personalities.

Love, brotherhood, cooperation, service, self-sacrifice, inclusiveness, freedom from doctrine, recognition of divinity —these are the characteristics of the citizen of the kingdom, and these still remain our ideals. Therefore the question of importance facing humanity today is, just what must be done in order to bring about the attainment of the three major objectives which Christ held before us. They remain objectives for all mankind, and are generally so recognised, even when their Christian interpretation is ignored, or when Christ remains unrecognised. How shall we perfect the human being, so that his handling of life, and his attitude to people and his environment, are correct and constructive? How shall we materialise on earth that state of consciousness, accompanied by that condition of living, the result of which would deserve to be recognised as the kingdom of God? How shall we arrive at an understanding of the problem of death, with the surmounting of the process of dying, and the achieving of resurrection? Christ has provided a definite answer and programme for the solution of the problem of human perfection, the problem of a new world, and the problem of immortality.

That humanity is on its way to great and vital events is generally recognised. We have in the past progressed through varying civilisations to the important present, and we are on our way to still greater achievements. The question, however, arises whether we may hasten the process; whether, by a right understanding of Christ and His teaching, we could so expedite matters that the kingdom and its laws may hold sway earlier than would otherwise be the case. No sacrifice on our part would be too great, if Christ was right in the position He took and in the teaching He gave as to the nature of man. The decision rests with us. The choice is ours. Therefore in the last analysis what is the decision we have to make? What is the question that we have to answer? Christ has said that man is divine. Was He right? If man is divine and a son of the Father, then let us proceed to express that divinity and claim our birthright. We have been occupied with much thought and discussion about God in the past. God transcendent has been both recognised and denied. God immanent is on the verge of recognition, and in that recognition may surely lie the way out for man. Are we divine? That is the all-important question.

If man is divine, if the testimony of the ages is true, and if Christ came to show us divinity in expression and to found the new kingdom, then the breaking down today of the old forms, and the wide-spread destruction of the familiar structures of society and religion, may simply be part of the process of instituting the new processes of life and the planned work of a vital evolving spirit. A reaction to the appearance of the kingdom may account for the unrest of the masses, and the general sensitive response to the new ideals may be due to the impact of the force of the kingdom upon the minds of the more advanced people of the world. The mystic and the Christian may talk in terms of the kingdom of God; philanthropists and philosophers may talk in terms of the world community, of the new civilisation, of the world federation of nations, of humanity as a body corporate, of community living and of internationalism and economic interdependence and world unity; but these are mere words and names which differing types of mind apply to the one great emerging fact of a new kingdom in nature arising out of the human kingdom, with its own principles of living, its laws of group welfare, and its brotherhood of man.

In the unfoldment of the human consciousness we are passing out of the necessary stage of individualism; we have temporarily lost sight of the deeper truths, the mystical values, and the one Life behind all forms. We have been too much occupied with material and selfish interests. But this has been a needed stage, even though it may well be that it has persisted too long. It is time for us to end the period of selfish individualism, permitting it no longer to be a controlling factor in our lives, time for us to begin to blend and unify the deeper elements of the world of reality with the outer life. The best minds of the age are now appreciating this, and on every hand the call is going out for a deepening of life, a recognition of the nature of and the need for a coherent understanding of the world processes, and their conscious intelligent integration into a recognisable world order. The disintegration in the world at this time is right and good, provided we understand why it is taking place and by what it should be succeeded. Destruction which is carried on with a view to eventual construction is right and proper, but the plans for the coming building must be somewhere understood, and some idea must exist as to subsequent reconstruction.

Our need today is to see the hidden thread of purpose which will lead us out of the apparent impasse; to isolate, out of the many theories, that basic theory which not only has its roots in the past, but is capable of application in a new way, in new terms, by those who are permeated with the new vision. We need what Dr. Schweitzer calls ". . . the recognition that civilization is founded on some sort of theory of the universe, and can be restored only through a spiritual awakening and a will for ethical good in the mass of mankind."[1] This awakening is already here, and the will to good is present. The teaching of Christ is not obsolete and out of date. It needs only to be rescued from the interpretations of the theologies of the past, and taken at its simple face value, which is an expression of the divinity of man, of his participation in the kingdom which is in process of being brought into recognition, and of his immortality as a citizen of that kingdom. What we are in reality passing through is "a religious initiation into the mysteries of Being,"[2] and from that we shall emerge with a deepened sense of God immanent in ourselves and in all humanity. The need for this revaluation is being impressed upon us constantly. It might be of value to us, therefore, to admit this possibility and consider practically our individual relation to the work which Christ expressed and inaugurated, and to deal with the problem of our individual perfecting, in order that we may help to found

[1] *The Decay and Restoration of Civilization,* by Albert Schweitzer, p. 78-79.

[2] *The End of Our Time,* by Nicholas Berdyaev, p. 105.

the kingdom and to develop those values which will warrant immortality.

Someone has remarked that our troubles at this time are due largely to the lack of intuitive perception on the part of those who can impress the masses and lead people forward. They seek to guide by mental processes and enforcements, and not by that intuitive presentation of reality which the child and the wise man can simultaneously recognise. It is vision that is needed, for "where there is no vision the people perish."[3] We have not lacked idealism, nor have we been too greatly unintelligent. Most people, faced with issues and problems, act with sincerity, even if their line of action may seem mistaken. But our outstanding error has been a failure to make those personality adjustments and sacrifices which would render realisation possible.

People ask for guidance; they demand right leadership; they hope to be led in the way that they should go; and yet all the time the guidance, leadership and direction have been given them. Christ blazed the trail and is still waiting for us to follow, not one by one, but—under inspired disciples—*as a race.* Like the children of Israel under Moses, we must go forth and find the "holy land." How then can those who have vision (and they are many) train themselves to aid in the right orientation of humanity? How can they become the leaders so sorely needed? By learning to be led themselves by Christ, and by following the guidance of the inner mystical Christ which will inevitably lead them direct to Christ the Initiator. As aspirants to the mysteries we must learn the way through obedience to the light which we may have, by love, and by becoming sensitive to inspiration from on high. There is no other way. We have no genuine excuse for failing, for others have gone ahead, and Christ made it all so clear and simple.

Obedience to the highest one knows, in small things as well as in great, is too simple a rule for many to follow, but it is the secret of the Way. We demand so much, and when a

[3] *Prov.,* XXIX, 18.

simple rule is given us, and we are told merely to obey the voice of conscience and to follow the glimmer of light which we can see, we do not find it sufficiently interesting to call forth prompt obedience. But this rule was the first which Christ followed, and even when a child, He said that He came to occupy Himself with His Father's business. He obeyed the call. He did as God told Him; He followed step by step the inner voice—and it led Him from Bethlehem to Calvary. But it took Him eventually to the Mount of Ascension. He has shown us what results from obedience, and He "learned obedience by the things which He suffered." He paid the price, and revealed to us what God in man could be and do.

The achievement of human perfection is not the simple matter of building a good character and being nice and kind. More than that is involved. It is a question of understanding and of a new and regulated inner attitude, one which is oriented to God because it is oriented to the service of man, in whom God is expressing Himself. "If we do not love our brother whom we have seen, how can we love God whom we have not seen?"[4] This is the question which St. John, the beloved Apostle, asks and which we have not yet, as a race, attempted to answer. The vital need is to return to the simple fundamental instruction which Christ gave, and to learn to love our brother. Love is not a sentimental, emotional state of consciousness. It takes into account the point in evolution and the development of character of those to be loved; but in spite of all, it is a love which sees truly, and which, because it sees so truly can act wisely. It is a love which realises that the world needs love, and that a spirit of love (which is a spirit of inclusiveness, of tolerance, of wise judgment and far-sighted vision) can draw all men together into that outward unity which is based upon a recognised inner relationship.

We are all so ready to take love. We are all so eager to be loved, because we realise, unconsciously if not consciously,

[4] *I St. John,* IV, 20.

that love means service, and we like to be served. The time has come when that selfish attitude to life must change, and we must learn to give love and not to ask love, to go out in service to all whom we contact day by day, and expect and exact nothing for the separated self. When this spirit (which is outstandingly the spirit of Christ and of those who know Him best) becomes more general, then we shall see a more rapid consummation of the desired changes. Theologically, we have said that "God is love," and then have interpreted Him in terms of our own hatreds, our own limited ideals, our narrow theologies, and our separative attitudes. We have recognised Christ as the great Server of the race, and have pointed to Him as the example of what is possible. But we accord no general service, and that quality is not yet the motivating power in the life of the world. It is motivating life more definitely than ever before, but the efforts that are now being made—twenty centuries after Christ left us with the command to follow in His steps—only serve to show how slow we have been, how much remains to be done, and how desperately men need to be served by those who have vision and the love of God in their hearts. It is obvious how little love there is used in the world at this time. The essential thing to remember is that the reason we can recognise God as a God of love is that we are ourselves, basically and potentially, God-like in quality. This in itself constitutes a problem, for unless the divine in us is somewhat awakened it is difficult for us to interpret love correctly, and it is impossible for the masses of men, who are yet upon the path of becoming, and in many cases are scarcely human beings, to understand the real significance of love.

The understanding of love and the expression of love are strictly personal matters. Love can remain indefinitely a theory or an emotional experience. It can become a motivating factor in life and something which we contribute to the whole. If each would think out for himself the meaning of love in his life, and if all would decide to give love and understanding (not emotional reactions, but steady, steadfast, understanding love), then the tangles in this troubled world of ours would straighten out, and it would be an easier place in which to live. The present chaos and turmoil would then more rapidly disappear. Love is essentially the realisation of brotherhood. It is the recognition that we are all the children of the One Father; it is pity and compassion and understanding and patience. It is the true expression of the life of God.

If the first requirement of the man who seeks to prepare himself for the Mysteries of Jesus is obedience to the highest which he can sense and know, and the second is the practice of love, the third is the development of that sensitivity and inner attention by means of which he can arrive at the significance and the condition of inspiration. This is not in any sense the development of psychic faculty as usually understood; it is present among God's children in many forms, from that of attention to the inner voice of conscience and duty (two of the lowest forms of inspiration) to that high spiritual attainment which finds expression in the inspired scriptures of the world.

Unless there is this inspiration, it is not possible for a man to enter into the temple and to commune with That which is introducing him to the subtle processes of initiation. The first Initiator is the soul itself, the divine self in man, the spiritual man, who stands behind the screen of the outer man, and who struggles to control and work through the outer personality. It is that soul or self which opens to man *the door* of inspiration and reveals to him the nature of his divine consciousness, attuning his ear to catch the sound of that "Voice which speaks in the silence"—when a man has quieted all the outer voices.

The attainment of the faculty of inspiration is essential to any progress upon the path of initiation, and it presupposes a development of intelligence which will enable a man to make the necessary differentiations. True inspiration is not in any sense the welling-up of the subconscious self or mind; nor is it the releasing in man of the flood of ideas and thoughts which are his—racial, national or family; it is not the tuning in on the world of thought which can so easily be done by those in whom a certain quality of telepathic rapport is developed. Nor is it listening to the many voices which can make themselves heard when a man succeeds in becoming so utterly negative and so emptied of all intelligent thought that the sounds, the ideas and the suggestions of the world of psychic phenomena very easily intrude. This happens usually when the standard of intelligence is of a relatively low order. Inspiration is something entirely different. It is a penetration into the world of thought and ideas to which Christ listened when He heard a Voice, and the Father spoke to Him. It is the intuitive response of an intelligent mind to impressions coming from the soul and from the world of souls. The speech of the kingdom then becomes familiar to us. We are in touch with those liberated souls who are functioning in that kingdom, and the waves of thought and the ideas which they seek to impress upon the minds of men find their way into circulation through the attuned minds of the disciples of the world. This is inspiration, and this is the faculty for which aspirants everywhere should begin to train themselves, and which must be attained in the world of everyday living. It is a power which is generated through the processes of right meditation; it is an expression of the soul, working through the mind, and thus actuating the brain with impulses which are purely spiritual. Inspiration is responsible for all the new ideas and the developing ideals of our modern world. The age of inspiration is not gone and past; it is present here and now. God still speaks to men, for this world of ours still provides adequate facilities for the development of those qualities which are characteristic of the Christ in the human heart, the soul, the son of God in incarnation, dwelling in this vale of tears, or as it has been called, this "vale of soul-making."

But to achieve this definite and conscious soul contact, the aspirant has to learn obedience through the things which he suffers, and he has also to practice the task of loving. This is not easy. It calls for discipline, for ceaseless effort and striving, for that conquest of self which means a daily crucifixion, and for that close attention which never takes its eyes from the goal, but which is always conscious of purpose, of progress and of orientation. The wonder of the process is that it can be carried forward here and now, in the situation in which we find ourselves, without demanding the least deviation from the place of duty and responsibility.

Such is the goal for the man who seeks to stand with Christ in the founding of the kingdom, thus fulfilling the will of God. There is no other objective worthy of man's attention, nor one which will so absorb every power he has, every gift and talent he possesses, and every moment of his being. Today the call is going forth for Servers of the race, and for men and women who will work at the task of perfecting the self in order that they may be better equipped to serve their fellow men and God in man.

We are told that when we enter the world of ideals, "the differences between religions become negligible and the agreements striking. There is only one ideal for man, to make himself profoundly human. 'Be ye perfect.' The whole man, the complete man, is the ideal man, the divine man." On the path of purification we discover how weak and faulty is the lower personal man; on the path of discipleship we work at the unfoldment of those qualities which are characteristic of the man who is ready to tread the Way and be born in Bethlehem. Then we shall know the truth about ourselves and God, shall know through attainment whether what we are told is fact or not. We are told that ". . . no one can rightly understand the historic truth of such documents as the Gospels unless he has first experienced within himself the mystical meaning which they contain . . . Angelus Silesius of the seventeenth century has already expressed the whole of the critical attitude toward this kind of investigation:

" 'Though Christ were yearly born in Bethlehem and never
   Had birth in you yourself, then were you lost for ever;

And if within yourself it is not reared again
The Cross at Golgotha can save you not from pain.' "[5]

Self knowledge leads one to God knowledge. It is the first step. Purification of the self leads one up to the portal of initiation, and then one can tread the Way that Christ trod from Bethlehem to Calvary.

We are human beings, but we are also divine. We are citizens of the kingdom, although we have not yet claimed and entered into our divine heritage. Inspiration is pouring in all the time; love is latent in every human heart. Only obedience is required at the first step, and when that is rendered, service, which is the expression of love, and inspiration, which is the influence of the kingdom, become a definite part of our life expression. This is what Christ came to reveal; it is the Word which He sounded forth. He has demonstrated to us our human and divine possibilities, and by accepting the fact of our dual but divine nature we can begin to aid in the founding and expressing of the kingdom.

The realisation must come to us that "the highest, purest and absolutely adequate expression of the mystery of man is Christ the God-man. He alone really and finally places human nature in the right light. His appearance in history entitles man to regard himself as more than a mere creature. If there is really a God-man there is also a Man-god, that is 'man' who has received the godhead into himself . . . the Man-god is collective and universal, that is to say, mankind as a whole or a world-church. For it is only in communion with all his fellow men that man can receive God."[6]

The individual attitude to the example of Christ is therefore obedience to the command that we achieve perfection. But the motive must be the one that incited Christ to all His divine activity—the founding of the new kingdom and the attainment of that state of consciousness on a universal and human scale which will make out of the human being

[5] Quoted in *The Way of Initiation,* by Rudolf Steiner, p. 46.
[6] *Wrestlers with Christ,* by Karl Pfleger, p. 235.

a citizen of the kingdom, consciously functioning therein, voluntarily subject to its laws, and striving steadfastly for its extension on earth. He is the messenger of the kingdom; and the raising of the consciousness of his fellow men, so that they can transcend themselves, becomes his self-appointed task. The sharing with them of the benefits of the kingdom, and the strengthening of them as they tread the difficult path to the gate which admits into that kingdom, become the only dear and immediate duty. The soul who has made contact with the lower expression, the personal self, sweeps that self on to the path of Service. The man cannot then rest until he has led others into the Way and toward the freedom of the sons of God which distinguishes the new and coming kingdom.

The new religion is on the way, and it is one for which all previous religions have prepared us. It differs only in that it will no longer be distinguished by dogmas and doctrines, but will be essentially an attitude of mind, an orientation to life, to man and to God. It will also be a living service. Selfishness and self-centred interests will finally be ruled out, for the kingdom of God is the life of the corporate whole, sensed and desired by all its citizens, and worked for and expressed by all who tread the Way. Initiation is nothing more than the process of developing within us the powers and faculties of this new and higher kingdom, which powers release one into a wider world, and tend to make one sensible of the organic whole in place of the part. Individualism and separatedness will disappear as that kingdom comes into being. The collective consciousness is its major expression and quality. It is the next definite and clearly indicated step upon the evolutionary Path, and there is no escape from this issue. We cannot prevent ourselves from finally becoming conscious of the larger whole, or actively participating in its unified life. However, it is possible to hasten the coming of the kingdom, and the need of the world at this time, and the general turning of men towards the world of ideas, would seem to indicate that the time has come for the making of that extra effort which will precipitate the appearance of the kingdom and bring forth into manifestation that which is awaiting immediate revelation. This is the challenge which today confronts the Christian Church. The need is for vision, wisdom and that wide tolerance which will see divinity on every hand and recognise the Christ in every human being.

As we grasp the significance of the kingdom of God we begin to understand what is meant by the Church of Christ, and the meaning of that "cloud of witnesses"[7] by which we are so constantly surrounded. The kingdom of God is not some one particular church with its own peculiar doctrines, its particular formulations of truth, its specialised method of government upon earth and of approach to God.

The true Church is the kingdom of God on earth, divorced from all clerical government and composed of all, regardless of race or creed, who live by the light within, who have discovered the fact of the mystical Christ in their hearts, and are preparing to tread the Way of Initiation. The kingdom is not composed of orthodox theologically minded people. Its citizenship is wider than that, and includes every human being who is thinking in larger terms than the individual, the orthodox, the national and the racial. The members of the coming kingdom will think in terms of humanity as a whole; and as long as they are separative or nationalistic, or religiously bigoted, or commerically selfish, they have no place in that kingdom. The word *spiritual* will be given a far wider connotation than that which has been given in the old age which is fortunately now passing. All forms of life will be regarded from the angle of spiritual phenomena, and we shall no longer regard one activity as spiritual and another as not. The question of motive, purpose and group usefulness will determine the spiritual nature of an activity. To work for the whole; to be occupied with the aiding of the group; to be cognisant of One Life pulsing through all forms, and to work in the consciousness that all men are brothers—these are the initial qualities which a citizen of the kingdom

[7] *Heb.*, XII, 1.

must show.   The human family is individually self-conscious and this stage of the separative consciousness has been a needed and useful one; but the time has arrived when we are aware of greater contacts, of wider implications, and of a more general inclusiveness.

How will this condition of God's kingdom materialise on earth? By the gradual and steady increase of the numbers of those who are citizens of that kingdom living their lives on earth and demonstrating the qualities and the consciousness which is characteristic of such citizens; by men and women everywhere cultivating the wider consciousness, and becoming more and more inclusive. "Any reflection," Dr. Hocking tells us, "that can infallibly break the walls of the Self, opens up at once an infinite World-field.   Set a second to my One, and I have given all the numbers."[8] And he gives us the clue to the process which must be cultivated in this work of essential unity by saying that ". . . the true mystic is he who holds to the reality of both worlds, and leaves to time and effort the understanding of their union."[9]   The kingdom of God is not divorced from practical daily living upon the level of everyday affairs.   The citizen of the kingdom is world-conscious and God-conscious.   His lines of contact are clearly delineated in both directions: he is interested not in himself, but in God and his fellow men, and his duty to God is worked out through the love he feels and shows for those around him.   He knows no barriers and recognises no divisions; he is living—as a soul—in every aspect of his nature, through his mind and his emotions, and on the physical plane of life.   He works through love and in love and because of the love of God.

A close study of the Gospel story and a spirited attention to the words of Christ will make apparent that the three outstanding characteristics of His work and the three main lines of His activity are intended to be ours also.   These three are, as we have seen, first, the achieving of perfection and its dem-

[8] *The Meaning of God in Human Experience,* by W. E. Hocking, p. 315.
[9] *Ibid.,* p. 399.

onstrating through the five great events which we call the crises in the life of Christ, the five major initiations of the Orient and of the esoteric schools; secondly, the founding of the kingdom—a responsibility which rests upon each of us, because, though Christ certainly opened the door into the kingdom, the rest of the work rests upon our shoulders; thirdly, the attaining of immortality, based on the development of that within ourselves which is of the nature of the real, which has true value and which deserves to stand the test of immortality. This last thought is one which warrants our attention. Arresting in its implication, it is sadly and deeply true that ". . . man, as he exists today, is not capable of survival. He must change or perish. Man, as he is, is not the last word of creation. If he does not, if he cannot, adapt himself and his institutions to the new world, he will yield his place to a species more sensitive and less gross in its nature. If man cannot do the work demanded of him, another creature who can, will arise."[10]

Such has always been the evolutionary plan. The life of God has constructed for itself vehicle after vehicle, in order to manifest, and kingdom has succeeded kingdom. The same great expansion is imminent today. Man, the self-conscious being, *can* differ radically from the forms of life in the other kingdoms because he can go forward upon the wave of God's life *in full consciousness*. He can share in the "joy of the Lord" as the wider reaches of consciousness become his; he can know the nature of that bliss which is the outstanding condition of God's nature. There is no need for human failure, nor for a definite break in the continuity of revelation. There is that in man which can enable him to bridge the gap between the kingdom in which he finds himself and the new kingdom on the horizon. Human beings who are citizens of both kingdoms—the human and the spiritual—are with us today as always. They move with freedom in either world, and Christ Himself gave us the perfect demonstration

[10] *The Supreme Spiritual Ideal*, by S. Radhakrishnan, in *The Hibbert Journal*, October, 1936, p. 33.

of that citizenship and told us that we could do "even greater things" than He had done. Such is the glorious future towards which man is oriented today, and for which all world events are preparing him.

The preparation for this kingdom is the task of discipleship and constitutes the arduous discipline of the five-fold way of initiation. The work of the disciple is the founding of the kingdom, and the primary characteristic of its citizens is immortality. They are members of a Deathless Race, and the final enemy which they overcome is death; they function consciously in or out of the body and care not which it is; they have life everlasting because there is in them that which cannot die, being of the nature of God. To be immortal because one's sins are forgiven seems an inadequate reason to an intelligent mind; to have everlasting life because Christ died two thousand years ago does not prove satisfactory to the man who is conscious of his own responsibility and his own identity; to live for ever because one is religious, or has accepted certain forms of belief, is a reason repudiated by the man who is aware of his own inner power and nature; to base one's faith in survival upon tradition or even upon an innate sense of persistence does not seem sufficient. We know much about the power and tenacity of self-preservation and the creative urge to self-perpetuation. Perhaps these two are simply carried forward in an idealistic sense as man faces finality.

Yet there is innate in humanity the sense of belonging elsewhere; there is a divine discontent which must surely have a basis in some natural inheritance which is the guarantee of our origin. This reaching out towards a larger and fuller life is just as much a human characteristic as the normal tendency of the individual to reach toward family life and social contacts. It is therefore just as capable of achievement as that tendency, and to this the testimony of the ages contributes. Personal salvation is, after all, of small importance unless it has place in a more general and universal salvaging. Promise is held out in the Bible that "he that doeth the will of God abideth for ever,"[11] and in these words we have the clue. There has been a tendency to think that when God created man His will to expression had been perfectly satisfied. There is surely no real basis for this belief. If God is not capable of producing something of far greater perfection than humanity, and if the life which pours through the natural world is not working towards something greater, finer and more beautiful than anything yet produced, then God is not divine in the sense in which this term is usually accepted. We demand of God far more than this—greatness beyond anything that has yet been shown us. We believe that this is possible. We rest back upon divinity, and are assured that it will not fail us. But revelation of the ultimate perfection, whatever that may be (and we should not limit God by any of our own pre-conceived ideas), may require the unfolding in man of powers and a mechanism which will enable him to recognise it, to share in its wonder and its larger sphere of contacts. We ourselves may have to change in order to express the divine as Christ expressed it, before God can go on to the manifestation of the beauty of the hidden kingdom. God needs man's cooperation. He calls for men to do His will. We have looked upon this as a way to our own individual good, which perhaps has been a wrong attitude. We may arise and carry forward the inner Plan by equipping ourselves towards perfection, in order that God may "see of the travail of His soul, and shall be satisfied."[12] We may constitute God's crucial experiment. The germ of divine life is in us, but we ourselves have something to do about it, and the time has come when humanity as a whole must apply itself to the fostering of the divine life within the racial form.

It is our immediate duty therefore, in the interests of the kingdom whose citizens are immortal, to unfold that which in ourselves is divine, and whose characteristics can be known by the sense of value, by the attribute of light, and by the nature of its love and loves. Full expression of the "Hidden

[11] *I St. John*, II, 17.
[12] *Isaiah*, LIII, 11.

Man of the Heart" is the need today. The revelation of the Self within the self is the demand. It is this self, nurtured, fostered, then trained and developed, which is the immortal aspect in man, and for this self are we responsible. There is no evading this, nor is there evading of the fact that we are part of a whole, and that only as Christ enters into recognition by the entire race and is expressed by humanity as a whole, shall we achieve that for which we have been created —the fulfilling of the will of God, as Christ fulfilled it. We need to transcend the inferiority complex which rises up in questioning when such words occur as the above phrase: "As Christ fulfilled it." A book earlier quoted states that this idea of a personal Christ must be eclipsed and superseded by Christ as the life and hope in all of us. It is only the uniquely significant who understand the true inner meaning of immortality. Those in whom the sense of values is subordinated to the values of the soul, whose consciousness is that of eternity, are eternal in their living processes. This we must remember.

Are we interested in the vital whole? Is the welfare of the race of real moment to us? Are we willing to sacrifice everything to the good of the whole? These are questions which are of importance to the individual aspirant, and which he must answer if he is to understand clearly what he is attempting to do. This process of giving deference to the whole has been summed up for us by Dr. Schweitzer, who presents to us such a wonderful picture of the kingdom of God. He says that:

"Civilization, put quite simply, consists in our giving ourselves, as human beings, to the effort to attain the perfecting of the human race and the actualization of progress of every sort in the circumstances of humanity and of the objective world. This mental attitude, however, involves a double predisposition: firstly, we must be prepared to act affirmatively toward the world and life; secondly, we must become ethical.

"Only when we are able to attribute a real meaning to the world and to life shall we be able also to give ourselves to such action as will produce results of real value. As long as we look on our existence in the world as meaningless, there is no point whatever in desiring to effect anything in the world. We become workers for that universal spiritual and material progress which we call civilization only in so far as we affirm that the world and life possess some sort of meaning, or, which is the same thing, only in so far as we think optimistically.

"Civilization originates when men become inspired by a strong and clear determination to attain progress, and consecrate themselves, as a result of this determination, to the service of life and of the world. It is only in ethics that we can find the driving force for such action, transcending as it does, the limits of our own existence.

"Nothing of real value in the world is ever accomplished without enthusiasm and self-sacrifice."[13]

No man who cannot attain to the consciousness of the true values is yet ready for the immortality which is the prerogative of the sons of God. The building of that inner structure which is the spiritual body is carried on by means of purification, perfecting, meditation and initiation, and above all else, by service. There is no other way. The true values to which the initiate gives his life are those of the spirit, of the kingdom of God, those which concern the whole and which lay no primary emphasis upon the individual. They are expressed through expansion, service and conscious incorporation in the whole. They are to be summed up in the one word Service. They are expressed through inclusiveness and non-separateness. It is here that the Church, as usually understood, meets its major challenge. Is it spiritual enough to let go of theology and become truly human? Is it interested enough to widen its horizon and recognise as truly Christian all who demonstrate the Christ spirit, whether they be Hindu, Mohammedan, or Buddhist, whether they are labeled by any name other than that of orthodox Christian?

Another basic thought emerges out of all that we have considered. It is whether or not we are today transiting out of the age of authority into the age of experience, and whether

[13] *The Decay and Restoration of Civilization,* by Albert Schweitzer, p. VIII, preface.

this transition does not indicate that the race is rapidly preparing for initiation. We are revolting from doctrines, having very little use for them, and the reason, Dr. Dewey tells us, is that ". . . adherence to any body of doctrines and dogmas based upon a specific authority signifies distrust in the power of experience to provide, in its own ongoing movement, the needed principles of belief and action. Faith in its newer sense signifies that experience itself is the sole ultimate authority."[14] It is obvious that this connotes not uniformity but a recognition of our essential unity.

2

Thus step by step we have followed the Christ in His stupendous task, and we have studied the task in its uniqueness. He did something of such significance for the race that only today are we in a position to grasp it. So occupied have we been with our own individual salvation and our own hope of heaven that the really unique things which Christ did have largely escaped our observation. That He followed in the steps of many of God's children who, in their day and generation, had served, suffered, and brought the world salvation, remains unquestioned; that He gave us an example of perfected humanity such as the world had never previously seen is equally unchallenged. The greatest of the previous sons of God, the Buddha, after much struggle arrived at illumination, and blazed the trail for humanity up to and through the portal of initiation. But Christ was perfect, having (dare we say during some previous cycle of lives?) learned obedience through the things which He had suffered. That He overcame death and opened the gates of immortality to all humanity is likewise true. But since the first dawn of human history men have always suffered for each other; they have again and again, here one and there another, achieved perfection and disappeared from human view. The divine spark in man has always rendered him immortal. Men have always

[14] Quoted in *Reality and Illusion*, by Richard Rothschild, p. 320.

sensed their divinity, and they have always reached out their hands and their hearts to God. The sons of the Father have never forgotten the Father's home, no matter how far away they may have wandered. God has always equally sought after us, and from century to century He has sent His messengers as an embodiment of His remembrance.

But Christ came as a special Messenger. He came to found the kingdom of God on earth and to institute a new and tangible expression of Deity upon our planet. His mission has not failed. The kingdom is now organised upon earth and is composed of those men and women everywhere who have lost sight of their own individual salvation and hope of heaven because they know that unless heaven can express itself here and now it is but a futile hope. They are occupied with the processes of self-perfection and self-purification because they seek to serve their fellowmen more efficiently and adequately, and thus "glorify their Father which is in heaven."[15] They are not interested in self-aggrandisement nor with the making of claims of any kind—beyond the one stupendous claim that they are sons of God, as are we all; they do not prate of initiation or call themselves initiates; they are satisfied to walk among men as those who serve and who are citizens of the kingdom of God. They are the world servers, and their only interest is in following the steps of Him Who went about doing good and proclaiming the tidings of the kingdom. They do not say that theirs is the only way into the kingdom, but to those who do not know Christ they say: "Little children, love one another." They do not condemn those who know nothing of Christ's sacrifice upon the Cross, but they say to those who seek the way; "Take up thy cross" and follow Christ. To their fellow disciples they bring constantly the reminder that "except a corn of wheat fall into the ground and die, it abideth alone," and they set themselves the goal of the new birth. The bulk of the thinking, well-meaning men and women of the world are today

[15] *Matt.*, V, 16.

going up from Nazareth in Galilee to Bethlehem. Some, per-haps more than one can estimate, are passing on their way to the Baptism in Jordan, whilst a few are valiantly climbing the Mount of Transfiguration. One here and there may be stead-fastly setting his face to go to Jerusalem, there to be crucified; but these are rare. Most of us are learning, in the daily dying to self, to fit ourselves for the final Crucifixion initiation, and by the constant renunciation of everything that holds back the expression of divinity qualifying for that tremendous spiritual experience which ever preceded the Resurrection, and which is called the Great Renunciation.

Let us vision clearly just where we stand upon the Path of Evolution. Have we yet set our feet upon the Path of Proba-tion, that difficult path of purification which is a necessary first step? Or are we definitely upon the Path of Discipleship, knowing what we are doing, cultivating the finer values and those distinctive qualities which are the hall mark of mani-festing divinity?

The only incentive which will be strong enough (or which ever has been strong enough) to enable a man to tread the fivefold way to the Centre from which the Word goes forth is a realisation of the deep and distressing need of our modern world for revelation, for pure example and for loving service. There is no way by which this sad and war-torn world of ours can be saved and men's lives transfigured except by a mani-festation of the spirit of God. Instead of waiting for God to take action and send some Saviour (Who would probably not be recognised any more than Christ was), the time has come, and mankind has evolved sufficiently, for the divine life within it to surge forth and up to God, calling forth His response, His recognition, which we have seen Him repeat time and time again. He is willing to accord. We are His children and we are beginning to live divinely, thinking (as He thinks) in terms of the whole and not in terms of the separative and selfish individual. Now is a time of crisis when all human beings are needed, and the call goes forth for each to make that extra effort towards unselfishness, and that mental push towards clarity of thought, which will transform us from well-meaning aspirants into clear-sighted disciples animated by a spirit of love and goodwill to all men, irrespective of race or creed or colour.

This religious will is in expression now, not turned to theology or to the formation of doctrines and occupied with their enforcement, but to love and service, forgetting self, giving the uttermost that is possible for the helping of the world. This will breaks down all barriers and elevates the children of men wherever the will to be so helped is found. And it is something that is organising slowly in the world today, its quality that of universality, and its technique that of loving service. Men everywhere are responding to the same inner spiritual impulse which is illustrated for us in the beautiful tale which is related of the Buddha. It runs as follows:

"In the belief that He had attained unto the last stage of perfection the Buddha was about to abandon existence in finite space and time, to relinquish all sorrow and suffering for the pure being of bliss universal and eternal.

"At that moment a buzzing gnat was snapped up by a passing bat.

" 'Stay,' mused the Enlightened One, 'the state of perfection I am entering is but perfection of myself, a unique perfection, my wholeness is a unique wholeness; not yet then am I a being universal. Other beings still suffer imperfection, existence, and resultant death. Compassion unto these still awakes within me when I contemplate their suffering.

" 'The way of life unto perfection I have, in truth and in deed, illuminated for them: but can they tread that way without me?

" 'The unique perfection of myself I dreamed, the perfection of my own character and personality is but imperfection while one other being—one single gnat—still suffers imperfection of its identical kind.

" 'No being may reach bliss alone: all must reach it together, and that, the unique bliss proper to each. For am I not in every other being and is not every other being in me?'

"With still small voice in every self thus speaketh the Buddha, by its inspiration to inner character, its aspiration to outer personality, perpetually transmuting this self into not-self, each reality dependent on the other, an everlasting way of life to tread to perfection of each, of all."[16]

Christ emphasises the same lesson, and always His disciples have sought, in their place and time, to teach the law of service.

Sometimes it seems as if the two extremes lived on in the consciousness of man—the notorious and ambitious, and the great world servers. Hitherto the sequence has been: service of ourselves, of our family, of those we love, of some leader, some cause, some school of politics or religion. The time has come when service must expand and express itself on broader and more inclusive lines, and we must learn to serve as Christ served, to love all men as He loved them and, by the potency of our spiritual vitality and the quality of our service, stimulate all we meet so that they too can serve and love and become members of the kingdom. When this is seen clearly, and when we are ready to make the needed sacrifices and renunciations, there will be a more rapid manifestation of the kingdom of God on earth. The call is not for fanatics or for the rabid devotee who, in attempting to express it, has so marred divinity. The call is for sane and normal men and women who can comprehend the situation, face what must be done, and then give their lives to expressing for the world the qualities of the citizens of the kingdom of Souls: love, wisdom, silence, non-separativeness and freedom from hatreds and partisan, creedal beliefs. When such men can be gathered together in large numbers (and they are gathering rapidly) we shall have the fulfilment of the angels' song at Bethlehem, *"On earth peace, good will toward men."*

[16] *Eros and Psyche*, by Benchara Branford, p. 355.

Training for new age
discipleship is provided
by the *Arcane School*.
The principles of the
Ageless Wisdom are
presented through esoteric
meditation, study and
service as a *way of life*.

*Write to the publishers
for information.*

INDEX